Free Press
v.
Fair Trial

Free Press v. *Fair Trial*

SUPREME COURT DECISIONS SINCE 1807

Douglas S. Campbell

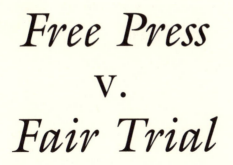

PRAEGER

Westport, Connecticut
London

For Betty Jane Spencer Campbell, my mother;
R. Douglas Campbell, my father;
Sandy, Connie, Bettie, and Sue, my sisters;
and Bill, my brother

Library of Congress Cataloging-in-Publication Data

Campbell, Douglas S.
    Free press v. fair trial : Supreme Court decisions since 1807 /
Douglas S. Campbell.
        p.   cm.
    Includes bibliographical references and index.
    ISBN 0-275-94277-5 (alk. paper)
    1. Free press and fair trial—United States—Cases.   I. Title.
KF9223.5.A52C36   1994
342.73'0853—dc20
[347.302853]   93-18241

British Library Cataloguing in Publication Data is available.

Library of Congress Catalog Card Number: 93-18241
ISBN: 0-275-94277-5

First published in 1994

Praeger Publishers, 88 Post Road West, Westport, CT 06881
An imprint of Greenwood Publishing Group, Inc.

Printed in the United States of America

∞™

The paper used in this book complies with the
Permanent Paper Standard issued by the National
Information Standards Organization (Z39.48-1984).

10 9 8 7 6 5 4 3 2 1

Shep.

CONTENTS

PREFACE

Few areas of law have attracted as much attention, confusion, and probably
disdain as the problems arising from the conflict between a free press and a
fair trial. These problems are as old as the press itself, and, for the past two
centuries, Americans have sought their own constitutionally acceptable
solutions. This book seeks to help non-lawyers understand the primary issues
of this conflict by taking an historical look at the attempts of the United
States Supreme Court to reconcile the protections of two, sometimes
incompatible amendments found in the Bill of Rights: the First and Sixth
Amendments.

Starting with *Burr* v. *United States* (1807), the historical survey highlights the thirty major United States Supreme Court cases devoted primarily
to this conflict and presents often-cited influential quotations from 70 supporting cases. Four areas of relevant information are presented for each major
case. First is the legal background. Examined in this section are the issues
that constitute the legal context of the case. Among the items covered are
relevant state and federal statutes, important lower court decisions and other
germane decisions by the Court, rules and regulations promulgated by the
American Bar Association, and opinions and evaluations from eminent jurists
and prominent scholars.

The circumstances surrounding the events giving rise to the case represent the second area of relevant information. This section is particularly helpful to a researcher because the Court is extremely reluctant to divulge factual
information about persons and events involved in any given case. Often the
Court will leave out first names, geographical locations, or details essential to
understanding the actions taken by a defendant who, as a result of such
actions, faced criminal charges. Nowhere in Estes v. *Texas* (1965), for example, does the Court reveal that Estes was selling nonexistent liquid fertilizer
tanks.

The third section presents detailed summaries of the cases. Majority,
plurality, concurring, and dissenting opinions are summarized using, wherever
efficacious, direct quotations. An analysis of the significance of a case forms

the last section. For the most part, this section points out what aspects of the Court's ruling are influential in subsequent cases.

Two brief notes about style are necessary. First, because docket numbers made no reference to years until 1974, I added the year to all the docket numbers assigned through the end of 1973. In addition to a page number, then, these docket numbers include all four digits in the numeral of a year: e.g., 1919-437. Those numbers with the year included by the Court use only the last two digits of the date: e.g., 86-636. Second, for those cases not yet published in the *United States Reporter,* I have cited page numbers from the *Lawyer's Edition.*

I close with a few words of thanks. I confess that these comments reflect my human inadequacy to express all the assistance I received, but they are sincere and heart-felt. First, I wish to thank my understanding and strongly supportive wife, Beverly, who never complained when I spent many nights away from home at distant universities researching matters far removed from her own professional responsibilities. Second, I thank Saundra K. Hybels, colleague, office mate for a few years, widely published and highly respected author, and, most of all, friend, who has provided much-appreciated and often badly needed encouragement of my research efforts. Finally, I take special care to mention Craig Dean Willis, an accomplished and enterprising university president, who fully supported my endeavors and took a genuine personal interest in my work.

Nor should I forget the Professional Development Committee of the Pennsylvania State System of Higher Education, which awarded me a grant to complete my research during the summer of 1992.

I owe a debt of gratitude to many, many librarians. I mention first Ester Jane Carrier, research librarian par excellence. I am sure she must have been tempted to hide every time I walked into the university library's reference section, but she always greeted me with a smile and she always found what I was seeking. In addition, I express gratitude for assistance from librarians at the law schools of Duke University, the University of North Carolina at Chapel Hill, and Dickinson University, and most especially for two very helpful and friendly persons at the University of Virginia Law School Library: Michael Klepper, Media Librarian, and Steve West, Television Production Specialist.

INTRODUCTION

The issues arising out of conflicts between a fair trial (guaranteed by the Sixth Amendment) and a free press (guaranteed by the First Amendment) are myriad, but one issue is primary and two others are extremely important. (See the end of this introduction for the texts of the First, Fifth, Sixth, and Fourteenth Amendments.)

Primary is the problem of assembling an impartial jury. In essence, this issue centers on the difficulty of finding prospective jurors who are not prejudiced unconstitutionally for or against a defendant because they were exposed to extrajudicial information from the media. While it is virtually certain that during a trial jurors will be exposed to information prejudicial to a defendant, it is also true that special safeguards regulate the introduction of testimony and evidence in a court of law. American constitutional law contains no such safeguards governing what extrajudicial information the media may disseminate about defendants. Consequently, jurists justly are concerned about unregulated publicity that may unfairly (and so unconstitutionally) prejudice prospective jurors before a trial begins.

Although the possibility exists that pretrial publicity could unconstitutionally prejudice prospective jurors to favor a defendant, in practice this is rare. The Court, however, did face at least two appeals on this basis. Convicted of polygamy, George Reynolds appealed the dismissal of prospective jurors who were also polygamists (*Reynolds* v. *U.S.* [1878]), and Mima Queen, who lost her suit to win freedom from slavery, appealed the dismissal of a prospective juror who said he detested slavery (*Mima Queen* v. *Hepburn* [1813]). Moreover, in 1992 a man charged with sending obscene letters asked a judge that his jury be made up of only nymphomaniacs and atheists because only these jurors would be free from unconstitutional prejudice against him. His request was denied.

Two other issues relevant to the conflict between a fair trial and a free press are extremely important: access and due process. Access is a double-edged sword. One edge cuts to the notion of citizen access to the media. This notion is only tangentially related to the conflict between a fair trial and a free press. The other edge, media access to the courts, is very closely related to the conflict. One very tempting way to solve the problem of a prejudiced juror is not to give information to the media. The media cannot publicize information they do not have. Moreover, denying the media information does not violate the strictest meaning—at least according to Blackstone and the Court in *Near* v. *Minnesota* (1934) —of the First Amendment. That is, denying information does not constitute prior censorship nor does it prevent the media from disseminating whatever information they possess. It may, however, threaten a free press in its broader sense. Few would argue against the notion that the right to print information becomes less valuable without a concomitant right to obtain information. Thus, it very well may be the case that denying access to the criminal courts or to some portion of the judicial process, in effect, censors the reporting of this nation's courts.

Another consideration raised by access is the media's traditional role as watchdog. Can citizens of a democracy be certain that justice is truthfully, fairly, and honestly administered if a criminal trial is not open to the public? Granting the media access to trials, therefore, provides an opportunity for the public to witness the criminal justice system in action. The Court has described this opportunity as prophylactic and therapeutic. Access is described as prophylactic because it is believed to prevent vigilantism or self-help. That is, the Court believes citizens would be less likely to seek revenge for a crime if they know that the courts will punish the criminals who committed it. Witnessing firsthand the courts declaring criminals guilty and sentencing them to prison, the Court is suggesting, may serve to discourage victims, the friends and relatives of victims, or simply Don Quixotes from righting what they perceive to be wrongs. In addition, citizens unaware of a particular crime also gain trust in the criminal justice system and allow it to operate unmolested in part because they believe that the mere existence of an opportunity to witness a trial keeps honest the judge, attorneys, and other participants.

The Court says witnessing criminal trials can be therapeutic because it may serve as a kind of catharsis. Not only can victims and their friends and relatives gain comfort from witnessing criminals declared guilty and sentenced to some sort of punishment, but all citizens are comforted by routine media reports that the courts are effective. Without the opportunity to witness trials, therefore, and without the opportunity to read news reports about them, the citizenry may lose confidence in the criminal justice system.

Technology, especially television, has dramatically changed media coverage of public trials, and it has given rise to a number of questions related to access, questions that the framers of the Constitution could not have contemplated. How many persons must witness a trial for it to be considered public or for the prophylactic and therapeutic values to gain significance? For example, do the constitutional guarantees of a public trial and of a free press mean that today's criminal trials may be—or even must be—televised? In contrast, do the psychological aspects associated with television threaten a fair trial by eliciting uncharacteristic behaviors from participants, including not only witnesses and jurors but also lawyers and judges?

Contempt is also an important issue relevant to the conflict between the First and Sixth Amendments. Judges are virtual dictators in the courtroom. They have enormous powers over trial participants and observers. Although they cannot forbid the press from printing information, they can regulate the behavior of journalists in the courtroom. Judges can force all trial observers to be quiet, for example, so that the jury can hear the testimony. Regulation of the behavior of journalists, however, may infringe on a free press. Since contempt is not relevant to juror prejudice, cases related to this topic are not included in the list of primary cases. Readers interested in contempt will find all the cases germane to this issue listed in the section devoted to supporting cases.

The notion of due process has acquired such importance that it has become essential to the Court's rulings on the conflict between a free press and a fair trial. Few jurists today would disagree that the Fifth Amendment right of not being deprived of life, liberty, or property without due process of law applies only to the federal government and does not grant state courts authority to enforce this right. Such agreement is the result of an early effort by John Barron—*Barron* v. *Baltimore* (1833)—to claim that, since the rights and liberties protected by the Bill of Rights belong to every citizen, they should inhibit the power of the states as well as that of the federal government. In essence, Barron was arguing that these rights and liberties are so fundamental to the notion of a true democracy that the states as well as the federal government should be prevented from violating them, even though the Constitution does not declare specifically that the first ten amendments limit state authority. The Court emphatically disagreed, saying that if these rights were to be applied to the states, then this amendment would contain explicit words to that effect.

The Fourteenth Amendment, however, says that states, like Congress, also may not deprive any person of life, liberty, or property without due process of law. This amendment, in effect, created what courts called dual citizenship: all citizens simultaneously hold citizenship in both the United States and in a particular state. A state, therefore, may not deny or abridge its citizens their rights granted to them as simultaneous citizens of the federal government, but a state may grant rights different from those inherent in federal citizenship. Thus, the total of citizens' rights will change from state to state, but all citizens enjoy a certain uniform, minimum set of rights regardless of the state they live in.

The distinction between the Fifth Amendment's notion of due process, which applies only to the federal courts, and the Fourteenth's, which applies also to state courts, is extremely important primarily because most criminal trials are held in state courts. When the Fourteenth Amendment was ratified in 1868, Barron's argument was revived. Clearly, the Fourteenth Amendment applied basic notions of rights and liberties to the states.

Exactly what constitutes these rights and privileges was not clear. In the Fifth Amendment and in the rest of the first ten amendments (known collectively as the Bill of Rights—although some limit the phrase Bill of Rights to the first eight amendments since the Ninth and Tenth Amendments do not list particular rights), rights exist that are not mentioned specifically in the Fourteenth; the courts have struggled ever since 1868 with the problem of how many (if any) of the rights enumerated in the Fifth Amendment or in the entire Bill of Rights are implied by the Fourteenth Amendment.

At first, the Court said no rights enumerated in the Bill of Rights were implicit in the Fourteenth Amendment. Later, it recognized the existence of what it called certain fundamental rights, especially those of the First Amendment, asserting that these rights could be applied to the states through the Fourteenth Amendment. Eventually, nearly all the rights of the first ten amendments were felt to be implicit in the due process clause of the Fourteenth Amendment, which, nevertheless, were still seen to be different from the due process rights of the Fifth Amendment.

What, then, is due process? In *Davidson* v. *New Orleans* (1878), the Court noted that Edward Coke's equivalent to "due process of law" is the phrase "law of the land" found in the Magna Carta (1215). Due process so conceived is what the law, and implicitly the citizenry who created this law, recognize as fair, impartial, equitable, just, proper, and acceptable, but not, as the Court said in *Davidson,* arbitrary, oppressive, or unjust. In essence, due process is fairness. Applied to criminal law, due process means that the administration of criminal justice must be fair.

Two forms of due process have been distinguished over the years. The first is called *procedural due process.* This phrase sounds more than a bit redundant, but it means, at bottom, that there must exist accepted procedures or rules that can be used to apply the law. In criminal law, procedural due process means, among other things, that the criminal courts must follow procedures or rules already in place. Trial and appellate judges cannot make up their own rules from day to day as they perform their duties. The second form is called *substantive due process.* This phrase means that the procedures or rules must be fair. The mere correct application of a rule on the books does not result in constitutional due process unless the rule itself is fair.

Therefore, judicial due process means, first, that the courts must establish rules before they apply them and, second, that these rules must be fair. Persons who are accused of a crime, for example, must be tried in a court of law operating under rules created before their trial commences. The rules cannot be created or changed after the start of a trial since to do so would not be a fair way to proceed. In addition, the rules themselves must be fair. There is no justice when courts are required to follow predetermined rules if the rules themselves are unjust.

Consequently, when persons convicted of crimes appeal on the basis of due process, they are making only one or two claims. First, using the notion of *procedural* due process, they may claim that the trial court did not use the correct rules or did not apply correctly the rules governing a criminal trial. In this case, defendants appealing on the basis of due process are asserting that the trial was unfair because the wrong rules were followed or the right rules were applied in an incorrect manner. These rules, it should be noted, are different among states and different between federal courts and state courts. Second, using the notion of *substantive* due process, appellants may claim that, even though the rules applied were correct and correctly applied, the rules themselves were unfair.

Since the rules of criminal procedures are voluminous, one way to narrow the scope of due process is to limit its application to constitutional requirements. Even here, there is widespread and deep disagreement—in spite of the best efforts by the United States Supreme Court—over what the Constitution requires as due process in the criminal courts. While it is clear, for example, that the Fifth Amendment prohibits federal courts from trying a person twice for the same crime, the definition of a valid trial is not clear, nor is it clear at what point a trial officially has begun.

The problem that has received the most attention, however, is determining which due process rights found in the first eight or ten amendments are applied to the states by operation of the Fourteenth Amendment. The Court noted in *Davidson* (1878) that the due process clause of the Fifth Amendment did not generate much attention in the first 100 years of the Court. But the Fourteenth Amendment, although ratified only a decade before *Davidson,* immediately crowded the docket. The Court speculated that high interest in the Fourteenth Amendment was based on a "strange misconception." Not surprisingly, losers of cases in the state courts looked to the Fourteenth Amendment as a way to test the constitutionality of the abstract legal principles or of the state legislation upon which their cases were decided.

At first, the Court said only those rights specifically mentioned in the Fourteenth Amendment itself limit state authority. Later, the Court said that there exist certain fundamental rights and liberties that are implicit in the Fourteenth Amendment and that the Fourteenth does apply them to the states.

During the late fifties, sixties, and early seventies the Court discovered a rather long list of fundamental rights that it said are implicit in the Fourteenth Amendment. By the time it ceased this process of discovery, it had discovered nearly all the fundamental rights and liberties that are mentioned in the Bill of Rights. Thus, even though the Court denies to this day that the Fourteenth Amendment applies all the rights and liberties of the Bill of Rights to the states, it has discovered a series of fundamental rights and liberties nearly identical to those mentioned in the first ten amendments and applied these fundamental rights to the states. It may not be completely inaccurate, therefore, to say that the Court today has come to accept the basic argument of John Barron. That is, by discovering in the Fourteenth Amendment fundamental rights and liberties that apply to the states, it, in effect, has applied almost all of the nearly identical rights and liberties of the Bill of Rights to the states.

FIRST AMENDMENT

Congress shall make no law respecting an establishment of religion, or prohibiting the free exercise thereof; or abridging the freedom of speech, or of the press, or the right of the people peaceably to assemble, and to petition the Government for redress of grievances.

FIFTH AMENDMENT

No person shall be held to answer for a capital, or otherwise infamous crime, unless on a presentment or indictment of a grand jury, except in cases arising in the land or naval forces, or in the militia, when in actual service in time of war or public danger; nor shall any person be subject for the same offense to be twice put in jeopardy of life or limb; nor shall be compelled in any criminal case to be a witness against himself, nor be deprived of life, liberty, or property, without due process of law; nor shall private property be taken for public use, without just compensation.

SIXTH AMENDMENT

In all criminal prosecutions, the accused shall enjoy the right to a speedy and public trial, by an impartial jury of the State and district wherein the crime shall have been committed, which district shall have been previously ascertained by law, and to be informed of the nature and cause of the accusation; to be confronted with the witnesses against him; to have compulsory process for obtaining witnesses in his favor, and to have the assistance of Counsel for his defense.

FOURTEENTH AMENDMENT (Ratified June 13, 1868) Section 1

All persons born or naturalized in the United States, and subject to the jurisdiction thereof, are citizens of the United States and of the state wherein they reside. No state shall make or enforce any law which shall abridge the privilege or immunities of citizens of the United States, nor shall any state deprive any person of life, liberty, or property, without due process of law; nor deny to any person within its jurisdiction the equal protection of the laws.

Burr v. U.S.

Aaron Burr
v.
The United States of America

Docket No. 14692g
25 Fed. Cas. 49 (1807)

Background

Unlike all other cases in this book, the Burr decision did not come to the United States Supreme Court through an appeal from a lower court. Rather, it constitutes a decision by Chief Justice John Marshall in his role as judge in a circuit court of original jurisdiction, a role assigned to him by the Judiciary Act of 1789. Yet, without doubt, Marshall's rulings on a pretrial motion in this case are commonly considered the first constitutionally important statements defining impartial jurors.

No one would question the assertion that the early post-Revolutionary American legal establishment, such as it was, based its notion of an impartial jury on William Blackstone's revisions of Sir Edward Coke's seminal definition in *The First Part of the Institutes of the Laws of England, or A Commentary upon Littleton, not the Name of the Author only, but of the Law Itself* (1656). By the beginning of the nineteenth century, Coke's definitive work was in its thirteenth edition. To understand the background of Marshall's rulings, therefore, it is necessary first to look at Coke and Blackstone.

Coke, in section 234 of what is popularly known as *Coke upon Littleton*, says an impartial juror has three "properties":

> First, he ought to bee dwelling most neere to the place where the question is moved. Secondly, he ought to bee most sufficient both for understanding, and competencie of estate. Thirdly, he ought to bee least suspicious, that is, to be indifferent as he stands unsworne: and then hee is accounted in the law *liber et legalis homo*; otherwise he may be challenged, and not suffered to be sworn. (156A)

The most famous of these conditions Coke repeats twice in section 234: "He that is of a jury, must be . . . also one that has such freedome of mind as he stands indifferent as hee stands unsworn" (155B).

The great seventeenth century jurist goes on to explain that a jury or individual prospective jurors perceived to be "unindifferent" can be challenged. He writes this of a challenge to the entire list of prospective jurors, "The challenge to the array is in respect of the cause of unindifferencie or default in the sherife or other officer that made the returne, and not in respect of the person returned" (156B, 157A). In other words, a challenge to the jury as a whole consists of questioning the procedure used by the sheriff to round up persons for jury duty. If the sheriff correctly follows the legal procedure—and the procedure as described by Coke is fairly complex, but precise—then a challenge to the jury as a whole cannot be upheld. Only if the sheriff fails to follow the correct procedure in some respect (by, for example, finding potential jurors living too distant from the location of the trial) could the jury as a whole be rejected as not legally constituted.

More relevant to the Burr case is what Coke and, later, Blackstone call a challenge to the polls; that is, a challenge to a particular juror. The first kind of challenge to an individual juror Coke terms "peremptorie." Of it he writes, "This is so called because he [the defendant] may challenge peremptorily upon his owne dislike, without shewing of any cause" (157A).

Perhaps in part because Coke was describing challenges in civil cases (like those between a landlord and a tenant), Blackstone expands upon the definition of a peremptory challenge when used in a criminal case. He writes in *Commentaries on the Laws of England in Four Books*:

> But in criminal cases, or at least in capital ones, there is, *in favorem vitae* (from a regard to life), allowed to the prisoner an arbitrary and capricious species of challenge to a certain number of jurors, without showing any cause at all; which is called a *peremptory* challenge: a provision full of that tenderness and humanity to prisoners for which our English laws are justly famous. This is grounded on two reasons. 1. As every one must be sensible, what sudden impressions and unaccountable prejudices we are apt to conceive upon the bare looks and gestures of another; and how necessary it is, that a prisoner (when put to defend his life) should have a good opinion of his jury, the want of which might totally disconcert him; the law wills not that he should be tried by any one man against whom he has conceived a prejudice, even without being able to assign a reason for such his dislike. 2. Because upon challenges for cause shown, if the reason assigned prove insufficient to set aside the juror, perhaps the bare questioning his indifference may sometimes provoke a resentment; to prevent all ill consequences from which the prisoner is still at liberty, if he pleases, peremptorily to set him aside. (IV, 353)

In other words, defendants are allowed to reject capriciously a potential juror. Blackstone gives two reasons for allowing such whimsical objections. The first is that "the bare looks and gestures of" potential jurors could make them appear hostile to a defendant. Since it is extremely important that defendants feel the jury is truly objective and not made up of persons prejudiced against them, Blackstone explains that defendants should be allowed to reject a certain number of potential jurors purely on the basis of speculation. To preclude the defense from never bringing the case to trial by issuing a never-ending series of peremptory challenges, Blackstone points out that a limit properly is placed on the number of such challenges.

The second reason Blackstone gives for allowing peremptory challenges is the danger of alienating jurors who have been unsuccessfully challenged for such insubstantial reasons. For example, a judge very well might reject the defense's challenge of a juror based on the sole reason that the juror's manner of dress makes it likely that this person would not be sympathetic to the defendant. In this situation, the unsuccessfully challenged juror might resent being challenged for such a trivial reason and so be more likely to arrive at a guilty verdict. Therefore, allowing defendants to reject potential jurors without giving a reason enables the defense to avoid alienating jurors unsuccessfully challenged for what these jurors might perceive to be a personal affront.

A second type of challenge to the polls—that is, to individual jurors—Coke calls "principall" because, "If it be found true, it standeth sufficient of it selfe without leaving any thing to the conscience or discretion of the triors" (157A). Under this category Coke lists what he calls "four heads," the third of which is most relevant to the Burr case and to twentieth century notions of an impartial juror. Coke calls this third type "affection or partialitie," and he lists two forms of it: "either by judgment of law without any act of his, or by judgment of law upon his owne act" (157B). Being a relative of the defendant is the most common example of what Coke calls "by judgment of law without any act of his [that is, without an act by the potential juror]" (157B). The learned jurist then gives two examples of "judgment of law upon his owne act" (157B). One consists of a person who was previously a juror in a case that was later reversed and is now being tried again; another consists of potential jurors who allow the defendant to buy them lunch. These are called principal challenges, says Coke, because the partiality of the potential jurors is clear to all. Thus, there is no need for the judge to determine whether or not favoritism or partiality toward the defendant is present; favoritism can be assumed when such "principalls" are involved.

What Coke calls challenges based on "affection or partialitie," Blackstone terms "*Challenge for prejudice.*—Jurors may be challenged *propter affectum*, for suspicion of bias or partiality" (III, 363). Like Coke, Blackstone divides this type of challenge into two forms, and he lists the same two illustrations as Coke. Of the first form he writes:

> A *principal* challenge is such, where the cause assigned carries with it
> *prima facie* evident [Coke's spelling] marks of suspicion, either of

malice or favour: as, that a juror is of kin to either party within the ninth degree; that he has been arbitrator on either side . . . : all these are principal causes of challenge; which, if true, cannot be overruled, for jurors must be *omni exceptione majores* (above all exception). (III, 363)

In short, Blackstone follows Coke in asserting that one form of challenge based on prejudice is distinguished by the fact that the bias is obvious. That is, the bias is so clear to both the defense and the prosecution that there is no need for the trial judge to rule officially whether or not bias is present; it is simply assumed to be present by all parties. The most common example of such bias is found in the bond between family members. A mother, for example, would probably be thought by all concerned parties to favor the defendant if her son or daughter were that defendant.

When favoritism is not so obvious, a challenge based on "affection or partialitie" is called a "challenge to the favour"; that is, a challenge based on an assertion that a potential juror too strongly favors or does not favor the defendant, what Coke calls "expressed favour or expressed malice" (157B). He describes the challenge as, "Challenge concluding to the favour, when either partie cannot take any principall challenge, but sheweth causes of favour, which must be left to the conscience and discretion of the triors upon hearing their evidence to find him favourable or not favourable" (158A).

Blackstone accepts Coke's notion of challenges *to the favour*. He describes them as objections to "some probable circumstances of suspicion, as acquaintance, and the like; the validity of which must be left to the determination of *triors*, whose office is to decide whether the juror be favourable or unfavourable" (III, 363). (He explains the complex process for selecting the triors, a process that has since been dropped and so is not relevant to a contemporary notion of an impartial jury.) Coke says "the causes of favour" are infinite, but a simple example of "circumstances of . . . acquaintance" would be a neighbor. A neighbor might prejudicially favor or disfavor the defendant. The existence of prejudicial favoritism and, if it exists, whether it favors or disfavors the defendant is not necessarily clear from the mere fact that a potential juror is a neighbor of the defendant. Some neighbors are closer than others. A trial judge, after questioning of the neighbor is complete, would be required in this example to rule officially whether this potential juror expressed prejudicial favor for or against the defendant.

Circumstances

The origins of Aaron Burr's trial for treason can be traced to his service in the Revolutionary War when he met, while serving on Benedict Arnold's staff, General James Wilkinson, who later was to betray him.

Another relevant event occurred when Alexander Hamilton, a long-time professional and political rival, made derogatory remarks about Burr during their hotly contended gubernatorial campaign in New York. Burr subsequently challenged Hamilton to a duel and eventually used a pistol to fatally wound his rival at Weehawken, New Jersey, on July 11, 1804.

Fleeing first to Philadelphia, Burr developed with Jonathan Dayton, former U.S. senator from New Jersey, his plans for what was described by his enemies to be a new empire. These plans were complex and ever-changing, but, at bottom, they involved the creation of a political area that included Mexico and much of the U.S. territory west of the Allegheny River.

Soon a coroner's inquest in New York declared Burr guilty of the murder of Alexander Hamilton, and a warrant was issued for his arrest. Upon hearing of the warrant, Burr went to see his daughter in South Carolina and later traveled to Washington where he presided in 1805 over the United States Senate during the last session of his term as vice president. There is no little irony in the fact that, during this session, Justice Samuel Chase of the Supreme Court was tried on articles of impeachment referred from the House of Representatives.

When his term ended, Burr undertook a western trip in order to evaluate the feasibility of his plans for a new empire. During his personal reconnaissance, he visited Wilkinson, now governor of the Louisiana Territory, and purchased more than a million acres of land there. When preparations were under way to go to Mexico, suspicions of treason began to grow. To stop the rumors, Burr hired Henry Clay, who twice cleared him in court of treasonable intent.

Then Wilkinson betrayed Burr in a letter to President Thomas Jefferson, who, thanks to the influence of Burr's New York rival Hamilton, narrowly beat the colonel in the electoral college on the 36th ballot. Eventually Burr was arraigned (for the fourth time) in Richmond, Virginia, and indicted (for the first time) for treason on June 24, 1807. Tried before Chief Justice John Marshall, Burr was acquitted on September 1.

The attorneys for both sides represented a virtual who's who of the time. Officially leading the prosecution was George Hay, U.S. attorney for the district of Virginia, son-in-law of soon-to-be president Monroe, and considered a firm supporter of Jefferson. (Many early scholars and trial observers thought that Jefferson was dictating the prosecution's strategy.) Hay was assisted, among others, by Alexander McRae, lieutenant governor of Virginia.

The defense was led ostensibly by Burr himself. His main attorney was Edmund Randolph, member of the former Continental Congress during the revolution, attorney general and secretary of state under George Washington, and governor and attorney general of Virginia. He was assisted, among others, by Luther Martin of Maryland, who previously had defended Judge Chase. Interestingly, Martin was described by observers as having a great memory, but he was considered coarse, ungrammatical, disorganized, and a drinker. He also possessed a speech defect that caused him to slobber.

Summary of the Court's Analysis

Not surprisingly, the trial was long and complex, but Marshall's rulings related to an impartial jury (recorded in a separate section) are clear and decisive. The trial itself is recorded in the section numbered 14,693. Special motions are dealt with in sections numbered 14,962a through 14,962h. Number 14,962g focuses on the concept of an impartial juror.

Marshall directs his words at the outset in 14,962g to the basic notion of what constitutes an impartial jury:

> The great value of the trial by jury certainly consists in its fairness and impartiality.
>
> I have always conceived, and still conceive, an impartial jury as required by the common law, and as secured by the constitution, must be composed of men who will fairly hear the testimony which may be offered to them, and bring in their verdict according to that testimony, and according to the law arising on it. This is not to be expected, certainly the law does not expect it, where the jurors, before they hear the testimony, have deliberately formed and delivered an opinion that the person whom they are to try is guilty or innocent of the charge alleged against him. The jury should enter upon the trial with minds open to those impressions which the testimony and the law of the case ought to make, not with those preconceived opinions which will resist those impressions. (50)

Here, Marshall simply outlines the generally accepted notions of the day, inherited for the most part from Coke and later Blackstone, that one prerequisite of an impartial juror is the possession of a mind open enough to be able to arrive at a verdict based solely on the evidence presented in court.

Echoing Coke and Blackstone, Marshall then goes on to point out that the reason relatives are not allowed to serve on a jury is that they can be presumed to have an insufficiently open mind upon entering the jury box so that they would be unable to base their verdict only upon the admissible testimony of witnesses. Instead, they would be perceived as basing their verdict on prior knowledge of the defendant.

Marshall focuses next on the value of juror avowals that they can render an unbiased verdict:

> It is admitted that where there are strong personal prejudices, the person entertaining them is incapacitated as a juror, but it is denied that

fixed opinions respecting his guilt constitute a similar incapacity. Why do a person's prejudices constitute a just cause of challenge? Solely because the individual who is under their influence is presumed to have a bias on his mind which will prevent an impartial decision of the case, according to the testimony. He may declare that notwithstanding these prejudices he is determined to listen to the evidence, and be governed by it; but the law will not trust him. Is there less reason to suspect him who has prejudged the case, and has deliberately formed and delivered an opinion upon it? Such a person may believe that he will be regulated by testimony, but the law suspects him, and certainly not without reason. He will listen with more favor to that testimony which confirms, than to that which would change his opinion; it is not to be expected that he will weigh evidence or argument as fairly as a man whose judgment is not made up in the case. (50)

Marshall expounds here upon an essential point—not addressed by Coke or Blackstone—that will occupy the Court's attention for the next century and a half. That point is determining the weight that should be given to jurors' assertions under oath that they can set aside any opinions of guilt or innocence brought with them to the jury box, and that they can arrive at a verdict based solely on evidence presented in court.

This next paragraph contains the most widely quoted words relating to the definition of an impartial jury:

Were it possible to obtain a jury without any prepossessions whatever respecting the guilt or innocence of the accused, it would be extremely desirable to obtain such a jury; but this is perhaps impossible, and therefore will not be required. The opinion which has been avowed by the court is, that light impressions which may fairly be supposed to yield to the testimony that may be offered, which may leave the mind open to a fair consideration of that testimony, constitute no sufficient objection to a juror; but that those strong and deep impressions which will close the mind against the testimony that may be offered in opposition to them, which will combat that testimony, and resist its force, do constitute a sufficient objection to him. Those who try the impartiality of a juror ought to test him by this rule. They ought to hear the statement made by himself or given by others, and conscientiously determine, according to their best judgment, whether in general men under such circumstances ought to be considered as capable of hearing fairly, and of deciding impartially, on the testimony which may be offered to them, or as possessing minds in a situation to struggle against the conviction which that testimony might be calculated to produce. The court had considered those who have deliberately formed and delivered an opinion on the guilt of the prisoner as not being in a state of mind fairly to weigh the testimony, and therefore as being disqualified to serve as jurors in the case. (50, 51)

Here Marshall presents his famous distinction between an acceptably impartial juror, who holds only "light impressions," and a biased juror, who holds "those strong and deep impressions which will close the mind against the testimony that may be offered in opposition to them, which will combat that testimony, and resist its force" (51). It is not unimportant to note here Marshall's focus on a juror's expression of an opinion formed before the trial. It is the content of this expression, not jurors' sworn avowals about their own open-mindedness, says Marshall, that the court is to consider when determining the impartiality of jurors.

Next Marshall takes up a somewhat technical legal question: What proportion or what segment of the case must jurors hold a firm opinion about before they are considered unconstitutionally biased? He writes, "The question now to be decided is whether an opinion formed and delivered, not upon the full case, but upon an essential part of it, not that the prisoner is absolutely guilty of the whole crime charged in the indictment, but that he is guilty in some of those great points which constitute it, does also disqualify a man in the sense of the law and of the constitution from being an impartial juror" (51).

Marshall answers his own question in general terms as follows:

> It would seem to the court that to say that any man who had formed an opinion on any fact conducive to the final decision of the case would therefore be considered as disqualified from serving on the jury, would exclude intelligent and observing men, whose minds were really in a situation to decide upon the whole case according to the testimony, and would perhaps be applying the letter of the rule requir-ing an impartial jury with a strictness which is not necessary for the preservation of the rule itself. But if the opinion formed be on a point so essential as to go far towards a decision of the whole case, and to have a real influence on the verdict to be rendered, the distinction between a person who has formed such an opinion and one who has in his mind decided the whole case appears too slight to furnish the court with solid ground for distinguishing between them. The questions must always depend on the strength and nature of the opinion which has been formed. (51)

Having set forth his general ideas about what constitutes an impartial juror, Marshall now applies these concepts to the case at hand:

> In the case now under consideration, the court would perhaps not consider it as a sufficient objection to a juror that he did believe, and had said, that the prisoner at a time considerably anterior to the fact charged in the indictment entertained treasonable designs against the United States. He may have formed this opinion, and be undecided on the question whether those designs were abandoned or prosecuted up to the time when the indictment charges the overt act to have been committed. On this point his mind may be open to the testimony.

Although it would be desirable that no juror should have formed and delivered such an opinion, yet the court is inclined to think it would not constitute sufficient cause of challenge. But if the juror have made up and declared the opinion that to the time when the fact laid in the indictment is said to have been committed the prisoner was prosecuting the treasonable design with which he is charged, the court considers the opinion as furnishing just cause of challenge, and cannot view the juror who has formed and delivered it as impartial, in the legal and constitutional sense of that term. (51)

In essence, Marshall says the determining factor in this case is chronology; that is, the essential question focuses on whether jurors hold the opinion that Burr's treasonous acts took place only before—and not also after—those actions described in the indictment.

In an attempt to make his point here a bit clearer and to, in part, call in the support of precedent, Marshall refers to the libel case that brought Justice Chase to impeachment, the case of *Callender* v. *U.S., 25 Fed. Cas. 239 (1800), number 14,709:*

With respect to the general question put in Callender's Case, the court considers it as the same with the general question put in this case. It was, "Have you made up and delivered the opinion that the prisoner is guilty or innocent of the charge laid in the indictment? . . . [I]n this case the opinion is formed on report and newspaper publications. (52)

According to Marshall, Chase, in the Callender case, said the jury can consider only the possible libel by James Thompson Callender that appears in the book in question (named *The Prospect Before Us*) and not other possible libelous statements Callender may have made before he wrote the tract. Likewise, the jury in the Burr case, said Marshall, can consider the possible treasonous character of only those acts mentioned in the indictment and of the actions he may have taken earlier, such as serving with Benedict Arnold.

A brief look at the arguments put forth by Burr's attorneys provides a helpful context for understanding Marshall's comments about a challenge to the array. The court reporter presents this summary of Martin's arguments:

Mr. Martin . . . insisted that the constitutional guaranty that every criminal shall be tried by an "impartial jury," required that the jurors should be perfectly indifferent and free from prejudice. He enforced with much power the position that a man who had formed an opinion as to the criminal intention of the accused, although not as to the act, could not be considered an impartial juror. He argued that Colonel Burr was not to be [i.e., should not be] denied a fair trial because the public mind has been so filled with prejudice against him that there was some difficulty in finding impartial jurors. He referred to the inflammatory article which had been published against colonel Burr in the

Alexandria Expositor and other newspapers, and inquired if he was to be held responsible for such publications. (49)

When taking up a challenge to the array, Marshall refers to two special periods of Scottish rebellion against the English. The first is the Jacobite revolution in 1715, when James Edward Stuart, known as the Old Pretender, led an unsuccessful rebellion against English rule. The second, in 1745, was led by his son Charles, known as the Young Pretender to his enemies and as Bonnie Prince Charles to his supporters in Scotland.

About the difference in difficulty between obtaining impartial juries during times of revolution and obtaining them in the face of widespread newspaper reports, Marshall writes:

> The argument drawn from the situation of England during the rebellions of 1715 and 1745, with respect to certain prominent characters whose situations made it a matter of universal notoriety that they were the objects of the law, is founded entirely on the absolute necessity of the case, and the total and obvious impossibility of obtaining a jury whose minds were not already made up. Where this necessity exists the rule perhaps must bend to it, but the rule will bend no further than is required by actual necessity. The court cannot believe that at present the necessity does exist. The cases bear no resemblance to each other. There has not been such open, notorious war as to force conviction on every bosom respecting the fact and intention. It is believed that a jury may be obtained composed of men who, whatever their general impressions may be, have not deliberately formed and delivered an opinion respecting the guilt or innocence of the accused. (52)

Here Marshall touches upon an issue that will become central to twentieth century solutions for guaranteeing an impartial jury: Can an event or a crime be so infamous that nearly every person in a given geographical area would have a prejudice against whomever is put on trial? In the last part of the nineteenth century, the notion of what was later termed *an infectious prejudice* was unequivocally rejected. When it was reconsidered in the middle of the twentieth century, however, this notion found great support in the Court.

Ruling

In the end, Marshall's ruling was very narrow and clearly congruent with the general law of the day:

> The opinion of the court is that to have made up and delivered the opinion that the prisoner entertained the treasonable designs with which he is charged, and that he retained those designs and was prosecuting

them when the act charged in the indictment is alleged to have been committed, is good cause of challenge. (52)

Significance

More than one phrase in Marshall's ruling is important. The first is that potential jurors who have "made up" their "opinion" before the trial started can be challenged successfully. By "made up" Marshall meant that the opinions held are so powerful that "the individual who is under their influence is presumed to have a bias on his mind which will prevent an impartial decision of the case, according to the testimony" (50). He described these thoughts as "[s]trong and deep impressions which close the mind against the testimony that may be offered in opposition to them, which will combat that testimony and resist its force" (51).

In contrast, impartial jurors who have not "made up" their minds could be defined, he said, as free from the dominating influence of knowledge acquired outside the courtroom. The key to his definition is the word *dominate*. Marshall indicated that jurors can be impartial if their thoughts based on information gathered outside the courtroom are free from "strong and deep impressions that close the mind" (50). He describes constitutionally acceptable thoughts formed before the trial as "light impressions . . . [that] may fairly be supposed to yield to the testimony that may be offered" (50). These thoughts "leave the mind open to a fair consideration of the testimony" and "constitute no sufficient objection to a juror" (50).

In short, Marshall said that some thoughts formed prior to the trial unconstitutionally prejudice a juror; others do not. He seems to label *opinions* unconstitutional and *impressions* constitutional. Marshall asserted that once formed, an opinion reached before the trial so dominates that it cannot be changed by evidence introduced in court. Impressions formed before the trial, contrarily, are so lightly held that they are quite capable of being changed by courtroom evidence. Thus, the essential distinction is the strength of pretrial thoughts as measured by their resistance to change when exposed to evidence and testimony introduced in court.

It was common practice then for courts to determine whether or not potential jurors were unconstitutionally prejudiced simply by asking them whether or not any opinions they may have formed would prevent them from rendering a verdict based solely on the evidence presented in court. Those who said yes could serve; those who said no could not.

This practice does not conform to Marshall's ruling. He asserted that even though a person "may declare that notwithstanding these prejudices he is determined to listen to the evidence, and be governed by it . . . the law will not trust him" (50). He writes, "Those who try the impartiality of a juror ought to test him by this rule. They ought to hear the statement made by himself or given by others, and conscientiously determine, according to their best judgment, whether in general men under such circumstances ought to be considered as capable of hearing fairly, and of deciding impartially, on the testimony which may be offered to them, or as possessing minds in a situation to struggle against the conviction which that testimony might be calculated to produce" (51). Thus Marshall felt that the trial judge should, through close questioning, evaluate the sincerity of statements by persons who avowedly have formed thoughts about the guilt of an accused.

Another significant aspect of the ruling is Marshall's observation that potential jurors must have "delivered the opinion" they "made up" before they can be considered unconstitutionally impartial. Coke hints at this idea when he defines challenge based on favor as "expressed favor or expressed malice." In addition to Coke's phrase, though, the insistence on expression seems to be accounted for by at least two other reasons. First, thoughts are considered lightly held until they are expressed, at which point they become opinions. The theory behind this notion is that if thoughts are important, then they will be expressed. If they are not important, then they fail to result in expression. Thus, once expressed, thoughts become, *ipso facto*, opinions too strong to resist being changed solely by evidence introduced in a courtroom.

Another reason for insistence on expression is that an opinion may not be capable of being known unless it is expressed. Marshall's assertions appear to support this notion. If persons who hold unconstitutional opinions fail to express them, then it may be impossible for the trial judge to know of these opinions and so evaluate their constitutionality. Persons who express their opinions, however, make it possible for the trial judge to evaluate their strength and so their constitutionality.

Finally, the last words of Marshall's ruling are significant. He points out that the opinions of potential jurors in this case are not unconstitutional unless these persons formed and expressed the opinion that the accused "entertained the treasonable designs with which he is charged, and that he retained those designs and was prosecuting them when the act charged in the indictment is alleged to have been committed" (51). The significance of these words is related not to the depth of thoughts held but to their comprehensiveness. The focus here is on what portions of the defendant's actions have potential jurors formed opinions about. To be unconstitutional, Marshall says, the opinions must be of the precise acts the indictment accuses the defendant of engaging in or of acts that substantially amount to the same thing.

Reid v. U.S.

The United States
v.
Thomas Reid and Edward Clements

53 U.S. 361, 13 L.Ed. 1023, 12 Howard 361 (1851)

Background

In the landmark case *Barron* v. *Baltimore* (1833), the Court ruled that the first ten amendments to the United States Constitution do not limit the power of the states. The Court wrote, "Had the framers of these [ten] amendments intended them to be limitations on the powers of the State governments they would have imitated the framers of the original Constitution and have expressed that intention" (250). Because most criminal statutes were passed by state legislatures, it is not surprising that for about its first sixty years of existence the Court found no opportunity to address the conflict between the First and Sixth Amendments.

In fact, *Reid* represents the first time the Court evaluated the impact on a fair trial of jurors reading a newspaper story about some aspect of a trial they were part of. It is an inauspicious beginning. The Court only reluctantly addressed the issue, declining to set down a "general rule." Yet, with some reticence, the justices did "receive" the sworn word of jurors saying the newspaper article did not influence their verdict. The importance of receiving these affidavits is tempered, however, by the Court's assertion that there was nothing substantive in the newspaper article that would have influenced these jurors' decision even if they did, in fact, read it as they swore in the affidavits that they did.

It would appear that the Court eventually was able to muster enough courage to suggest that two conditions may be worthy of consideration when contemplating denying a request for a new trial on the basis that one or more jurors had read a newspaper account of at least part of the original trial. The first condition is whether the content of the newspaper article about the trial is such that it would not influence the jurors' opinions even if they did read it. The second is whether the jurors are willing to swear that reading the information did not influence their verdict.

The amount of attention the justices gave to this point should not go unnoticed. Although the Court conducted a fairly substantial investigation into the background of a separate issue in this case, it based its ruling on the question of juror prejudice solely on its own cursory analysis of the facts. Indeed, it was not until twenty-seven years later that the Court would undertake any sort of historical analysis as a basis for its opinion on juror prejudice.

Circumstances

Thomas Reid and Edward Clements were tried separately for shooting and stabbing to death John Heeney while on the American ship *J. B. Lindsey*. The first count charged by the grand jury said the two men on January 29, 1850, "not having the fear of God before their eyes, but being moved and seduced by the instigation of the devil, . . . with force and arms . . . piratically, feloniously, willfully, and of their malice and aforethought did . . . strike, penetrate, and wound said John Heeney . . . one mortal wound of the depth of four inches, and of the breadth of half an inch."

A jury found Reid guilty on December 17, and on December 23 he was sentenced to be executed on January 31, 1851. On January 14, Reid moved on two grounds for a new trial. The first was that he was not allowed to call as a witness Clements, who was declared incompetent (that is, the law did not permit Clements to testify because he was being tried for the same crime as Reid). The second ground was juror prejudice. In particular, Reid objected to two jurors, each of whom had read a newspaper account about certain aspects of the trial.

The first juror, after being selected, read an article in a newspaper his relatives brought to him. The newspaper originated from his place of employment where he had received it each day as a subscriber. It contained an account of evidence being introduced into the trial. This juror said in a voluntary affidavit that he at first read only part of the report. Later, during deliberations, he took the paper out of his pocket and read the whole story. He also said he read the story out of curiosity, only to see if it was accurate and to refresh his memory. Eventually, he concluded it was indeed accurate but said it did not influence his verdict because he had made up his mind before he read it the second time.

The second juror said he read the newspaper in the courtroom after being sworn. He said he looked at only a few sentences before concluding that it was not an accurate report. He also said it "had not the slightest influence on his judgement" (361). Neither juror discussed the newspaper article with the others on the panel.

Summary of the Court's Analysis

Chief Justice Roger B. Taney writes for the Court.
Justices John McLean, James M. Wayne, John Catron,
John McKinley, Peter V. Daniel, Samuel Nelson,
Robert C. Grier, and Benjamin R. Curtis join.

Chief Justice Taney devotes a great majority of his words to the issue of whether or not Clements, who also was accused of the same murder, should be permitted to be a witness for Reid. At the time, federal rules of evidence said persons jointly indicted cannot be witnesses for each other. This aspect of the opinion concerns an apparent conflict between the Judiciary Act of 1789 and a Virginia statute of 1849 asserting that a person on trial for a crime cannot be forbidden to call as a witness another person who is a joint defendant.

The apparent conflict is reconciled in two ways. First, Taney says the Virginia law applies only to civil, not criminal, cases. Second, after a long historical analysis going back to Coke, the Chief Justice states, "No law of a state made since 1789 can affect the mode of proceedings or the rules of evidence in criminal cases; and the testimony of Clements was therefore properly rejected, and furnished no ground for a new trial" (366).

The issue of juror prejudice is dealt with much more quickly by the Court. The question it addresses is simply whether or not the two jurors' voluntary affidavits, which Taney feels would impeach their verdict, should be received as evidence of prejudice. He asserts that it is not necessary to answer this question because, even if the testimony in the affidavits were true, it is not sufficient grounds for ordering a new trial. He writes, "There was nothing in the newspapers calculated to influence their [the two jurors'] decisions, and both of them swear that these papers had not the slightest influence on their verdict" (366).

Ruling

Taney writes:

It is the opinion of this court, 1st. That the . . . refusal of the court to admit his [Clements'] testimony does not entitle the prisoner [Reid] to a new trial; and 2d. That the facts stated in the affidavits of the jurors do not entitle the prisoner to a new trial. Whereupon it is now here ordered and adjudged by this court, that it be so certified to the said Circuit Court [of the United States for the Eastern District of Virginia]. (367)

Significance

At first the Court's words appear to be rather insignificant because the justices appear uncomfortable addressing the issue of juror prejudice resulting from reading extra-trial information. Seen in the light thrown by later cases, however, this one takes on some significance because the Court felt it necessary to mention two items: (1) the jurors swore the newspaper did not influence their verdict, and (2) the content of the news story about the trial did not contain material that could unconstitutionally prejudice the jurors.

The Court's willingness to give mere notice of the sworn word presented by jurors takes on added significance in the very next case to consider this issue, *Reynolds* v. *U.S.* (1878), even though the opinion of that case is not delivered until twenty-seven years later. Indeed, the significance of the decision simply to acknowledge the affidavits becomes clear when one considers the historical fact that for several decades afterward the Court accepted as sufficient evidence of no unconstitutional prejudice what trial courts judged to be a juror's honest assertion of impartiality.

The Court's other point related to extra-trial publicity received little attention for nearly a century. Nineteenth century courts chose not to evaluate the content of newspaper articles as a basis for determining whether or not the articles would prejudice unconstitutionally a juror. As the jurors' sworn word by itself became less and less authoritative in the twentieth century, however, the courts did begin to consider the content of the information available to all prospective jurors and of the news stories read by individual jurors. An excellent, if somewhat brief, historical review of this point can be found in *Mu'Min* v. *Virginia* (1991).

The Court's notice that the *Reid* jurors did not discuss their reading of the newspaper article with others on the panel is worth a short comment. The fact there was no discussion is pointed out by the Court as evidence that no other jurors were exposed to the newspaper article describing the admission of evidence into the trial, and so the other jurors were thought free from whatever taint may have resulted from such reading.

Reynolds v. U.S.

George Reynolds

v.

United States

Docket No. 1878-180
98 U.S. 145, 25 L.Ed. 244, 8 Otto 10 (1878)

Motion submitted February 13, 1878. Decided February 18, 1878.
Argued November 14, 15, 1878. Re-decided January 4, 1879.
Modified May 5, 1879.

Background

Reynolds v. *U.S.* contains the Court's first historical analysis of what constitutes an impartial juror and the very first guidelines governing the process for determining the constitutionality of a juror's opinion about the guilt or innocence of an accused. In *Reid* v. *U.S.* (1851) the Court only reluctantly addressed this issue, declining to set down a "general rule." Therefore, before *Reynolds,* the primary guidance from the Supreme Court came from Chief Justice John Marshall's ruling seventy years earlier in his role as judge in a circuit court of original jurisdiction, a role assigned to him by the Judiciary Act of 1789.

Marshall asserted that the trial judge must not take the word of prospective jurors that they have not formed an unconstitutional opinion about the accused's guilt. Instead, he said the judge should "test" jurors' assertions of impartiality by asking them to declare their lack of bias in court and then evaluating firsthand the truth of their statements. Thus Marshall felt that the trial judge should, through close questioning, evaluate the sincerity of statements by persons who had avowedly formed thoughts about the guilt of an accused.

Marshall also felt that prospective jurors must have "delivered the opinion" they "made up" before they could be considered unconstitutionally impartial. Chief Justice Morrison R. Waite noted that, while unexpressed opinions tend to indicate opinions that are lightly held, at times, unconstitutionally strong opinions do remain unexpressed by a juror.

The primary focus of the case, however, was not jury prejudice but religion. George Reynolds, personal secretary to Brigham Young, asked the Court to assert that Mormon polygamy was protected by the free exercise clause of the First Amendment. He challenged the constitutionality of a section of the Morrill (or Land Grant) Act passed by the United States Congress in 1862. Although best known for establishing land grant colleges, the Morrill Act also outlawed polygamy. The relevant section reads: "Every person having a husband or wife living, who shall marry any other persons . . . in a Territory of the United States . . . shall . . . be adjudged guilty of bigamy" (Act of 1 July 1862, Sec. 1, 12 Stat. 501). Reynolds was testing this act.

Circumstances

Nine years after marrying Mary Ann Tuddenham, on July 22, 1865, at the close of the Civil War, George Reynolds married Amelia Jane Schofield on August 3, 1874, without first divorcing Tuddenham. In October 1874, he was convicted of bigamy by the District Court of the Third District of the Territory of Utah. He said he married a second time because, as a member of the Church of Jesus Christ of Latter-Day Saints (the Mormon Church), it was his religious duty, and he saw no immorality in polygamy. He also said he received permission from "recognized authorities in the church." He challenged the conviction on several grounds, one of which was a prejudiced jury.

Summary of the Court's Analysis

Chief Justice Morrison R. Waite writes for the Court.
Justices Nathan Clifford, Samuel F. Miller, William Strong,
Ward Hunt, Noah H. Swayne, Stephen J. Field, Joseph P. Bradley,
and John Marshall Harlan join.

Waite lists six questions into which he says the "assignments of error" can be grouped. The second and third are the most relevant to a conflict between a free press and a fair trial.

(1) Was the indictment bad because found by a grand jury of less than sixteen persons?

(2) Were the challenges of certain petit jurors by the accused improperly overruled?

(3) Were the challenges of certain other jurors by the Government improperly sustained?

(4) Was the testimony of Amelia Jane Schofield given at a former trial for the same offense, but under another indictment, improperly admitted in evidence?

(5) Should the accused have been acquitted if he married the second time, because he believed it to be his religious duty?

(6) Did the court err in that part of the charge which directed the attention of the jury to the consequences of polygamy? (53)

Was the indictment bad because found by a grand jury of less than sixteen persons? The problem raised by the fifteen-member grand jury is simply whether an Act of Congress entitled "In Relation to Courts and Judicial Officers in the Territory of Utah," which was passed June 23, 1874 (18 Stat. at L. 253) and which did not specify a particular number of jurors, governs this case, or whether Section 808 of the Revised Federal Statutes, which specified a jury of no fewer than sixteen members, governs this case. Waite asserts that Section 808 regulated only circuit and district courts, not territorial courts, and so the Court affirms the fifteen-member grand jury.

Were the challenges of certain petit jurors by the accused improperly overruled? Waite begins his discussion of "the challenges of certain petit jurors" with two references: one to the Sixth Amendment's assertion of an accused's right to an "impartial jury" and another to Coke's famous statement that a juror must be as " 'indifferent as he stand sworn' " (154). One way to determine a prospective juror's impartiality, Waite notes, is examination "on his *voir dire*" (155).

The prospective jurors were all challenged here, according to the Court, "for principal cause"; that is, the jurors were challenged because they were felt to hold malice toward Reynolds. Waite says that a challenge based on a belief "that a juror has formed an opinion as to the issue to be tried" is on "good ground" (155). He notes that, although courts have not agreed about the "knowledge which the opinion must rest on in order to render the juror incompetent," and although they do not all agree that malice or ill will must be present, they do agree "it [a juror's opinion of the accused's guilt or innocence] must be founded on some evidence, and be more than a mere impression" (155). Among the descriptions of a firm opinion are "fixed," "positive," "decided and substantial," "deliberate and settled" (155). Contrarily, there is agreement, Waite says, that, if the opinion is merely "hypothetical," then the "partiality is not so manifest as to necessarily set the juror aside" (155).

After quoting Marshall's words from *Burr* (1807) about impartial jurors, Waite writes, "Every opinion which he [a juror] may entertain need not necessarily have that effect [of eliciting partiality]" (155). "In these days of newspaper enterprise and universal education, every case of public interest is almost, as a matter of necessity, brought to the attention of all the intelligent people in the vicinity, and scarcely any one can be found among those best fitted for jurors who has not read or heard of it, and who has not some impression or some opinion in respect to its merits" (155, 156).

Since most jurors will have formed some sort of opinion, the trial judge, writes Waite, "will practically be called upon to determine whether the nature and strength of the opinion formed are such in law necessarily to raise the presumption of partiality. The question thus presented is one of mixed law and fact" (156).

Once the judge makes these decisions, however, they are to be respected. Waite then pens the now-famous words, which set extremely important precedent, "The finding of the trial court upon that issue ought not to be set aside by a reviewing court, unless the error is manifest" (156). He adds, "It must be made clearly to appear upon the evidence the court ought to have found the juror had formed such an opinion that he could not in law be deemed impartial. The case must be one in which it is manifest the law left nothing to the 'conscience or discretion' of the court" (156).

Waite reviews the testimony given by the challenged juror, Charles Read, in this case and concludes:

> [T]aken as a whole, it [the evidence] shows that the juror "believed" he had formed an opinion which he had never expressed and which he did not think would influence his verdict on hearing the testimony. We cannot think this is such a manifestation of partiality as to leave nothing to the "conscience or discretion" of the triers. The reading of the evidence leaves the impression that the juror had some hypothetical opinion about the cases, but it falls far short of raising a manifest presumption of partiality. (156)

Waite points out that appeals courts should be mindful that jurors often try to use prejudice as an excuse for getting out of jury duty. Then he writes these words that influenced the courts for more than a century, "The manner of the juror while testifying is oftentimes more indicative of the real character of his opinion than his words" (156, 157). He continues:

> Care should, therefore, be taken in the reviewing court not to reverse the ruling below upon such a question of fact, except in a clear case. The affirmative of the issue is upon the challenger. Unless he shows the actual existence of such an opinion in the mind of the juror as will raise the presumption of partiality, the juror need not necessarily be set aside, and it will not be error in the court to refuse to do so. (157)

Before moving on to other issues, Waite comments on the fact that juror Read did not express his opinion. He writes, "The fact that he had not expressed his opinion is important only as tending to show that he had not formed one which disqualified him. If a positive and decided opinion had been formed, he would have been incompetent even though it had not been expressed" (157).

Were the challenges of certain other jurors by the Government improperly sustained?   The third question taken up by the Court is the validity of the trial court's dismissal of all prospective jurors who admitted they

were or had been living in polygamy. Reynolds did not challenge the government's right to determine the jurors' marital state; rather, he challenged only
the judge's ruling dismissing them because it was based on principle, not
favor. Coke, and later Blackstone, asserted that a challenge for principle is
distinguished by the fact that the bias is obvious—that is, prejudice is so clear
there is no need for the trial judge to justify its presence by questioning
prospective jurors; it is simply assumed to be present. The most common
example of such bias is the bond between family members.

When impartiality is not so obvious, however, then Coke and Blackstone
call this a challenge to the favor, namely, a challenge based on an assertion
that a prospective juror is too strongly favoring or not favoring the defendant—what Coke calls "expressed favor or expressed malice" (Coke 157B).
Coke, and Blackstone after him, provide that challenges to the favor are
given to "the conscience and discretion of the triors upon hearing their
evidence to find him [a prospective juror] favourable or not favourable"
(Coke 158A). United States law, Waite observes, does not provide for separate triers of challenges to favor. Instead, the judge is the trier for all
challenges. While the judge here may have upheld the challenge for principle
when he should have upheld it for favor, the mistake is not sufficient to
overrule the verdict because there did exist sufficient reason to believe a
challenge for favor would have been upheld.

Waite writes:

> It needs no argument to show that such a jury could not have gone
> into the box entirely free from bias and prejudice, and that if the
> challenge was not good for principal cause, it was good for favor. A
> judgment will not be reversed simply because a challenge good for favor
> was sustained for cause. As the jurors were incompetent and properly
> excluded, it matters not here upon what form of challenge they were set
> aside. (157)

In other words, the trial judge upheld the challenge for principle when
he should have upheld it for favor. Nevertheless, the judge's error is not
sufficient to reverse the verdict. Polygamy of prospective jurors, for instance,
constitutes sufficient evidence to support a challenge for favor, even if the
judge improperly based his ruling on principle. [See the "Circumstances"
section of *Hopt* v. *Utah* (1887), p. 31, for a relevant discussion of the differences between actual and implied prejudice.]

**Was the testimony of Amelia Jane Schofield given at a former trial
for the same offense, but under another indictment, improperly admitted in evidence?** Amelia Jane Schofield was Reynolds's second wife. She
had testified in an earlier case where he was also tried for polygamy. She was
subpoenaed to testify at this trial, but the sheriff was unable to find her. The
prosecutor, therefore, asked that her testimony from the previous trial be

admitted into evidence. Reynolds objected, citing his Sixth Amendment right to confront witnesses. Since the trial judge felt that Reynolds knew where she was but would not tell, he ruled that her testimony from the previous trial would be admitted. The Court agrees. Waite, after tracing the law to *Lord Marley's Case* (6 State Trials 770) in England in 1666, noted that Reynolds "had full opportunity to account for the absence of the witness . . . or to deny under oath that he had kept her away" (160). But he did not.

Should the accused have been acquitted if he married the second time, because he believed it to be his religious duty? The discussion of this question begins with the notion of criminal intent. Was there any criminal intent in Reynolds's act of marrying a second wife if he sincerely believed that he was fulfilling a religious obligation of his faith? Waite asserts that Reynolds's lack "of evil intent" or "of understanding on his part that he was committing a crime, did not excuse him" (162). Instead, his deliberate second marriage "implies" criminal intent.

Next the Court addresses the issue of separation of church and state. After a substantial discussion focusing for the most part on the framers of the Constitution, Waite concludes, "Congress was deprived [by the First Amendment] of all legislative power over mere opinion, but was left free to reach actions which were in violation of social duties subversive of good order" (164). Therefore, "In our opinion the statute immediately under consideration [forbidding polygamy] is within the legislative power of congress" (166).

"The only question which remains," Waite writes, "is whether those who make polygamy a part of their religion are excepted from the operation of the statute. If they are, then those who do not make polygamy a part of their religious belief may be found guilty and punished, while those who do must be acquitted and go free" (166). The Court cannot accept such a distinction, he asserts, because "to permit this would be to make the professed doctrines of religious belief superior to the law of the land, and in effect to permit every citizen to become a law unto himself" (167). Waite presents an example: "Suppose one believed that human sacrifice were a necessary part of religious worship, would it be seriously contended that the civil government under which he lived could not interfere to prevent a sacrifice?" (166).

Returning to the notion of criminal intent, Waite writes, "Every man is presumed to intend the necessary and legitimate consequences of what he knowingly does" (167). He ends the discussion of this point with these words: "When the offense consists of a positive act which is knowingly done, it would be dangerous to hold that the offender might escape punishment because he religiously believed the law which he had broken ought never to have been made" (167).

Did the court err in that part of the charge which directed the attention of the jury to the consequences of polygamy? Reynolds claimed that part of the judge's charge to the jury unconstitutionally appealed to the jurors' passions and prejudices. The trial judge's charge contained these words:

> You should consider what are to be the consequences to the innocent victims of this delusion. As this contest goes on, they multiply, and there are pure-minded women and children. . . . These are to be the sufferers; and as jurors fail to do their duty, and as these cases come up in the Territory of Utah, just so do these victims multiply and spread themselves over the land. (167, 168)

Of these words, Waite writes, "All the [trial] court did was to call the attention of the jury to the peculiar character of the crime for which the accused was on trial, and to remind them of the duty they had to perform. There was not appeal to the passions, no instigation of prejudice" (168).

Ruling

Waite writes, "Upon a careful consideration of the whole case, we are satisfied that no error was committed by the court below, *and the judgment is consequently affirmed* [Waite's emphasis]" (168).

Justice Stephen J. Field writes a concurring opinion.

Field's separate opinion concurs with the Court in every aspect but one. He feels that the testimony of Amelia Jane Schofield should not have been admitted because "a sufficient foundation" was not "laid for its introduction" (168).

(On the petition for rehearing, Reynolds asked that the sentence to imprisonment at hard labor be reduced only to imprisonment. The Court granted his request.)

Significance

Three parts of this ruling are particularly significant to understanding the conflict between a fair trial and a free press. The first is that not all opinions formed outside the courtroom—including those formed from reading a newspaper—necessarily make a juror incompetent or unconstitutionally prejudiced. Deep opinions do; light ones do not. The Court used Marshall's words when it said that light opinions are "hypothetical" and are defined as those that do not prevent the juror from rendering a verdict based solely on the evidence presented in court. Deep opinions, in contrast, are so strongly held that they resist pressures from the evidence to change. Worth mentioning are Waite's comments that unexpressed opinions tend to be indicative of lightly held ones, although he admitted that, at times, unconstitutionally strong opinions remained unexpressed by a juror.

The Court also stated unequivocally that prospective jurors who have formed an opinion about the guilt of the accused may be challenged. It said that while there exists no universal agreement about the "knowledge which the opinion must rest on in order to render a juror incompetent," there is widespread agreement that an unconstitutional juror's opinion of the accused's guilt "must be founded on some evidence, and be more than a mere impression" (155).

Second, the Court asserts the trial judge is best qualified to determine as a mixed question of fact and law whether a prospective juror is impartial because only this judge can observe the juror's "manner" or demeanor. Manner, Waite asserted, is often more important in determining the truth and strength of an opinion than is testimony. Appeals courts, therefore, can overrule only if a "clear" or "manifest" error was committed.

More than a century later, in *Patton* v. *Yount* (1984), the Court disagreed about the scope of these two questions and about the meaning of granting deference to a trial court's answers. Stevens in dissent asserted there that the question of fact is to be limited to a determination of whether the juror's testimony is true; the determination of how strongly an opinion is held, he said, is a matter of law. He also said only the trial court's finding of truth is due the deference of fact. The majority, however, said that the question of fact includes determining both the truthfulness and the depth of a juror's opinion; whereas the question of law centers upon applying the correct standard of impartiality. The deference to fact, according to the *Patton* Court, applies, therefore, to both the truthfulness and the depth of a prospective juror's opinion about the guilt of an accused.

Third, since a juror is to be presumed impartial, the burden of showing prejudice falls upon the challenger.

This case gains considerable significance because it set forth the first guidelines governing the process for determining a juror's partiality. The Court issued three primary sets of directions. The first is that not all opinions formed outside the courtroom are necessarily unconstitutionally prejudicial. Second, the trial judge is to determine juror impartiality as a matter of fact and law, and appeals courts can overrule only if a "clear" or "manifest" error was committed. Third, the presumed impartiality of a juror means the burden of showing prejudice rests upon the challenger.

Hopt v. Utah

Frederick Hopt

v.

People of the Territory of Utah

Docket No. 1887-1099

120 U.S. 430, 30 L.Ed 708, 7 S.Ct. 614 (1887)

Submitted January 21, 1887. Decided March 7, 1887.

Background

The Sixth Amendment guarantees defendants a fair trial by an impartial jury; it does not guarantee trial by unopinioned jurors. A distinction can be drawn between jurors who are unconstitutionally prejudiced against a defendant and jurors who merely hold an opinion that the defendant is guilty. This distinction is built on the premise that actual prejudice against a defendant is too strong to be overcome by evidence presented in court, but a mere opinion of guilt can be so "lightly" held that jurors could overcome their opinions after hearing courtroom evidence.

Who draws these distinctions in criminal trials and on what basis they are drawn are two important questions raised by *Hopt* v. *Utah*. The Court says here the trial judge draws the distinctions on the basis of guidelines in state criminal statutes.

Circumstances

Frederick Hopt was convicted four times (the last in September 1885) and first sentenced to death for the murder of John F. Turner on July 3, 1880. Three times the Court reversed his conviction; in this case he seeks to extend his record to four. Hopt bases his requests primarily on four points: prejudiced jurors, improper evidence, improper jury instructions given by the trial judge, and an improper reference to one of his former trials by the district attorney.

Hopt says four jurors were unconstitutionally prejudiced. When challenged for actual (as contrasted to implied) bias, three of the jurors were excused by the trial judge. The fourth, however, was ruled not to hold an actual bias and thus was deemed to be an impartial and competent juror.

Implied bias means the jurors are biased *de jure,* or by law; that is, the law defines them as biased even before they are questioned about their knowledge of a defendant. An example of a person declared by law to hold an implied bias is a close relative. The mother of a defendant is defined by law as unconstitutionally biased and so cannot serve on the jury of her son or daughter. Coke used the termed "affection" to describe implied bias. In contrast, actual bias is *de facto,* or factual, bias, what Coke called bias by favor. Actual bias is determined by the trial court only after the questioning of prospective jurors.

Passed in 1878, an Act of the Territory of Utah in Section 241 defined actual bias of a juror as " 'The existence of a state of mind, on the part of a juror, which leads to a just inference in reference to the case that he will not act with entire impartiality' " (432). Another law governing prejudiced jurors in Utah was an Act of the Territory passed in March 1884, which reads in part:

> No person shall be disqualified as a juror by reason of having formed or expressed an opinion upon the matter or cause to be submitted to such jury [juror], founded upon public rumor, statements in public journals, or common notoriety; provided it appear to the court, upon his declaration under oath or otherwise, that he can and will, notwithstanding such an opinion, act impartially and fairly upon the matters submitted to him. (432-433)

In other words, this act appears to assert that jurors who hold opinions based on rumors or news stories about the guilt of a defendant can still be seated as long as they convince the judge they are sincere and competent when they say they can base their verdict solely on evidence presented in court.

Summary of the Court's Analysis

Justice Stephen Johnson Field writes for the Court.
Chief Justice Morrison Remick Waite and
Justices Samuel Freeman Miller, Joseph P. Bradley,
John Marshall Harlan, William Burnham Woods,
Stanley Matthews, Horace Gray, and Samuel Blatchford join.

At the outset Justice Field lists the four errors claimed by Hopt:

> (1) the ruling of the trial court upon challenges to several jurors; (2) the admission in evidence of the opinion of a witness, as to the direction from which the blow was delivered which caused the death of the deceased; (3) the instruction to the jury as to the meaning of the words

"reasonable doubt;" (4) the reference on the argument by the district attorney, to previous trials of the case. (430)

Starting with the first assigned error, Field examines the opinions held by all four challenged jurors even though three were successfully peremptorily challenged and never allowed to pass judgment. Only a juror referred to as Gabott, who was "challenged for both actual and implied bias" (434), served on the jury and so voted for conviction. Thus, only Gabott, says Field, "can properly be assigned as error here; and . . . that ruling was in our judgment correct" (436). In other words, only Gabott's participation in the verdict as a prejudiced juror can be used by Hopt as a possible basis for suggesting that his trial was unconstitutional. Since the three other jurors were not seated, their prejudices and opinions are irrelevant to this case.

Field begins his analysis of Gabott's state of mind by summarizing the juror's knowledge obtained from sources outside the trial. Field writes:

> He [Gabott] had heard of the case through the newspapers, and read what was represented to be the evidence; that he had talked about it since that time; that he did not think he had ever expressed an opinion on the case, but that he had formed a qualified opinion; that is, if the evidence were true, or the reports were true; that he had an opinion touching the guilt or innocence of the accused, which it would take evidence to remove; but that he thought he could go into the jury box and sit as if he had never heard of the case, and that what he had heard would not make the least difference. On his cross examination, he testified that he knew nothing about the case, except what he had read from time to time in the public press; that, if what he had heard turned out to be the facts in the case, he had an opinion, otherwise not; and that, according to his present state of mind, he could sit on the jury and determine the case without reference to anything he had heard; that he was not conscious of any bias or prejudice that might prevent him from dealing with the defendant impartially and that he thought he could try the case according to the law and the evidence given in court. On his re-examination he further stated that he would be guided by the evidence altogether, without being influenced by any opinion he might then have, or may have previously formed. (434)

Field concludes that, according to the "express terms of the Statute of 1884," Gabott "could not be disqualified as a juror for an opinion formed or expressed upon statements in public journals, if it appeared to the court upon his declaration . . . that he could and would, notwithstanding such an opinion, act impartially and fairly upon the matter submitted to him" (434–435). Field says the newspaper Gabott read qualified as a "public journal" and the judgment of the trial judge "upon the competency of the juror in such cases is conclusive" (435). In other words, Field says that, when a juror forms an opinion based upon comments in a newspaper, Utah territorial law gives the trial judge the right to determine that juror's prejudice based upon the judge's observation of the juror's sworn testimony that the newspaper did not prejudice his verdict. The judge's evaluation, Field asserts, is to be respected by the Court.

The Court also stated that, because Hopt left unused "several" peremptory challenges, "If, therefore, the ruling of the court in disallowing the challenges to the two for bias, actual or implied, was erroneous, no injury to the defendant followed" (436).

The Court made short work of Hopt's second assigned error: "the admission in evidence of the opinion of a witness, as to the direction from which the blow was delivered" (436). Field writes, "The evidence was admissible; and . . . if not admissible, the error was cured by the evidence being stricken out with the accompanying instruction [to the jury to disregard it]" (437). He adds, "The trial of a case is not to be suspended, the jury discharged, a new one summoned, and the evidence retaken, when an error in the admission of testimony can be corrected by its withdrawal with proper instructions from the court to disregard it" (438).

Hopt's third objection relates to the judge's explanation of reasonable doubt, and focuses on the word "abiding" in this passage of the court's instructions to the jury: "If . . . you can truthfully say that you have an abiding conviction of the defendant's guilt, . . . you have no reasonable doubt" (439). Field writes curtly, "We are satisfied that the defendant was in no way prejudiced by the instruction of the court" (441).

The reference during closing argument by the district attorney to a previous trial constitutes Hopt's last assigned error. Field writes, "There was, in fact, no reference to any verdict on a previous trial, but merely a mention of the times the case had been before the court, so as to magnify its importance" (442). He concludes, "We do not see that the defendant was in any way prejudiced by such reference" (442).

Ruling

Field writes, "The judgment of the court below is affirmed" (442).

Significance

Two items addressed by the Court in this case are worthy of comment. First is the Court's acceptance of the 1884 Act of the Territory as a constitutionally adequate guide to determining juror impartiality. The germane section says jurors who have formed opinions about a case on the basis of newspaper reports can be seated if the trial judge believes the jurors' assertion that they can render a verdict solely on the basis of the evidence presented in court. Here the judge rules a juror to be competent, apparently believing his assertion that, even though prior to the trial he had formed an opinion about the guilt of Hopt on the basis of a news story, it was a qualified opinion because he said he could render a verdict guided solely by the evidence "without being influenced by any opinion he . . . may have previously formed."

The Court, in other words, recognized a difference between opinion and prejudice by accepting as constitutional the statute's assertion that an opinion formed on the basis of news reports does not prejudice a prospective juror. This statute implied that a distinction can be drawn between jurors who are unconstitutionally or actually prejudiced against a defendant and jurors who merely hold an opinion that the defendant is guilty.

The second item addressed by the Court is a bit of common sense handed out by Field. He said that the verdict could not be changed on the basis of challenged jurors who were excused and who did not sit in judgment as long as there remained unused peremptory challenges. The Court seems to be saying here that, as long as Hopt left unused some peremptory challenges, he was not injured unconstitutionally by being forced to challenge peremptorily jurors whom he says should have been excused for cause.

Spies v. Illinois

In the Matter of August Spies, et al.

Docket No. 1887-09
123 U.S. 131, 31 L.Ed. 80, 85 S.Ct. 21 (1887)
Argued October 27, 28, 1887. Decided November 2, 1887.

Background

The words in the Fourteenth Amendment are much too close to those in the Fifth Amendment not to tempt defense attorneys to apply the Bill of Rights to the states. The Fifth Amendment prevents the federal government from violating certain personal liberties, such as the right not to incriminate oneself, but the Fourteenth Amendment protects liberties from the states, and most criminal statutes are passed by state legislatures. Consequently, soon after ratification of the Fourteenth Amendment defendants began to argue that the rights implied in the Fifth Amendment's due process clause were identical to those in the due process clause appearing in the Fourteenth Amendment. Indeed, not content to rest with the Fifth Amendment, others argued that all of the rights enumerated in the entire Bill of Rights— including, for example, the right to a fair trial and the right to trial by jury—were also applied to the states through the Fourteenth Amendment.

The *Spies* case is thought by historians to represent the first significant attempt to assert that the effect of the Fourteenth Amendment is to apply at least some of the personal rights listed in the Bill of Rights to the states as well as to the federal government. One of these rights asserted by *Spies* is the right to a fair trial, guaranteed by the Sixth Amendment; another is the right not to be compelled to be a witness against oneself, guaranteed by the Fifth Amendment. The "immunities and privileges" mentioned in the Fourteenth Amendment apply these rights, Spies claimed, to citizens of the states as well as to citizens of the federal government.

The Court avoids addressing the issue by asserting that it is irrelevant because Spies did in fact receive a fair trial. That is, the Court felt it was unnecessary to rule on the assertion that the Fourteenth Amendment applies these two personal liberties in the Fifth and Sixth Amendments to the states because neither of these liberties was violated.

Later, the Court would be forced to face the issue. At first it denied the Fourteenth Amendment applied the liberties listed in the Bill of Rights to the states. Then it said that certain fundamental liberties similar, but not identical, to those in the first ten amendments do exist and these liberties are applied to the states through the Fourteenth Amendment. Then it said that the liberties of the First Amendment, and not just similar fundamental liberties, are applied to the states through the Fourteenth Amendment. Eventually, the Court ruled that the Fourteenth Amendment does apply all of the fundamental liberties in the Bill of Rights to the states, including the right to assistance of counsel; to remain silent; to an impartial jury; to confront and cross-examine witnesses; and to a speedy, public, and fair trial.

Circumstances

The years 1884–1886 have been described as the "great upheaval," and 1886 has been called a "revolutionary year" (H. David, 3). Certainly, it can be said in truth that this case literally exploded upon the scene. On May 4, 1886, during a meeting in Haymarket Square, Chicago, Illinois, organized to protest the actions of police taken against striking factory workers the night before, someone threw a bomb at the nearly 200 police officers who arrived as the meeting was winding down. A riot ensued killing seven or eight members—reports vary—of the police department and two other persons in the crowd. Subsequently, eight anarchists were tried on a variety of charges; among the eight were August Spies and Samuel Fielden, who were convicted of murder.

Born February 25, 1847, Samuel Fielden, treasurer of the Chicago American Group of the IWPA (International Working People's Association) in 1884, was a native of Lancashire, England. He went to work in mills at the age of eight and became a strong Methodist. After arriving in the United States at age 21, not long after the end of the Civil War, he moved to Chicago where he earned a living hauling stone. Soon thereafter he became a socialist and in 1880 a charter member of the first teamsters' union in Chicago. He was elected vice president of that union in 1883. He joined the IWPA in July 1884, becoming treasurer of the Chicago American Group.

Spies was born in central Germany, December 10, 1855, and emigrated to America in 1872, going to Chicago a year later where he worked as an upholsterer. In 1875 after hearing a speech, he became a socialist and eventually joined the Socialistic Labor Party (SLP) and ran for local office on the SLP ticket.

In 1880 Spies was asked by the Socialistic Publishing Company to manage the *Arbeiter-Zeitung* (Workers' Newspaper), then on the verge of bankruptcy. He did, and in a few years the *Arbeiter-Zeitung* achieved the highest circulation of any German newspaper in Chicago. In 1884 Spies became editor, remaining in that office until the day of his arrest. By 1886 the newspaper had 20,000 readers.

The foundation for that fateful May 4, 1886, Haymarket Square meeting was laid as early as 1884 when a weak federation of national trade unions (called then the Federation of Organized Trades and Labor Unions of the United States and Canada, but later named the American Federation of Labor and known widely by the abbreviation AFL) began pushing for a campaign to win an eight-hour working day by May 1, 1886.

On May 3, 1886, an outdoor meeting was held near the McCormick Harvester Company plant where a strike was in progress. Although police were on hand to guard strikebreakers working at the plant, replacement workers who left the building after their shift was over were attacked by strikers. Police intervened with the result that one striker was killed and several others were injured. A meeting was called for the following evening, May 4, at Haymarket Square to protest what some strikers said was police brutality.

Although organizers hoped for tens of thousands of participants (Haymarket Square could accommodate 20,000 persons), only about 3,000 appeared at the square, and all but about 300 of them left before the police arrived. Two of the speakers were Spies and Fielden. Mayor Carter Harrison, present during the early speeches, left sometime between nine and ten o'clock, stopping by a nearby police station where he termed the meeting "tame." He was dressing for bed when he heard the explosion.

Spies, expecting to speak to the crowd in German, arrived after 8 p.m. because speakers using German usually appeared last. Yet, when he arrived, the small crowd in the square was still waiting for the speeches to begin. It was not until after 9 p.m. that the first speaker arrived and began his speech.

When the first speaker finished, Fielden starting talking—it was around 10 p.m. and some time after Mayor Harrison had left. Ten minutes into his speech it began to look like rain, so Fielden said he would finish quickly. Many supporters left anyway. Yet two detectives hurried away and reported to the police chief that Fielden was using inflammatory language when he spewed forth the following words:

> "You have nothing more to do with the law except to lay hands on it
> and throttle it until it makes its last kick. It turns your brothers out on
> the wayside and has degraded them until they have lost the last vestige
> of humanity, and they are mere things and animals. Keep your eye upon
> it, throttle it, kill it, stab it, do everything you can to wound it—to
> impede its progress." (Avrich 205)

Lead by Inspector John ("Black Jack") Bonfield of the Chicago police and a Captain Ward, the police ran to the square. Bonfield formed his men into ranks and marched them to the meeting where Ward commanded the participants to disperse. Fielden protested that the meeting was peaceable. When Ward repeated his command, Fielden agreed to leave and began to step down from the wagon on which he was speaking. At that moment a bomb exploded in the ranks of the police. Officers responded by shooting into the crowd with their pistols. When Fielden was hit in the knee by a bullet, he ran and made his way to a drugstore where he had his wounds dressed. Spies, climbing down from the wagon behind Fielden, escaped to a tavern. Eventually nearly 1,000 officers reached the square, but the "riot" was over in less than five minutes.

Thirty-one persons were indicted on sixty-one counts, and eight were brought to trial for murder (June 21–August 20, 1886) before Judge Joseph E. Gary in Cook County Criminal Court. Among other things, the demonstrators were charged with the murder of policeman Mathias J. Degan and conspiracy to commit murder.

Although the identity of the bomb maker never was discovered, Judge Gary ruled that since Degan had been killed in pursuance of a conspiracy that used force to overthrow law, the defendants were guilty. All but Oscar Neebe, who was known to be a bomb builder but was not proved to be the maker of this particular bomb, were sentenced to hang; Neebe got fifteen years.

The trial is thought by most historians to be the most celebrated in the late nineteenth century. The courtroom was crowded with spectators including reporters from out-of-town newspapers. Chicago newspapers demanded the eight defendants be hanged. Most historians say Judge Gary favored the prosecution; he even allowed the spectators to applaud at the end of State Attorney Julius S. Grinnell's closing argument. Jury selection took twenty-one days, with 981 prospective jurors questioned in an attempt to find twelve veniremen who would not admit to a prejudice against the defendants. A relative of one of the slain policemen was accepted by Gary for service on the jury.

Many famous persons, including William Dean Howells, Henry Demarest Lloyd, and Samuel Gompers, objected to the verdict. The sentence attracted worldwide attention. On November 8, 1887, more than 16,000 persons in England meeting in forty-nine clubs denounced the hanging scheduled to take place three days later.

The convictions were upheld by the Illinois Supreme Court on September 14, 1887, and the U.S. Supreme Court ruled on November 2, 1887, that it had no jurisdiction in the case. On the day of the hanging, Governor Richard J. Oglesby commuted to life imprisonment the sentences of Samuel J. Fielden and Michael Schwab, saying they were "good" men at heart. On November 11, 1887, Spies and three others were hanged. Louis Lingg committed suicide in his cell early that day when he blew off the lower half of his head by holding a small bomb in his mouth.

Nina Van Zandt, the daughter of a wealthy family, married Spies by proxy during his trial while he was in jail, some think in a futile attempt to prevent his conviction or, failing that, his execution. After Spies was executed, she married an affluent Italian and moved to Italy for four years before returning, without her husband, to lecture for a living.

Acting on a petition with 60,000 signatures, Governor John Peter Atgeld (the first Democratic governor in Illinois since the Civil War) on June 26, 1893, pardoned three of the anarchists still in prison, including Fielden, saying they were not fairly tried. The governor said the jury was packed, that Judge Gary was biased, and no proper conviction could be sustained unless the bomb thrower could be identified. A conservative uproar against Atgeld's action helped to end his political career, and he lost his attempt at reelection. In a reference to, among others, Vachel Lindsey and Edgar Lee Masters, historian and economist Henry David writes of Atgeld's pardon, "It also served to bury the name of John Peter Atgeld beneath a flood of odium and abuse from which the songs of poets and the labors of admirers have not yet been able to rescue it" (488).

The purpose of the Court's action here is to determine not the validity of Spies's assertions, but merely whether Spies's claims of errors are truly federal questions that come under the authority of the Court.

Summary of the Court's Analysis

Chief Justice Morrison R. Waite writes for the Court.
Justices Samuel F. Miller, Stephen F. Field, Joseph P. Bradley,
John M. Harlan, William B. Woods, Stanley Matthews,
Horace Gray, and Samuel Blatchford join.

Justice Waite says he has two initial concerns arising from section 709 of the Revised United States Statutes. First, did Spies in a state court ask a federal "question reviewable here . . . made and decided in the proper court below," and, second, was that question "of a character to justify us in bringing the judgment here for re-examination" (166)? In short, did Spies claim in the proper way at the proper time and place that a constitutional right was denied to him by a court? Waite asserts that the Court does not want to waste time by allowing an appeal to be brought before it when the members know in advance that they will deny all the arguments in it. He says that because "in the present case we have had the benefit of argument in support of application, we are able to determine as a court in session, whether the errors alleged are such as justify us in bringing the case here for review" (166).

Next Waite lists what he feels are the five main considerations related to the Court's determination of its jurisdiction. The first is an attack on the constitutionality of the Illinois statute governing the selection of a jury. The second is a claim by Spies that he was not given a fair trial by the State of Illinois, a right guaranteed by the Sixth Amendment. The third claim, the constitutional "right, privilege and immunity of trial by an impartial jury," Spies says, applies to the states through the Fourteenth Amendment. Spies, in his fourth argument, says he was unconstitutionally compelled to be a witness against himself. Finally, he says he was denied "equal protection of the laws," a right also guaranteed him by the Fourteenth Amendment. The particular provisions of the Constitution Spies says he was denied are found in Amendments Four, Five, Six, and Fourteen.

Waite writes in response, "That the first ten articles of amendment were not intended to limit the powers of state government in respect to their own people, but to operate on the National Government alone, was decided more than a half century ago" (166). Spies, he notes, argues against this position, "Yet in so far as they secure and recognize fundamental rights—common-law rights—of the man, they make them privileges and immunities of the man as a citizen of the United States, and cannot now be abridged by a State under the Fourteenth Amendment" (166). Waite adds, "It is also contended [by Spies] that the provision of the Fourteenth Amendment which declares that no State shall deprive 'any person of life, liberty, or property without due process of law' implies that every person charged with crime in a State shall be entitled to a trial by an impartial jury and shall not be compelled to testify against himself" (166, 167).

Waite says, however, that before the Court addresses the meanings and implications of the Fourteenth Amendment, it should determine whether there is, in fact, any evidence to suggest that the jury was impartial or that Spies was compelled to testify against himself.

Spies's charge of failure to provide an impartial jury, says Waite, focuses on the constitutional sufficiency of the Illinois law governing the selection of a jury. Consequently, the Court quotes at length from the statute, approved March 12, 1874. The key passage reads as follows:

> In the trial of any criminal cause, the fact that a person called as a juror has formed an opinion or impression based upon rumor or upon newspaper statements (about the truth of which he has expressed no opinion), shall not disqualify him to serve as a juror in such case, if he shall upon oath state that he believes he can fairly and impartially render a verdict therein in accordance with the law and the evidence, and the court shall be satisfied of the truth of such statements. (167)

Before addressing the constitutionality of this law, Waite outlines the limitations of its application to Spies. The justice notes that *Hopt* v. *Utah* (1887) and *Hayes* v. *Missouri* (1887) limit Spies's appeal in this case to only seated jurors: namely, Theodore Denker and H. T. Sanford, who was called after all of Spies's peremptory challenges were used.

The trial judge interpreted this law in his instructions, Waite points out, to mean, among other things, the following:

> "Although a person called as a juryman may have formed an opinion based upon rumor or upon newspaper statements, but has expressed no opinion as to the truth of the newspaper statements, he is still qualified as a juror if he states that he can fairly and impartially render a verdict thereon in accordance with the law and the evidence, and the court shall be satisfied of the truth of such statement." "It is not a test question whether the juror will have the opinion he has formed from newspapers changed by the evidence, but whether his verdict will be based only upon the account which may here be given by witnesses under oath." (168)

This interpretation of the statute, says Waite, does not render it importantly different from similar laws already held constitutional by the Court. In particular, Waite points to the Utah statute reviewed in the *Hopt* case. He also finds no constitutionally significant ("material") differences between the Illinois statute and similar ones in New York, Michigan, Nebraska, and Ohio.

From this analysis, the Court asserts, "We agree entirely with the Supreme Court of Illinois . . . that the statute on its face, as construed by the trial court, is not repugnant to section 9 of article 2, of the Constitution of that State [Illinois]" (170). Since the Illinois constitution is "substantially" similar to the U.S. Constitution, Waite concludes that the law is not unconstitutional even if the Fourteenth Amendment required application to the states of the Sixth Amendment's guarantee of a trial by an impartial jury.

That principle having been settled, Waite turns his attention to the questioning of the two relevant jurors in order to determine if the trial judge correctly applied the constitutionally valid Illinois statute to these two persons. This section of the opinion quotes at length from the *voir dire* of the jurors, starting with Denker. Part of that questioning focused on Denker's avowed expression of the opinion he said he had formed after reading the newspaper. The trial court asked him the question: "Did you in any conversation that you had say anything as to whether you believed or not the account which was in the newspapers which you read? A[nswer]. No, Sir; I never expressed an opinion in regard to whether the newspapers were correct or not" (170, 171).

Spies's attorney asked this question:

> "That is, you have now made up your mind, or at least you have formed an opinion; you have expressed that freely to others. Now, the question is whether when you listen to the testimony you will have in your mind the expression which you have given to others and have to guard against that and be controlled by it in any way. A. No, sir; I don't think I would. I think I could try this case from the testimony regardless of this." (173)

Denker was then unchallenged and accepted by attorneys for both sides.

When juror Sanford was being questioned, Spies's attorney engaged in this exchange with him:

> "Q. I do not care very much what your opinion may be now, for your opinion is made up of random conversations and from newspaper readings, as I understand? A. Yes.
>
> Q. That is nothing reliable. You do not regard that as being in the nature of sworn testimony at all, do you? A. No.
>
> Q. Now, Mr. Sanford, if you should be selected as a juror in this case, do you believe that, regardless of all prejudice or opinion which you now have, you could listen to the legitimate testimony introduced in court and upon that and that alone render and return a fair and impartial, unprejudiced and unbiased verdict? A. Yes." (177)

Since Spies's peremptory challenges were exhausted at this point, Sanford was challenged for cause. Before the trial court ruled, the state questioned Sanford, asking him, among many other things, "'Q. Have you ever said to anyone whether or not you believe the statements of facts in the newspapers to be true? A. I have never expressed it exactly in that way, but still I have no reason to think they were false'" (178).

According to Waite, the trial court then overruled Spies's objection for cause and seated Sanford as a juror since Spies had no peremptory challenges left. Neither side objected. After quoting at some length from *Reynolds* v. *United States* (1878), Waite asserts that the Court cannot overrule the seating of Sanford and Denker and their acceptance as jurors unless "the error complained of is so gross as to amount in law to a denial by the State of a trial by an impartial jury" (180). "We are unhesitatingly of opinion," Waite writes, "that no such case is disclosed by this record" (180).

Turning now to Spies's assertion that he was compelled in violation of the Fifth Amendment to be a witness against himself, Waite writes, "He voluntarily offered himself as a witness in his own behalf, and by so doing he became bound to submit to a proper cross examination under the law and practice in the jurisdiction where he was being tried" (180).

In the matter of unreasonable search and seizure of a letter, Waite points out, "It still remains uncontradicted that objection was not made in the trial court to its admission" (181). "If the right was not set up or claimed in the proper court below, the judgment of the highest court of the State in the action is conclusive, so far as the right of review here is concerned" (181).

Next, Waite says that the claims by Spies and Fielden that they were denied rights due them by treaties with the United States since they were born in other countries were not made in either of the courts below and so "they cannot be raised in this court for the first time" (182).

Finally, Waite has little sympathy for claims by Spies and Fielden that they were not present when their sentence was given since the official record shows that they were indeed present. If they were, in fact, not present, then, asserts Waite, they should have corrected the record in the lower courts, not at this late stage.

Ruling

Waite writes, "Being of opinion, therefore, that the federal questions presented by the counsel for the petitioners, and which they say they desire to argue, are not involved in the determination of the case as it appears on the face of the record, we deny the writ. *Petition for writ of error is dismissed*" (182).

Significance

One significant aspect of this case is a clear and strong reaffirmation of the ruling in *Hopt* v. *Utah* (1887) that a defendant is not injured if a court wrongly fails to dismiss a juror for cause when peremptory challenges remain unused. This ruling poses serious problems for defending attorneys. If they use all their peremptory challenges too quickly just to preserve the right to appeal a failure to dismiss for cause, then they may not have a peremptory challenge available at the end of the *voir dire* when it is badly needed. The Court expresses little sympathy for the plight of defending attorneys, however, reaffirming its earlier stance (*Reynolds* v. *U.S.* [1878]), that the trial judge who rules on the validity of a challenge for cause should be given great respect for his judgment and fairness.

This case gains not a little historical significance as the first in a long series asserting that the Fourteenth Amendment applies the Sixth (and others) to the states. Spies contended, at bottom, that the provision of the Fourteenth Amendment declaring no state shall deprive "any person of life, liberty, or property without due process of law" implies that all persons charged with crime shall be entitled to a trial in all states by an impartial jury. The Court avoids ruling on such implications of the Fourteenth Amendment by asserting that because Spies failed to present evidence showing that the jury was in fact impartial, there is no need to look at an alleged requirement that his jurors be without bias.

The Court then focused on the constitutional sufficiency of the Illinois statute governing the selection of a jury, finding the law not importantly different from similar laws (in other states) already held constitutional by the Court. Thus, by asserting that the Illinois statute is substantially similar to constitutionally sufficient statutes in other states, the Court avoids directly addressing Spies's claims that the Fourteenth Amendment limits the states as well as the federal government.

Although not directly related to the conflict between a free press and a fair trial, *Spies* is also significant because Waite asserts that the Court will not rule on issues from state courts unless these issues are "set up or claimed in the proper court below" (181). The very next year (1888), for example, the Court, quoting from *Spies,* said in *Chappell* v. *Bradshaw,* "To give this court jurisdiction to review the judgment of a state court under section 709 of the Revised Statutes, because of the denial by a state court . . . , it must appear on the record that such title, right, privilege, or immunity was 'specially set up or claimed' at the proper time and in the proper way" (132).

Simmons v. U.S.

James A. Simmons

v.

United States

Docket No. 1891-1296
142 U.S. 148, 35 L.Ed. 968, 12 S.Ct. 171 (1891)

Argued December 11, 1891. Decided December 21, 1891.

Background

One of the many questions raised by the conflict between a free press and a fair trial is who has the legal authority to decide when a jury has been so strongly influenced by information gained from outside the trial that an unprejudiced verdict cannot be achieved. Another is what kind of information is so important that exposure to it would prevent a jury from rendering an unprejudiced verdict. These two questions are addressed in this case.

The Court ruled as early as *Mima Queen* v. *Hepburn* (1813) that defendants do not have a right to jurors who are prejudiced in their favor because "it was desirable to submit the case to those who felt no bias either way, and therefore the court exercised a sound discretion in not permitting him [a juror] to be sworn" (297). The nine justices supported a trial court's authority and "sound discretion" in dismissing a juror who said he would find it difficult to rule against a slave like Mima Queen since he was against slavery. In *Perez* v. *U.S.* (1824) the Court asserted that trial judges who exercise "sound discretion" possess "the authority to discharge a jury from giving any verdict, whenever in their opinion . . . there is a manifest necessity for the act, or the ends of public justice would otherwise be defeated" (580). Here the Court extends the authority of a trial court to include discharging a jury that a judge who exercised "sound discretion" feels has been exposed sufficiently to evidence outside a trial so that it cannot render an unprejudiced verdict.

Circumstances

Peter J. Classen, who was the president of Sixth National Bank of the City of New York, was convicted in late 1890 of "converting to his own use" on January 22, 1890, $622,000 worth of bonds and written obligations from certain railroad companies. In the circuit court for the Southern District of New York, under section 5209, Revised Statutes, James A. Simmons was charged with aiding and abetting Classen in return for $60,000. After Simmons was arraigned and pleaded not guilty, jury selection started on January 26, 1891.

When evidence was presented that juror eleven lied about knowing Simmons, Judge Charles L. Benedict adjourned the trial on February 9 just before one of Simmons's attorneys was scheduled to cross-examine Classen, an event highly anticipated by spectators. The judge later dismissed the jury and rescheduled the trial after rejecting a plea by Simmons for acquittal. A second jury found Simmons guilty on March 11, and he was sentenced on June 26 to six years in the Erie County Penitentiary.

This bizarre series of events was set into motion February 6 when a Charles M. Ward presented an affidavit to Edward Mitchell, U.S. attorney for the southern district of New York. In the affidavit Ward said he collected rent for his mother, who owned units numbered 165 and 167 Broadway, a double office building known as the Parmly Building. According to Ward, Simmons leased a suite of offices, labeled rooms A and B, on the fourth floor for four or five months during 1884. The eleventh juror, William E. Goodnow, rented at about that same time an office in a room, labeled C, adjoining Simmons's suit, and Ward said he often saw them talking.

Simmons responded to the charges by attacking Ward's motives, saying the broker wanted to hurt him as a result of a quarrel they had years ago. The defendant said he had a squabble with Ward about rent, with the result that Ward secured a writ of "ejectment." When the agent served the writ, Simmons said he paid up and left "to avoid further trouble."

Richard S. Newcombe, who, along with Charles A. Hess, was counsel for Simmons, wrote a letter to D.A. Mitchell, saying he had been interviewed by a reporter from the New York *Herald*. Because the reporter planned to print information he received from Ward's affidavit, Newcombe said he had written a letter to the newspaper presenting Simmons's view of events.

When presented with a motion to dismiss juror Goodnow, Judge Benedict went a step further. He discharged the entire jury. Benedict said the publication of the letter in the newspaper "affords, in my opinion, a sufficient ground to discharge the jury at this time" (142). He explains, "The statement made by Ward, conveyed to the jury by the publication of the letter of the defendant's counsel, makes it impossible that in the future consideration of this case by the jury there can be no true independence and freedom of action on the part of each juror which is necessary to a fair trial of the accused" (142). He said he takes this extreme action, among other reasons, "in order to prevent the defeat of the ends of justice," and "to preserve the rights of the accused to be tried by a jury, every member of which can render a verdict free from constraint" (142).

In short, Judge Benedict said publication of the letter in the newspaper so prejudiced the jury that its members could not render a verdict based solely on the evidence presented in court.

Summary of the Court's Analysis

Justice Horace Grey writes for the Court.
Justices Joseph P. Bradley, Ward Hunt, John M. Harlan,
Samuel Blatchford, Lucius Q. C. Lamar, David J. Brewer,
Henry B. Brown, and Chief Justice Melville W. Fuller join.

The first issue taken up by Justice Grey is the authority of the trial court to dismiss a jury without permission of the defendant. Grey quotes extensively from a very early opinion rendered by Justice Joseph Story in *Perez* v. *U.S.* (1824): "We think . . . the law has invested courts of justice with the authority to discharge a jury from giving any verdict, whenever in their opinion . . . there is a manifest necessity for the act, or the ends of public justice would otherwise be defeated" (142). Story warns that the judges should "exercise discretion" and should use this authority "with the greatest caution," but that "it is impossible to define all the circumstances which would render it proper to interfere" (142).

Grey said one adequate reason for justifying the discharge of a jury is that a court would feel "outside influences brought to bear it" would produce "such bias or prejudice as not to stand between the government and the accused" (142). Grey then quotes Justice Benjamin R. Curtis, who writes in *Morris* v. *U.S.* (1 Curt, 23, 37), "It is . . . a mistake to suppose that either party can have a vested right to a corrupt or prejudiced juror" (142).

Noting that the jury (including Goodnow) admitted reading the letter in the newspaper, Grey said the trial judge "was fully justified in concluding that such a publication . . . made it impossible for that jury . . . to act with the independence and freedom on the part of each juror requisite to a fair trial of the issue between the parties" (142). Moreover, Grey asserts that, having made such a determination, "It was clearly within his [the trial judge's] authority to order the jury to be discharged" (142).

Ruling

Writes Grey, "Judgment affirmed" (142).

Significance

The Court asserts that trial judges do have the authority to discharge a jury that has been exposed sufficiently to evidence outside a trial so that it cannot render an unprejudiced verdict. One such piece of evidence is a letter, published in a newspaper and read by at least some on the jury, attacking an assertion that a juror lied when he said he did not know the defendant. Newspapers publishing such information, it would appear, are putting in jeopardy the continuation of a trial because no one has the right, said the Court, to a corrupt or prejudiced juror.

Of significance also is the Court's continued support of the trial court's evaluation of the facts. In effect, the Court extended the authority of a trial court to include discharging a jury that a judge who exercised "sound discretion" feels has been exposed sufficiently to evidence outside a trial so that it cannot render an unprejudiced verdict.

The first attacks on the respect rendered to the evaluations of trial courts in these matters did not occur until the middle of the next century. In *Shepherd* v. *Florida* (1951) a concurring opinion said pretrial publicity may be so great that, instead of looking at the trial court's evaluation of individual juror prejudice, the Court could merely assume all prospective jurors were unconstitutionally prejudiced. Then in *Sheppard* v. *Maxwell* (1966) the Court outlined a number of steps a trial judge should take to protect defendants from the unconstitutional prejudice that may be elicited by pretrial publicity. Finally, dissenting justices in *Mu'Min* v. *Virginia* (1991) bitterly attacked the notion that trial courts do not need to make a minimal analytical effort to earn "special deference" to their "sound discretion."

Mattox v. U.S.

Clyde Mattox
v.
The United States

Docket No. 1892-1008

146 U.S. 140, 36 L.Ed. 917, 13 S.Ct. 50 (1892)

Submitted October 31, 1892. Decided November 11, 1892.

Background

Two unusual events influenced the deliberations of the jury in this case. The first was an unsolicited conversation with the bailiff in charge of the jury after closing arguments had been completed and deliberations were about to begin. The second was the reading of a newspaper article during deliberations by some members of the jury. Jurors attempted to submit affidavits related to these events.

The affidavits themselves raised a number of troubling questions. Should the Court accept them, and, if so, should the justices regard them as evidence that the jury verdict was invalid? These questions were first raised in *Reid* v. *U.S.*, 1851, where the Court avoided addressing them. A note to *Doss* v. *Tyack* (55 U.S. 297, 12 L.Ed. 428, 14 Howard 297, 1852) cites several cases in support of not receiving such documents: "Affidavits or testimony of jurors will not be received to impeach their verdict, or to explain the grounds of their verdict" (428). Another short discussion of this topic can be found in *Clinton* v. *Englebrecht*, 80 U.S. 434, 20 L.Ed. 659, 13 Wall 434 (1872).

Circumstances

A grand jury in Wichita, Kansas, indicted Clyde Mattox on September 7, 1891, for shooting in the breast, back, and abdomen John Mullen, described as a colored man, in what was then commonly called the Oklahoma Indian Territories of Kansas.

After the jury had been charged and retired to deliberate, a bailiff made within its hearing comments prejudicial to Mattox. Among them was the assertion that "'This is the third fellow he has killed'" (140).

In addition, a news story from the October 8, 1891, edition of the Wichita, Kansas, *Wichita Daily Eagle,* was read by the jury from a newspaper purchased by a juror. The article, like the bailiff, made comments clearly prejudicial against Mattox. Here are the most blatant:

> If he is not found guilty of murder he will be a lucky man, for the evidence against him was very strong, or at least appeared to be to an outsider.
>
> It was expected that their [the jury's] deliberations would not last an hour before they would return a verdict.
>
> The lawyers who were present and the court officers also agree that it [the closing argument by prosecuting attorney Ady] was one of the best and most logical speeches Mr. Ady ever made in this court. It was so strong that the friends of Mattox gave up all hope of any result but conviction. When the jury filed out, Mattox seemed to be the most unconcerned man in the room.
>
> His mother was very pale and her face indicated that she had but very little hope. She is certainly deserving of a good deal of credit for she has stuck by her son, as only a mother can, through all his trials, and this is not the first one by any means, for Clyde has been tried for his life once before.
>
> Nobody saw him do the killing and the evidence against him is purely circumstantial, but very strong, it is claimed by those who heard all the testimony. (141)

Summary of the Court's Analysis

Chief Justice Melville W. Fuller writes for the Court.
Justices Stephen Johnson Field, John Marshall Harlan, Horace Gray,
Samuel Blatchford, Lucius Quintus Cincinnatus Lamar,
David Josiah Brewer, Henry Billings Brown, and George Shiras join.

Chief Justice Fuller begins by stating why the Court feels it has the authority to review Mattox's request for a new trial. Put simply, he asserts that because the district court did not consider the affidavits of jurors when it reviewed his "application" for retrial, the Court now can address it.

Fuller's first comments about the affidavits is that they differ from those submitted by jurors in *Reid* v. *U.S.* (1851). The jurors from Mattox's trial "confined their statements to what was said by the one [the bailiff] and read from the other [the newspaper]" (147). They did not, he took care to note, "state what influence, if any," the bailiff or the newspaper had on their verdict.

In *Reid,* however, the jurors asserted that the newspaper "had no influence on their verdict" (147). Because in the *Reid* case the court, although reluctantly, did receive the affidavits, which Fuller says is against "public policy, which forbids the reception of affidavits, depositions or sworn statements of jurors to impeach their verdicts" (147, 148), a precedent had been set. Still, the Court avers, such affidavits should be used only "with great caution" (148).

Aware that he has taken the first step down a slippery slope, Fuller carefully seeks to outline the ways affidavits from jurors may be used to impeach verdicts. First, he accepts the distinction drawn by Justice Brewer in *Perry* v. *Bailey,* 12 Kan. 539. There Brewer asserts that the "'personal consciousness'" of one juror cannot be used to overturn a verdict because it would allow the "'secret thought'" of one person to overrule the actions of the other eleven. Since "'overt acts . . . are accessible to the knowledge of all the jurors,'" however, they can be used by a court to evaluate the constitutional validity of a verdict (148).

Fuller points out that this same notion is supported by Justice Grey in *Woodward* v. *Leavitt,* 107 Mass 453. He writes, "'The evidence of jurors as to the motives and influences which affected their deliberations, is inadmissible either to impeach or to support the verdict. But a juryman may testify to any facts bearing upon the question of the existence of any extraneous influence, although not as to how far that influence operated upon his mind'" (149).

Since Fuller feels that affidavits may indeed be received if they are confined to "overt acts," then the next step to be taken is to determine whether the affidavits offered in this case are "material," that is, whether they are significantly relevant to overt acts affecting the jury.

One clear overt act that is "absolutely forbidden," Fuller notes, is "private communications, possibly prejudicial, between jurors and third persons, or witnesses, or the officer in charge" (150). He points out that the mere "presence of an officer during the deliberations of the jury is such an irregular invasion of the right of trial by jury as to absolutely vitiate the verdict in all cases without regard to whether any improper influences were actually exerted over the jury" (150). He concludes, "information that this was the third person Clyde Mattox had killed, coming from the officer in charge" was clearly "prejudicial" (150). Having established the relevance of the comments made by the bailiff, Fuller moves to a discussion of the newspaper articles.

The jury began deliberations on October 7 and read the newspaper article the morning of October 8 before they had reached a verdict. Fuller writes, "It is not open to reasonable doubt that the tendency of that article was injurious to the defendant" (150). Not content with this assertion, Fuller then takes pains to review what exactly in the newspaper article could be considered prejudicial against Mattox:

Statements that the defendant had been tried for his life once before; that the evidence against him was claimed to be very strong by those who had heard all the testimony; that the argument for the prosecution was such that the defendant's friends gave up all hope of any result but conviction; and that it was expected that the deliberations of the jury would not last an hour before they would return a verdict. (150, 151)

From the issue of affidavits, Fuller moves to the trial court's refusal to consider testimony related to the declaration of a dying person. The lower court was not willing to admit the victim's testimony as the declaration of a dying person because this testimony would favor Mattox, and previously the courts had ruled that such testimony could be received only if it tended to convict a defendant. In this case the victim, who knew he was close to death, said he knew Mattox and also said that, although he did not know who shot him, he did know it was not Mattox. Writes Fuller, "Dying declarations are admissible on a trial for murder . . . in favor of the defendant as well as against him. We regard the error thus committed as justifying the awarding of a new trial" (153).

Ruling

Writes Fuller, "Dying declarations are admissible on a trial for murder . . . in favor of the defendant as well as against him. We should, therefore, be compelled to reverse the judgment because the affidavits were not received and considered by the court" (151).

Significance

For at least three major reasons, courts understandably are reluctant to accept from jurors after a trial affidavits asserting they have changed their mind. Affidavits related to jurors' motives for voting (1) would be extremely difficult for a judge to evaluate, (2) would be the result of thinking or conversation outside the trial itself, and (3) would hold the tremendously burdensome prospect of creating a great number of retrials. Thus, from the first, courts were reluctant to receive from jurors affidavits attesting to their personal reasons for voting one way in court and later wanting to vote another.

Here, though, the Court recognizes an important distinction between two kinds of information attested to in a juror's affidavit: personal motive and overt act. Whereas personal motive may grant to one person the power to overrule an action of the other eleven, overt acts are observable by all members of the jury. Consequently, Fuller asserts that affidavits attesting to overt,

observable actions taken may be received by a court considering the constitutional validity of a verdict.

One such overt act is the reading of a newspaper article about the trial.
Although jurors may testify that the act of the reading did occur, Fuller says,
they may not testify about how much the newspaper article influenced their
verdict. Testimony about influence is too much like personal motive. While
he does not actually say so, Fuller implies by his actions that the Court itself
will evaluate the impact a newspaper article may have upon the deliberations
of a jury. Here he was following the precedent of Chief Justice Roger B.
Taney in *Reid* v. *U.S.* (1851). Taney asserted that it mattered not if one or
two of the jurors in Reid's trial read a newspaper article because "there was
nothing in the newspapers calculated to influence their decisions" (366). In
other words, Taney was willing to accept the jurors' affidavit asserting they
did in fact read a newspaper article about the case they were trying, but he
asserted that he, not a juror who did the reading, would be the person who
would evaluate whether the content of the article could threaten a fair trial.

The Court's assertion of its prerogative here is extremely significant
because it represents an important distinction. Justice Marshall first set forth
this distinction when he said, "Those who try the impartiality of a juror
ought to test him" (*Burr* v. *U.S.*, at 50, 1807). His test is summarized in his
assertion, "They [judges] ought to hear the statement made by himself [a
juror stating impartiality] . . . and conscientiously determine, according to
their best judgment, whether in general men under such circumstances ought
to be considered as capable of hearing fairly, and of deciding impartially"
(*Burr* v. *U.S.*, 51).

Taney and Fuller likewise are unwilling to accept jurors' statements about
the impact of a newspaper article upon their verdict. These two justices
reserved to themselves the power to determine whether or not the content
of the newspaper would be likely to prejudice a jury. Taney ruled the content
of the article in *Reid* did not contain information that would prejudice
unconstitutionally a jury, whereas Fuller ruled that the content of the article
in this case was indeed unconstitutionally prejudicial.

A great deal of significance, therefore, lies in the authority the justices
consistently reserved for themselves. While, as a matter of law, a Court may
receive affidavits from jurors attesting to overt acts relevant to the purity of
their deliberations, it may not receive statements evaluating the influence
such acts had upon determining a verdict. The Court will be the sole arbiter
of the fact of unconstitutional prejudice.

Thiede v. Utah

Charles Thiede

v.

People of the Territory of Utah

Docket No. 1895-633
159 U.S. 510, 40 L.Ed. 237, 16 S.Ct. 62 (1895)
Submitted October 21, 1895. Decided November 11, 1895.

Background

The Court heard this case without benefit of arguments or a brief filed by an attorney. While in prison, Thiede simply asked the Court to review the more-than-400 pages of proceedings and make rulings based on his assignment of errors. Although the Court discussed five of the assigned errors, only one is relevant to the conflict between a free press and a fair trial.

Four jurors admitted they had read newspaper stories about the murder for which Thiede was convicted. They also stated that, on the basis of these news stories, they had indeed formed "some impressions" (515), but they asserted they could "lay aside any such impressions and could try the case fairly and impartially upon the evidence presented" (516). The only question for the Court, therefore, was whether or not the jurors' declarations fell within the relevant law of the Territory of Utah, a law which it had previously declared constitutional, in *Hopt* v. *Utah* (1887).

Circumstances

Charles Thiede, 33, owner of a brewery and an adjacent saloon, said he woke up a Jacob Lauenberger about 1 A.M. on Tuesday, May 1, 1894, telling Lauenberger that his [Thiede's] wife, Mary, was lying dead at a corner of his saloon with her throat cut. Later testimony indicated that her head was nearly "severed" from the body by a large knife. About thirty feet away was a pool of blood and signs of a struggle. Blood stains led from that point to the body. A large knife often used by Thiede was never found.

Thiede, who had been in the saloon that night and who had blood on his hands and clothing, went with Lauenberger to find a physician. During the trial several witnesses said Thiede had mistreated his wife for some years, and that he had argued with her Sunday, the night before her death. Lauenberger testified that Thiede's wife said after the argument that she feared her husband would kill her. A neighbor identified only as Mr. Soderholm said he earlier saw Thiede chase Mary, catch her, throw her down violently, kick her, and then drag her back to the house by her hair. He said her face was always bruised and often bloody. Mrs. Soderholm said she had seen Thiede beat his wife with a stick. Another neighbor, a Mrs. Anderson, said she often heard a woman's screams coming from the Thiede house late at night.

Thiede was indicted on September 24, arraigned on September 28, tried on October 10, convicted of uxoricide on October 21, and sentenced on November 5 to be hanged. After the Supreme Court of the Territory of Utah affirmed his conviction, Thiede appealed to the United States Supreme Court.

Summary of the Court's Analysis

Justice David J. Brewer writes for the Court.
Chief Justice Melville Weston Fuller and
Justices Stephen Johnson Field, John Marshall Harlan,
Horace Gray, Henry Billings Brown, George Shiras,
Howell Edmonds Jackson, and Edward Douglas White join.

The first alleged error taken up by the Court is Thiede's "objection to going to trial on October 10, 1894, on the ground that the evidence taken at the preliminary hearing had not been transcribed, certified, and filed with the district court, as provided by law" (512).

Section 4883 of the 1884 *Compiled Laws of Utah* does indeed require that shorthand notes of a preliminary hearing "be transcribed into longhand by the [court] reporter within ten days after the close of the examination" (512). The transcription never took place, however, because Fred McGurrin, who took the shorthand notes, refused to do so. It seems that in a prior case neither the county nor the territory paid him for his transcription, and when he sued for his money, he lost the case. He was not about to do another transcription for free.

Brewer begins his analysis of the situation with these words:

A preliminary examination is not indispensable to the finding of an indictment or a trial thereon; and if the examination itself is not indispensable it would seem to follow that no steps taken [such as transcriptions of shorthand into longhand] in the course or as part of it can be. The statute nowhere expressly places the filing of this transcript as something necessary happening intermediate the examination and the trial, nor does it make the latter [that is, the trial] dependent upon a preliminary examination. (513)

Brewer also notes that Thiede was not denied any item of value from the preliminary hearing even though the shorthand was not transcribed. Thiede could have subpoenaed McGurrin, for example, Brewer writes, and "compelled [him] under oath to develop from his notes any testimony taken on preliminary examination" (514).

In dismissing the first alleged error, Brewer writes in summary, "We conclude, therefore, that the law does not forbid a trial before the filing of this transcript, nor was, in this case, the failure so to file an error working substantial injury to the rights of the defendant" (514).

The second error Thiede claims is that he was not given a list of the names of witnesses who were to testify until the trial was under way. Brewer points out here that, while there does in fact exist a United States statute requiring a list of witnesses to be delivered to defendants accused of murder, there is no similar statute in the Utah Territory. He concludes, "In the absence of some statutory provision there is no irregularity in calling a witness whose name does not appear on the back of the indictment or has not been furnished to the defendant before trial" (515). He continues, "There is no suggestion that the defendant was surprised by the calling of any witness or the testimony that he gave. This allegation of error, therefore, is without foundation" (515).

It is Thiede's third alleged error that is relevant to the conflict between a free press and a fair trial. He asserts, "The court erred in overruling defendant's challenges for cause directed against four jurors on the ground that on the *voir dire* they showed themselves incompetent to serve" (515). The jurors to whom Thiede objects admitted during questioning before the trial that, not only had they read newspaper accounts of the murder, but they also had formed "some impressions" on the basis of the news stories. Brewer notes, "Each [juror] stated that he could lay aside any such impression and could try the case fairly and impartially upon the evidence presented" (516).

Brewer then quotes from the relevant statute (Section 5024, *Compiled Laws of Utah*):

No person shall be disqualified as a juror by reason of having formed or expressed an opinion upon the matter or cause to be submitted to such jury, founded upon public rumor, statements in public journalism, or common notoriety: *Provided,* It appears to the court, upon his declaration, under oath or otherwise, that he can and will act impartially and fairly upon the matters submitted to him. (516)

He concludes, "The testimony of these jurors clearly placed them within the terms of this statute, and there was no error in overruling the challenges" (516).

Thiede also objects to the partiality of juror Joseph Smith. Smith said he "had no prejudice against him [Thiede], but simply against the business of saloon keeping" (516), yet that his prejudice "would not influence him in any way in passing the guilt or innocence of the defendant [Thiede]" (516). Moreover, Brewer notes, "The juror was . . . excused by the defendant before all his peremptory challenges were exhausted" (516).

Thiede says the fourth error was "admitting irrelevant, incompetent, and immaterial testimony" (516). After reviewing the testimony at some length, Brewer writes, "We cannot say that the testimony was absolutely immaterial; at any rate, we cannot see how it, in any manner, tended to prejudice the defendant" (519).

Nor did Thiede approve of juror Louis Gronosky serving as an interpreter for witness Lauenberger, who spoke only German. To this objection Brewer writes, "The juror certainly heard all that the witness stated, and was therefore fully prepared to act with the other jurors in considering the testimony, and as his interpretation of the witness's testimony was with the consent of the defendant, the latter cannot now question its propriety" (519, 520).

Finally, Thiede objects to the judge's refusal to present to the jury twenty-two paragraphs of instructions that Thiede prepared at the close of testimony. Writes Brewer in response, "Obviously, they were too late" (520).

Ruling

Brewer writes, "We find nothing in the record of which the defendant has any just complaint, and therefore the judgment is affirmed" (529).

Significance

This case is significant for the most part because it clarifies and reaffirms much of what the Court asserted earlier in relation to the existence of impartiality in a juror.

First, the Court did not question the constitutionality of the Utah Territorial Statute stating that jurors who have "formed or expressed an opinion" after reading a newspaper shall not be "disqualified" if the trial judge feels they "can and will act impartially." In other words, the Court is asserting once more that not all opinions formed by reading a newspaper prior to the trial necessarily make a juror unconstitutionally prejudiced.

Second, the Court felt it significant that the jurors asserted they were impartial even though they had formed an opinion. One piece of evidence the judge should consider, the Court reaffirmed, when determining whether or not a juror is prejudiced is the juror's mere assertion of impartiality.

Third, the Court reaffirmed its earlier ruling, *Reynolds* v. *U.S.* (1878), that the trial court shall be primary judge of whether or not prospective jurors are telling the truth when they assert that they can be impartial even after having formed an opinion based upon a news story.

Finally, the Court reaffirmed a holding in *Spies* v. *Illinois* (1887) when it pointed out that it is difficult upon appeal to rule a juror prejudiced when the defendant did not ask that very same juror to be excused before the trial began. Thiede did not use all his peremptory challenges, which allow him to dismiss a juror for no reason. If he did not dismiss a juror when he had the opportunity to do so without the requirement of giving a reason, then, the Court asked, how can he now, after the trial, claim, based on some newly discovered reason, that the juror should not have been allowed to sit in judgment?

Holt v. U.S.

James H. Holt
v.
The United States

Docket No. 1910-231

218 U.S. 245, 54 L.Ed. 1021, 31 S.Ct. 2 (1910)

Argued October 13 and 14, 1910. Decided October 31, 1910.

Background

By the beginning of the twentieth century the Court had clearly established the notion that prospective jurors who had formed an opinion about
the guilt of an accused were not necessarily unconstitutionally prejudiced. If
they were able to change their minds and arrive at a verdict based on only
evidence admitted into court, then they were considered competent. If their
impressions of guilt or innocence were too deep to be changed by the evidence, however, then they were considered partial and so incapable of
rendering a fair verdict.

The Court had also clearly established the notion that a trial judge was
competent to determine the fact of unconstitutional prejudice, mainly because the judge could observe the demeanor of jurors while they were declaring their impartiality (see *Hopt* v. *Utah* [1887]). An appellate court, therefore, was not to overrule trial judges unless they made a "manifest" or clear
error in fact when determining partiality (see *Reynolds* v. *U.S.* [1878]).
Justice Oliver Wendell Holmes, Jr., strongly reaffirmed here the Court's continued confidence in jurors to arrive at an impartial verdict even though they
may have formed an opinion from reading a newspaper and its confidence in
the trial judge's ability to evaluate the impartiality of prospective jurors.

Circumstances

On May 8, 1908, James H. Holt killed Henry E. Johnson by striking
him on the head three times with an iron bar known as a fish plate. Both
men were soldiers in the Coast Artillery Corps of the U.S. Army, stationed
at the Fort Warden Military Reservation on the northwestern coast of Puget

Sound, Washington. When off duty, Corporal Johnson, a member of the band, was a cobbler with a shop in the basement of the band barracks. Holt, 21 and a first-class gunner of 108th company, was serving as assistant cook at the Fort.

Since May 8 was payday, Thomas H. Knight, a civilian tailor, and a person identified in the trial only as "one Grieble," murdered Johnson to take his $39 salary. Holt invited the cobbler to his room on the pretext of making payment for work on his shoes; while there, he asked for a receipt. As Johnson bent down to write one, Holt hit him three times on the back of the head. After he fell face downward on the table, Holt struck him twice more.

The three companions then went to nearby Port Townsend where—according to the trial transcript—they "spent the money riotously." Knight became hopelessly drunk, so Holt and Grieble returned to the basement and put Johnson's body in the heating furnace at 5:45 A.M. the next morning. It was discovered only a few hours later in a charred, but recognizable, condition. The men returned to Port Townsend and were arrested at about 8 A.M.

During an investigation, two Captains showed Holt a coat covered with soot marks and asked him to put it on. After he did and saw that it fit, he admitted it was his. He also admitted the gunner's badge on a blouse burned in the furnace was his, although at trial he denied ownership of both. In addition, when the captains testified to this incident in court, Holt's attorney asserted that, because Holt was an enlisted man, the instructions "by his superior officers to do a thing, left him no exercise of his own discretion or his own free will in the matter, and, in effect, compelled him to do so."

Holt was tried before a jury in the circuit court of the United States, Western District of Washington, Northern Division, starting December 8, 1908. The jury separated on Friday, December 18, after all evidence had been presented and both sides rested, but before closing arguments. That Sunday morning local newspapers published an article stating, in the main, that the defendant would take the stand in his own behalf Monday morning, that the government would call a witness from Chicago, and that Holt had made a confession the judge ruled inadmissible. Holt's lawyer later claimed that the prosecution had an employee of the district attorney's office put the newspaper before the jury.

Prior to closing arguments on Monday, the court in the presence of the jury interrogated the reporter who wrote the story (which the jurors knew, from being in court themselves, was inaccurate) and elicited from him an admission that he had been misinformed in regard to some of the facts in the article. The court then admonished and advised the jurors to be careful not to give heed to unreliable statements published by the papers, and on each subsequent adjournment the judge warned the jurors to refrain from talking about the case or any subject connected with it.

After Holt was convicted and sentenced to life imprisonment, he appealed to the Court for a new trial based on numerous alleged errors.

Summary of the Court's Analysis

Justice Oliver Wendell Holmes, Jr., writes for the Court.
Chief Justice Melville Weston Fuller and Justices John Marshall Harlan,
Edward Douglas White, Joseph McKenna, William R. Day,
William Henry Moody, Horace Harmon Lurton,
and Charles Evans Hughs join.

Justice Holmes notes that some of Holt's objections are "meticulous," and these will be dealt with "summarily" (247), but, nevertheless, he shall take up the allegations of error in the same order that Holt submitted them.

First, Holmes declares the indictment "well enough" and then adds that the trial court was correct in refusing to allow Holt to withdraw his plea of not guilty.

Holt's objection to "not sustaining a challenge for cause to a juryman" elicits lengthy comment (247). Holmes writes:

> On his examination it appeared that this juryman had not talked with anyone who purported to know about the case of his own knowledge, but that he had taken the newspaper statements for facts; that he had no other opinion other than that derived from the papers, and that evidence would change it very easily, although it would take some evidence to remove it. He stated that if the evidence failed to prove the facts alleged in the newspapers, he would decide according to the evidence at the trial, and that he thought he could try the case solely upon the evidence, fairly and impartially. (248)

Having summarized the nature of the juror's opinion, Holmes turns to the trial judge's evaluation of its depth: "The finding of the trial court upon the strength of the juryman's opinion and his partiality or impartiality ought not to be set aside by a reviewing court unless the error is manifest, which it is not in this case" (248). Here Holmes alludes to the famous words of Justice Waite, who asserted, "The finding of the trial court upon that issue [juror impartiality] ought not to be set aside by a reviewing court, unless the error is manifest," *Reynolds* v. *U.S.* (1878) at 246.

Since the judge in this case said he was "unwilling to exclude the jury from any part of the proceedings in the trial" (249), he did not dismiss them while the attorneys argued about the inadmissibility of evidence, some parts of which were described as "'confessions'" (249). Holt's objections elicit from Holmes comments about what is termed the trustworthiness and competency of the jury. Here, Holmes was considering the capabilities of the jury to discount evidence they were aware of, but ruled inadmissible. Part of the evidence came from outside the trial (a newspaper); part of the evidence came from inside the trial (a prosecutor's arguments for introducing statements termed "confessions").

When explaining why the Court would not rule the jury unconstitutionally tainted after hearing the prosecutor argue unsuccessfully for the admission of "confessions" into evidence, Holmes writes, "Moreover, the judge said to the jury that they were to decide the case on the testimony as it came from the witnesses on the stand; not what the counsel might say or the newspapers publish; that he was not excluding them because he assumed they were men of experience and common sense and could decide the case upon the evidence that the court admitted" (249). Although Holmes admitted that "the more conservative course is to exclude the jury during the consideration of the admissibility of confessions" (249), he asserts, "We cannot say that he [the trial judge] was wrong in thinking that the men before him were competent for their task" (250).

Holmes gave the same reasons for not assigning error to the district attorney's opening statement in which the attorney characterized as "confessions" Holt's admissions he owned "a coat with soot marks upon it, and a gunner's badge" (250).

The next issue was the judge's decision to allow the jury to "separate" after each day's testimony was finished, with the result that some "read the Seattle daily papers with articles on the case, while the trial was going on" (251). This action, Holmes says, raises the "question how far the jury lawfully may be trusted to do their duty when the judge is satisfied that they are worthy of the trust" (249). Holmes says the possibility that the jurors would read these articles after leaving the courthouse each day "is so obvious" that "it may be assumed that they did so in this case" (250). Nevertheless, he asserts, their actions do not warrant a new trial. Using words often quoted in the twentieth century, he writes, "If the mere opportunity for prejudice or corruption is to raise a presumption that they exist, it will be hard to maintain jury trials under the conditions of the present day" (250). "We do not see in the facts before us," he concludes, "any conclusive ground for saying that his expressed belief that the trial was fair and the prisoner has nothing to complain of is wrong" (250).

An ingenious attempt to rely on the Fifth Amendment is described by Holmes as "an extravagant extension" (252). Holt objected to his being forced to try on a "blouse" in court. The jurist responds, "But the prohibition of compelling a man in a criminal court to be witness against himself is a prohibition of the use of physical or moral compulsion to extort communications from him, not an exclusion of his body as evidence when it may be material" (252).

The final two objections focus on the judge's charge to the jury. Holt objected to the judge's descriptions of reasonable doubt and presumption of innocence. Holmes summarily dismisses these complaints.

Ruling

Holmes writes, "We have dealt with all that seem to us to deserve mention and find no sufficient reason why the judgment should not be affirmed. Judgment affirmed" (254).

Significance

Having survived hand-to-hand combat during the Civil War, Holmes was not a timid man, and evidence of his fortitude is clearly exhibited in this opinion. In the main, this case is significant because of the trust placed in the jury to discard inadmissible evidence when arriving at a verdict.

Holmes affirmed the trial judge's confidence in the jury members to ignore whatever they may read in a newspaper after the end of each day's testimony. He, in fact, said that the decision allowing jurors to "separate" each night and to leave the courthouse is in itself an act of confidence in the ability of the jurors to ignore all evidence not admitted into trial. Indeed, the stalwart jurist made the trustworthiness and competency of jurors a central issue in this case, describing them as "men of experience and common sense . . . [who] could decide the case upon the evidence that the court admitted" (249).

The trial court won the Court's confidence even though the judge did not disqualify a prospective juror who, prior to the trial, had read the newspaper and formed an opinion based on what he read and even though the judge presented an opportunity for seated jurors to read newspapers during the trial after they separated at the end of the day. Consequently, Holmes reaffirmed both Waite's famous ruling that the trial judge's evaluation of the impartiality of a juror should not be overruled unless manifestly in error, *Reynolds* v. *U.S.* (1878), and Marshall's ruling that not all persons who read the newspaper and form an opinion are necessarily unconstitutionally prejudiced for or against the accused, *Burr* v. *U.S.* (1807).

To these famous rulings, Holmes adds his own eventually very wellknown words when he asserts that the "mere opportunity" for prejudice should not be equated with the existence of prejudice. In other words, Holmes was asserting that what jurors read about a trial would not necessarily make them unconstitutionally prejudiced. He also affirmed the notion that jury impartiality is a question of fact that no one is more capable of determining than is the trial judge.

Stroud v. U.S.

Robert F. Stroud
v.
The United States of America

Docket No. 1919-276
251 U.S. 15, 64 L.Ed. 103, 40 S.Ct. 50 (1919)

Argued October 22, 1919. Decided November 24, 1919.

Background

Changing the location (change of venue) of the trial is a solution to the problem of finding an impartial jury that can be traced back at least as far as to Coke. Here, however, instead of changing the location of the trial, the judge simply excluded citizens of a certain county from serving as jurors (change of venirepersons).

Circumstances

Robert F. Stroud is better known as "the Bird Man of Alcatraz" after a 1955 book by Thomas E. Gaddis and a 1962 film starring Burt Lancaster. The name is a bit of a misnomer, however, since Stroud was forced to give up his birds when transferred in 1942 from the federal prison at Leavenworth, Kansas—for disciplinary reasons—to Alcatraz. Although he had only a third grade education, he taught himself French, Spanish, and Greek, and he earned diplomas in mechanical drawing, engineering, music, theology, and mathematics from the Kansas State Agricultural College's extension division.

Stroud's work with birds can be traced to a single incident at Leavenworth Federal Prison. After being blown to his knees in the prison yard by a strong wind during a thunderstorm, he found himself face-to-face with a nest of four sparrows, which he then took to his solitary cell. There he applied a splint made out of a toothpick to one of the birds, which he named Runt. Eventually he was caring for as many as 300 birds (nearly all of them Roller Canaries), and he had built many cages and a crude laboratory in his cell to help him study bird diseases. In 1943 a 60,000-page manuscript he had written, called *Stroud's Digest of Diseases of Birds,* was published by Webb

Publishers. Financed by his brother and highly acclaimed, it was 500 pages in length and included 87 plates, nearly all hand drawn by Stroud. He also published a number of articles on birds in the *Roller Canary Digest;* the articles were often based in part on birds he dissected at first with his fingernails.

Born June 28, 1890, in Seattle, Washington, Stroud ran away from home at the age of 13, and by 18 he wound up in Alaska building a railroad for a company that abandoned the project when the port at one end of the line appeared, upon reflection, to be inadequate. Stroud, unemployed, contracted pneumonia and was nursed back to health by a dance-hall girl and prostitute who was twice his age and who called herself Kitty O'Brien. After a friend from the railroad, F. V. "Charlie" von Dahmer, beat up Kitty one January night in 1909 and tore from her neck a locket with the picture of her daughter in it, Stroud shot Dahmer to death. He turned himself in to the city marshal at Juneau, and later was sentenced to 12 years at McNeil Island prison, Puget Sound, Washington.

Because at McNeil Island he stabbed another prisoner who turned him in for stealing food from the kitchen, he was transferred in 1912 as one of fifty hard-core prisoners to the newly completed prison at Leavenworth, surrounded by a mammoth brick wall that reached 40 feet high in places. There Stroud stabbed and killed a guard named Andrew F. Turner during a fight on March 26, 1916, in the prison cafeteria.

Key evidence against the prisoner came from a letter he wrote to his mother. It reads in part as follows (the many spelling errors are left without remark):

> Sunday, March 26th at the noon meal I got up from the tabel and walk up the aisle to where a guard was standing and started to talk to him. We talked very quitly and stood very close together but any one looking at our faces could see that our words must be very intence—we all at once brake away from each other the guard reaching for his club which was under his left arm with his right hand and my self making a very quick movement with my left hand which had been at my side—Then we both stepped back and the guard seemed to be sick. He caught at the tabel behind him, staggered a littel and slipped to the floor. He died shortly aftwards of heart failure—The [unintelligible word] seems to hold that his heart was alright befor I made that move with my left hand—It wasnt and I will have to prove that when I go to trial. When they give the dead guard the once over they found that he had a dagger wound avout six inches deep that passed through his heart. (From Stroud's Trial Brief)

Stroud was convicted of first-degree murder May 16 and sentenced by Judge John C. Pollock to be hanged July 21. Because Kansas law does not give a judge the right to order the death penalty, however, the United States district attorney presented a "confession of error," and so the circuit court of appeals "reversed the judgment" (16).

On May 28, 1917, Stroud was convicted again, but this time "without capital punishment" (17). When Stroud appealed the second conviction, Solicitor General John W. Davis of the United States willingly "confessed error," in order to have another chance at the death penalty. At a third trial, on June 28, 1918, another jury found Stroud guilty of murder in the first degree, but made no recommendation to dispense with capital punishment. Therefore, a "sentence of death was pronounced," which Stroud also appealed. It is Stroud's appeal of the death sentence that provides the occasion for the Court's opinion. Although his appeal was denied, his mother was able, after indefatigable effort, to persuade President Woodrow Wilson on April 15, 1920, to commute his sentence to life just eight days before Stroud was to be hung in a gallows he watched being built from his prison cell.

He was transferred to the Medical Center for Federal Prisoners at Springfield, Missouri, in 1959, where he died November 21, 1963, of a heart attack. He had spent 42 of his 54 prison years in solitary confinement.

Summary of the Court's Analysis

Justice William R. Day writes for the Court.
Chief Justice Edward Douglas White and Justices Joseph McKenna,
Oliver Wendell Holmes, Jr., Willis Van Devanter, Mahlon Pitney,
James Clark McReynolds, Louis D. Brandeis, and John H. Clark join.

Justice Day says it is because Stroud's appeal focuses on "assignments of error alleged to involve the construction and application of the Constitution of the United States" that this case "is brought directly to this court" (17). He adds, "We shall dispose of such assignments of error as we deem necessary to consider in justice to the contentions raised in behalf of the plaintiff in error" (17), making it clear that the Court will pick which of the many alleged errors it will devote its time to.

Not surprisingly, the first one taken up by the Court is double jeopardy, a procedure forbidden by the Fifth Amendment. Writes Day, "The plaintiff in error himself invoked the action of the court which resulted in a further [third] trial. In such cases, he is not placed in second jeopardy within the meaning of the constitution" (18). In short, the Court said Stroud should not complain about being tried more than once for the same crime when he—and not an official of the government—is the one who asked for the additional trial.

The next claimed error addressed by the Court is the absence of an impartial jury. According to Day, Stroud asserted, "The testimony for the government in the former trials had been printed and commented upon by the local press" (18). Day writes that Stroud claimed the following:

> That the evidence published was only such as the government had introduced, and its wide circulation by the medium of the press created prejudice in the minds of the inhabitants of Leavenworth county against him [Stroud], and that the prejudice existed to such an extent that the jury impaneled to try the case, though not inhabitants of Leavenworth county, were influenced more or less by the prejudice existing in that county against him. (18, 19)

Stroud was also displeased that the prospective jurors during the week of May 20, 1918, heard certain statements read in open court. Among these statements was one by the trial judge, who said that Stroud's attorneys "had acted unprofessionally by not being there in court" (20). According to Day, Stroud said these statements "were commented upon by the public press of Leavenworth county, and created prejudice against defendant and his attorneys" (20).

After Stroud requested the jurors who heard these statements be "discharged" and that the trial be moved to another location, the trial judge simply excluded citizens of Leavenworth county from the jury. Writes Day of this action, "Matters of this sort are addressed to the discretion of the trial judge, and we find nothing in the record to amount to abuse or discretion such as would authorize an appellate court to interfere with the judgment" (20).

Next the Court looks at jurors challenged for cause on the basis "that they were in favor of nothing less than capital punishment in cases of conviction for murder in the first degree" (20). Day says that the challenge to one of these jurors "may well . . . have been sustained" (20, 21). He then points out, though, "This juror was peremptorily challenged by the accused [Stroud], and did not sit upon the jury" (21). Moreover, he notes that, since Stroud was given two more peremptory challenges than the minimum twenty required, his peremptory challenges were not "abridged to his prejudice" (21) by having to use up one on this juror. Day writes, "We are unable to discover anything which requires a reversal upon this ground" (21).

The last alleged error discussed by the Court is a set of letters written by Stroud which Day said Stroud wrote "voluntarily" after the murder. When Stroud tried to mail them, the letters, following the "established practice" of the prison, were turned over to the warden. The warden gave them to the district attorney. These letters, according to Day, contained "expressions tending to establish the guilt of the accused" (21). Thus, Day concludes, "There was neither testimony required of [i.e., forced from] the accused, nor unreasonable search and seizure in violation of his constitutional rights" (21, 22).

Of the other claimed errors, Day writes curtly, "We do not find it necessary to discuss them" (22).

Ruling

Day writes, "We are unable to find that any error was committed to the prejudice of the accused. Affirmed" (22).

Significance

The primary significance related to the conflict between a free press and a fair trial is the Court's approval of the trial judge's solution for avoiding a change of venue when citizens in a given county were exposed to a substantial amount of pretrial publicity. Instead of changing the location of the trial, his solution was to exclude citizens of a certain county from serving as jurors.

The Court's assertions about peremptory challenges is also of some significance to this conflict. Even though a trial judge may err by failing to sustain a juror properly challenged for the cause of holding unconstitutional prejudice resulting from pretrial publicity, the Court asserted that no reversible error has been committed if the defendant peremptorily challenges the juror and if the defendant has been granted more peremptory challenges than the minimum. In other words, forcing the defendant to use a peremptory challenge to excuse a juror who should have been excused for cause does not unconstitutionally injure defendants who are given more than the minimum number of statutorily required peremptory challenges. The rationale is that defendants in such situations still have the minimum number of legally required peremptory challenges even after being forced to use one unnecessarily. This ruling on peremptory challenges extends similar reasoning found in *Hopt* v. *Utah* (1887) and *Spies* v. *Illinois* (1887).

Shepherd v. Florida

Samuel Shepherd and Walter Irvin
v.
State of Florida

Docket No. 1951-420
341 U.S. 50, 95 L.Ed. 740, 71 S.Ct. 549 (1951)
Argued March 9, 1951. Decided April 9, 1951.

Background

After a fairly long hiatus in addressing issues related to the conflict between the free press and a fair trial, the Court enters the discussion once again in 1951, but this time through the back door. Although the ruling did not mention this conflict, a concurring opinion of two justices did focus on one particular aspect of it: intensive pretrial publicity.

In a *per curiam* decision, the Court—writing only a four-word sentence —reversed the conviction of two African Americans (then called Negroes) who had been tried for rape. The reversal appears to have been based exclusively on a belief that African Americans were "intentionally excluded" from a grand jury, and so the ruling appears at first blush unrelated to the definition of a free press.

In a concurring opinion, however, Justice Robert H. Jackson, joined by Felix Frankfurter, indicated that he was of a mind to reverse on the additional grounds of unconstitutionally prejudicial pretrial publicity. The newspaper coverage was so intense, according to Jackson, that implementing due process would have required moving the trial to a place unaffected by the influence of this publicity. Thus, expressed in this case is one of the major concerns about pretrial publicity—the level of its intensity. The proposed solution is a change of venue.

This concern for the jury as a whole represents a new consideration for the Court. Prior to 1951, the primary concern for fairness centered on the individual juror. Consideration of the entire jury was not reflected in a ruling until after World War I, when racial prejudice began to manifest itself more openly. Then, the Court recognized the power of intense and pervasive community prejudice when it ruled that five African Americans in Philips County, Arkansas, could not receive a fair trial there because anyone who would have acquitted them would have found it impossible to live in that location thereafter, *Moore* v. *Dempsey* (1923). Here the Court recognizes that such prejudice is not necessarily purely an immutable, indigenous phenomenon; it can be inflamed by the press.

Circumstances

A newly married seventeen-year-old white girl (with initials N. P.) in Lake County, Florida, reported on July 16, 1949, that she had been raped "at the point of a pistol, by four Negroes" (50). Samuel Shepherd and Walter Irvin, both then 22, and Charles Greenlee, then 16, were arrested that same day, indicted July 20 by a grand jury, arraigned August 12, and put on trial September 1. Three days later, the jury convicted all three—Shepherd and Irvin without recommendation of mercy—and the judge sentenced the two older men to death by electrocution. Their conviction and sentence were upheld by the Supreme Court of Florida.

Not surprisingly, there was a great deal of pretrial publicity. One of the stories that prejudiced the community against the two men pointed out that the sheriff said the two men had confessed. No one, including the sheriff, repudiated the story. An editor of one local paper said of the confession story, "The article . . . appeared to the best of my recollection in a number of daily newspapers and was not denied for a period of three days. I don't think they were ever denied" (50). According to Justice Jackson, "Witnesses and persons called as jurors said they had read or heard of this statement. However, no confession was offered at the trial" (51).

At a pretrial hearing Shepherd and Irvin said they were beaten by prison officials and did indeed confess, but only because they feared further beatings. Judge T. G. Futch would not let Dr. Nelson W. B. Spaulding, a physician, testify at the hearing about their physical condition, which their attorneys said would give clear evidence of the beatings.

The press also exploited other pretrial activities. A mob gathered outside the jail and demanded that Shepherd and Irvin be handed over to it. Another mob burned the home of Shepherd's father and mother. A reporter stated at a pretrial hearing that six white men drove to a small café in Groveland, called the Blue Flame and owned by African Americans, got out of their car, and fired about eight to ten shots into the rear door of the café from a distance of ten to fifteen feet away. Lawless mobs were reported to be roaming the county looking for the defendants and burning indiscriminately the homes of African Americans. One paper printed the assertion that if the two were not found guilty, then a mob would lynch them.

Nearly the entire community of African Americans fled the area before the trial, fearing for their lives and abandoning homes, farms, and businesses. National Guard units were called in to patrol the streets of Lessburg, Eustis,

Groveland, and Mascotte from July 17 to July 27. These events were reported, often repeatedly, and sometimes sensationally in the press. According to Jackson a cartoon was published in one newspaper "picturing four electric chairs and headed, 'No compromise—Supreme penalty'" (53).

Recognizing the potential for trouble, trial Judge Futch had the defendants transferred from the county jail at Tavares to the State Prison at Raiford, 100 miles from Lake County. He also promulgated a number of special rules:

> [He] limited the number of visitors to those that could be seated, allowed no one to stand or loiter in the hallways, stairways, and parts of the courthouse for thirty minutes before court convened and after it recessed, closed the elevators except to officers of the court . . . , required each person entering the courtroom to submit to search, [and] prohibited any person from taking a "valise, satchel, bag, basket, bundle or other such item" to the courtroom floor of the courthouse. (54)

Judge Futch charged the sheriff to enforce the rules and authorized him to use as many deputies as would be necessary.

Harry E. Gaylord was appointed by the court on August 12, the day of the arraignment, to be Shepherd and Irvin's attorney. By August 22, the NAACP had secured for them attorney Alex Akerman, Jr., of Orlando assisted by Franklin H. Williams of New York. Akerman immediately asked that the trial, scheduled for August 29, be delayed. Instead, jury selection began that day, and opening statements were given September 1. In addition, a hurricane struck Orlando shortly thereafter and Akerman lost two nights and one full day of preparation for the case. On September 3 the men were convicted and sentenced to death.

Akerman introduced into a pretrial hearing evidence of sensational news coverage from a great many newspapers, including the following: Orlando *Morning Sentinel,* Orlando *Evening Star, Sunday Sentinel Star,* Clermont and South Lake *Press,* Clermont and Groveland *News Topic,* Mount Dora *Topic,* Tampa *Tribune,* Miami *Herald, Eustis Lake Region News,* Lake County *Citizen,* and Leesburg *Commercial.*

Summary of the Court's Analysis

In a *per curium* decision, the Court made only the following comment, "The judgment is reversed. *Cassell* v. *Texas* (1950)" (50).

From this ruling, the only clue to the Court's reasoning can be found in its citation to *Cassell* v. *Texas* (1950), which was decided the year before. In *Cassell* the Court reversed the conviction of Lee Cassell, an African American, because, the Court said, "Negroes" were purposefully discriminated against in the selection of the grand jury that indicted him. This discrimination was manifested, according to the Court, in the fact that the Dallas County Commissioners who impanelled the jury said they simply did not know any African Americans whom they could select for jury duty. To the Court this lack of acquaintance with persons constituting such a large minority of the population is clear evidence of a conscious effort to exclude African Americans from grand juries.

Likewise, only one African American was a member of the grand jury that indicted Shepherd and Irvin, even though 4,500 of the 18,000 adults in the county were of African American heritage. In the memory of court officials, this one person was the only African American ever to serve on a jury in that county.

Justice Robert H. Jackson writes a concurring opinion.
Justice Felix Frankfurter joins.

Justice Jackson writes to point out that racial discrimination is not the only reason he would cite for reversing Cassell's conviction. Intense prejudicial pretrial publicity is another. He summarizes the problem with such pretrial publicity this way:

But prejudicial influences outside the courtroom, becoming all too typical of a highly publicized trial, were brought to bear on this jury with such force that the conclusion is inescapable that these defendants were prejudged as guilty and the trial was but a legal gesture to register a verdict already dictated by the press and the public opinion which it generated. (51)

Jackson then moves to the specific constitutional problems raised by publication of a newspaper story saying Shepherd and Irvin had confessed, even though no confession was produced at the trial. He writes:

If the prosecutor in the courtroom had told the jury that the accused had confessed but did not offer to prove the confession, the court would undoubtedly have declared a mistrial and cited the attorney for contempt. If a confession had been offered in court, the defendant would have had the right to be confronted by the persons who claimed to have witnessed it, to cross-examine them, and to contradict their testimony. . . . When such events take place in the courtroom, defendant's counsel can meet them with evidence, arguments, and requests for instructions, and can at least preserve his objections on the record. (51, 52)

But the court cannot control the admission of "evidence" into the newspapers. The result, writes Jackson, is that "rights of the defendant to be confronted by witnesses against him and to cross-examine them are thereby circumvented" (53). He adds, "It is hard to imagine a more prejudicial influence than a press release by the officer of the court charged with defendants' custody stating that they had confessed" (53). Moreover, this statement, which was "unsworn to, unseen, uncross-examined and uncontradicted was conveyed by the press to the jury" (52). He summarizes his objections to such activities in a single sentence: "Newspapers, in the enjoyment of their constitutional rights, may not deprive accused persons of their right to fair trial" (53).

Jackson's proposed solution is simple. He writes, "The judicial process must be protected by removing the trial to a forum beyond its probable influence" (53). In this regard, he took note of two motions by the defense: "one to defer the trial until the passion had died out and the other for a change of venue. These were denied" (53).

Although pleased that the trial judge took precautions to see that the trial itself was conducted in a calm atmosphere, Jackson notes, "Such precautions, however commendable, show the reaction that the atmosphere which permeated the trial created in the mind of the trial judge" (54). He adds, "This trial took place under conditions and was accompanied by events which would deny defendants a fair trial before any kind of jury" (55). In an undisguised attack on the press coverage, he writes, "The case presents one of the best examples of one of the worst menaces to American justice" (55).

The consequences of such actions are clear to Jackson, "These convictions, accompanied by such events, do not meet any civilized conception of due process. That alone is sufficient, in my mind, to warrant reversal" (52).

Significance

This case gains significance not from the Court's truncated ruling but from Justice Jackson's concurring opinion presenting a highly significant analysis of the increasing danger posed to a fair trial by unregulated publicity promulgated by a mass medium: newspapers. He noted that such publicity can threaten a fair trial not only by influencing the opinion of a particular juror who may read information in the press about the defendant but also by informing so often and so strongly the opinions of the general populace in a given geographical area so that it would be nearly impossible to find any potential juror unaffected by the publicity.

The focus of his analysis is the existence of unconstitutionally prejudicial statements disseminated in pretrial publicity by area newspapers. Jackson pointed out, on the one hand, courts can—indeed are required to—control the evidence given to the jury during a trial. In fact, a large number of very complicated rules have been developed over the years in a deliberate attempt to prevent the admission into trials of "prejudicial" material. These rules are designed to protect defendants' Sixth Amendment rights to a fair trial.

Like defendants in a criminal trial, the press, on the other hand, are also protected by a constitutional amendment: the First. Consequently, in spite of the elaborate rules developed to assure the Sixth Amendment's guarantee of a fair trial, jurors and prospective jurors could gain access to constitutionally nonadmissible (prejudicial) information by reading it in a newspaper. The general problem illustrated in the concurring opinion of this case, then, concerns a conflict between two constitutional amendments. The problem facing the Court is how to satisfy the requirements of each amendment without abridging the rights proclaimed in either one. Jackson's common-sense solution is to remove the jury from the influence of prejudicial pretrial publicity by moving the trial to a location where no such publicity appeared.

It is important to note that Jackson did not address the motion for a continuance, although the Court would eventually suggest continuances as a valid method to counter potentially prejudicial pretrial publicity. Here the reason for the continuance is not to allow time for passions to cool down but to allow the defense time to prepare its case. Shepherd and Irvin secured counsel of their choice on August 22. A hearing on pretrial motions began August 25, and jury selection began on August 29. In addition, a hurricane hit Orlando during this time, making it impossible for the defendants' attorneys to work for two nights and a day. That leaves only a few days for trial preparation for defendants housed in a prison more than 100 miles away from their attorneys.

The general problem of the dangers inherent in pretrial publicity can be illustrated specifically by the publication of a confession in a newspaper. Indeed, later cases are to focus narrowly on the difficulties raised by this particular conflict. Jackson noted several threats to a fair trial arising from publication in the press of a confession. The defendants do not have an opportunity to confront those persons who claim to have witnessed it, to cross-examine these witnesses, or even to contradict their testimony, all rights guaranteed by the Sixth Amendment.

One other aspect of the concurring opinion deserves mention. Jackson hinted at the dangers of contempt arising from publicizing statements asserting the existence of a confession that was never entered into evidence at a trial. He observed that if the prosecutor in a courtroom had told the jury that the accused had confessed but did not offer to prove the confession, the court would undoubtedly have declared a mistrial and cited the attorney for contempt.

Referring to a court's contempt powers, Jackson lamented that three recent cases had "gone a long way to disable a judge from dealing with press interference with the trial process" (52), citing *Craig* v. *Harney* (1946), *Pennekamp* v. *Florida* (1945), and *Bridges* v. *California* (1941). Jackson further noted that in *Nye* v. *U.S.* (1941), the Court ruled contempt is not to be imposed unless the "interference" "takes place in the immediate presence of the court" (52). Nevertheless, Jackson asserts, the trial judge, even though not possessing contempt power in this situation, is not without authority to "protect" defendants from an "out-of-court campaign to convict" (52). This authority is the power to change the venue.

In summary, this case gains a great deal of significance from Jackson's concurring opinion outlining the problems of securing an unprejudiced jury after a community has been exposed to intense pretrial publicity. Jackson recognized that demonstrating the prejudice of an individual juror is not necessary when an entire community is subjected to such intense prejudicial publicity that it is highly unlikely anyone could escape its influence.

Stroble v. California

Fred Stroble

v.

State of California

Docket No. 1952-373
343 U.S. 181, 96 L.Ed. 872, 72 S.Ct. 599 (1952)
Argued March 6, 1952. Decided May 12, 1952.

Background

Stroble continues an interest that first attracted the attention of the Court shortly after the end of World War I: concern for the impartiality of the jury as a whole, not simply with the possible prejudice of an individual juror. Initially, this new interest focused primarily on the racial prejudice of a community from which prospective jurors were selected. Perhaps nowhere is this interest better expressed than in the concurring opinion by Justice Robert H. Jackson—joined only by Justice Felix Frankfurter—in *Shepherd* v. *Florida* (1951). Jackson recognized the possibility that prejudice infecting an entire community is not necessarily purely an immutable, indigenous phenomenon; it can be inflamed by the press. In *Stroble* v. *California,* a year later, the Court turns from the racial aspect of jury impartiality and focuses specifically on the impact of the mass media and more narrowly on the ramifications for a fair trial of publishing confessions.

Perhaps because in *Shepherd* Jackson pointed out several threats to a fair trial arising from the publication in the press of a confession, Stroble's attorneys claimed he did not receive a fair trial as a result of his numerous confessions being widely published. Indeed, while Stroble was in the very process of confessing, the district attorney was releasing portions of his statements to the press. Jackson noted in *Shepherd* that some of the dangers of publishing confessions are that defendants do not have an opportunity to confront those persons who claim to have witnessed it, to cross-examine these witnesses, or even to contradict their testimony, all rights guaranteed by the Sixth Amendment.

The Court, however, drew important distinctions between Stroble's plight and the situation of the three young African Americans convicted of rape in rural central Florida. Stroble, for example, failed to ask for a change of venue, whereas Shepherd many times requested a different trial location.

In addition, Stroble simply asked the Court intuitively to recognize the existence of community prejudice; Shepherd presented thoroughly documented evidence of intense, sensational, prejudicial coverage by the local and regional press. Finally, unlike Stroble's statements, which were admitted into evidence, the so-called confessions by the three young African American men were printed in the press but ruled inadmissible as evidence in the trial. In short, the Court told Stroble that persons who claim a trial is unfair must shoulder the burden of proof.

For support of essential points related to Stroble's claims of denial of due process, the Court reaches back to *Lisenba* v. *California* (1941). The Court takes from *Lisenba* general notions of due process and applies them to Stroble's situation, including the statements or confessions attributed to Stroble published prior to his trial. Major Raymond Lisenba, a.k.a. Robert S. James, was convicted of murdering his wife by blindfolding her, tying her to a table, and then causing a rattlesnake to bite her. When she did not die from the rattlesnake bite, Lisenba drowned his wife by forcing her head under water at the edge of a fish pond. Lisenba said that bringing the snakes into the courtroom and submitting them as evidence deprived him of the Fourteenth Amendment's right to due process, which includes a fair trial by the state. To his argument, the Court replied, "The fact that evidence admitted as relevant by a court is shocking to the sensibilities of those in the courtroom cannot, for that reason alone, render its reception a violation of due process" (229).

Lisenba also argued that his confessions were involuntary and so the use of them as evidence in the trial deprived him of due process. The Court said in response, "The aim of the requirement of due process is . . . to prevent fundamental unfairness in the use of evidence whether true or false" (236). Using a now-famous phrase quoted in *Stroble,* the Court continued, "As applied to a criminal trial, denial of due process is the failure to observe that fundamental fairness essential to the very concept of justice. In order to declare a denial of it we must find that the absence of that fairness *fatally infected* [emphasis added] the trial; the facts complained of must be of such quality as necessarily prevent a fair trial" (236).

Two more points made by the Court in *Lisenba* are relevant to *Stroble.* The first is that the Court asserts it will "accept the determination of the triers of fact, unless it is so lacking in support in the evidence that to give it effect would work that fundamental unfairness which is at war with due process" (238). The second is that the Court said its "duty, then, is to determine whether . . . the admission of the confession [is] so fundamentally unfair, so contrary to the common concept of ordered liberty as to amount to a taking of a life without due process of law" (238). The phrase "ordered liberty" was taken from *Palko* v. *Connecticut* (1937), but it is not repeated in *Stroble*; instead, the Court focuses exclusively on the notion of fundamental rights.

In *Stroble,* the Court uses from *Lisenba* the notion of "that fundamental fairness essential to the very concept of justice" to determine if "newspaper accounts aroused such prejudice in the community" that they "fatally infected" the community such that due process was denied (236). It further asserts that Stroble must shoulder the burden of proving that the trial judge's admission of the confession denied him due process.

Circumstances

Born in Austria in 1881, Fred Stroble, was described by his lawyers as having weak and impaired mentality. He came to the United States in 1901 and eventually found a trade, working as a baker for twenty-one years from 1925 until 1946. On Tuesday, November 14, 1949, one of the most extensive and publicized manhunts in California history began when Stroble, at the age of sixty-eight, fled the home of his daughter, Sylvia Hausman, after molesting and murdering Linda Joyce Glucoft, the playmate of his six-year-old grandaughter, Rochelle.

Linda, then also six years old, told her mother at about 3:30 P.M. on November 14 that she was going next door to play with Rochelle. Rochelle's mother (Stroble's daughter, Sylvia Hausman), however, had already left her house at 2003 South Crescent Heights, Los Angeles, taking Rochelle to a party.

From Stroble's many confessions (which took up ninety-four pages in the trial transcript), it was learned that, when Linda came to the house after Rochelle and her mother had left, he gave her a chocolate bar and took her into Fred (his grandson) and Rochelle's bedroom where he kissed and hugged her and put his fingers in her vagina. Because she objected and began to scream, he squeezed her throat until she was quiet. After she revived, Stroble took one of Fred's knitted neckties from a rack on the dresser and tied it around Linda's neck.

Using a blanket to move her body, Stroble became aware she was not dead, so he hit her on the temple with a ball peen hammer he found in the kitchen. He then continued dragging her body through the house and outside to the incinerator. Still not sure she was dead, he went back to the kitchen for an ice pick. Feeling for her heart, he pushed in the pick from front and back, later telling police he wanted to make sure he got the heart so she would not suffer.

Afraid she might yet have some life left in her, Stroble went to the garage where he found an axe, which he used to hit her a couple of times on the head and the backbone with the flat part of the blade. Remembering at that point a bull fight he saw in Mexico a few years earlier, he thought he finally discovered a way to make sure she was dead. He returned to the kitchen, where he got a knife with a blade about two inches wide and stabbed her in the back and in the back of her neck.

Before running away, Stroble returned to the bedroom to retrieve Linda's panties. He threw the panties into the incinerator, covered Linda's body, and left home. The next day he was identified in a bar by a private citizen, William Martin Miller, who then summoned a uniformed patrol officer, Arnold W. Carlson, to make an arrest. While the police were driving him to the station house, Stroble gave his first confession, saying he had considered jumping into the ocean to commit suicide. Eventually, Stroble was questioned by District Attorney William E. Simpson, who released during and after the questioning a recorded interrogation of Stroble's descriptions of the ghastly event. Included in Stroble's statements were descriptions of the attempted molesting, the choking, the dragging, the ice pick stabbing, the axe bludgeoning, and the knifing at the back of the skull. After printing all these lurid details, The Los Angeles *Herald Express* dubbed Stroble the Werewolf.

Stroble's trial started on January 3, 1950, and just over two weeks later, on January 18, the jury began deliberations. Stroble had, on many previous occasions, molested female children; in fact, at the time he murdered Linda, he was a fugitive from justice, having jumped bail on a charge of molesting young girls. He had used the Hausman home before for what he described as a "hide out."

When Linda did not return home by five o'clock the afternoon of the murder, her parents notified the police who began a search. Her body was found early the next morning behind the incinerator of the Hausman home. It was wrapped in a blanket and covered with paper and wooden boxes. An axe was standing upright against the incinerator, a knife was stuck in a pile of lumber nearby, an ice pick was laying on a shelf in the garage, and a ball peen hammer rested on the ground behind a pile of wood. Her torn panties were found in the incinerator, and her hair and blood were found on the weapons.

An autopsy revealed the cause of death as asphyxia due to strangulation. A knitted, red necktie was wound twice around her neck. In addition to a mass of contusions and abrasions about her head, chest, and back, the autopsy also revealed a laceration extending deep into her neck, passing between the sixth and seventh cervical vertebrae and lacerating the spinal cord. Her external genitalia showed irritation. The right chest showed two puncture wounds. In the opinion of the examining physician all the wounds, with the exception of the deep laceration in the back of the neck, were inflicted while she was alive.

After deliberating less than twenty-four hours, the jury found Stroble guilty of murder in the first degree. The following day a hearing on Stroble's sanity started. On February 6 the judge found him sane and sentenced him to death. His conviction was upheld by the Supreme Court of California.

Summary of the Court's Analysis

Justice Tom C. Clark writes for the Court.
Chief Justice Fred M. Vinson, Justices Stanley F. Reed,
Robert H. Jackson, Harold H. Burton, and Sherman Minton join.

Justice Clark notes at the outset that Stroble lists five reasons for overturning his conviction, all based on a failure to receive due process. He says Stroble claims the following:

(1) that his conviction was based in part on a coerced confession;

(2) that a fair trial was impossible because of inflammatory newspaper reports inspired by the District Attorney;

(3) that he was in effect deprived of counsel in the course of his sanity hearing;

(4) that there was an unwarranted delay in his arraignment; and

(5) that the prosecuting officers unjustifiably refused to permit an attorney to consult petitioner [Stroble] shortly after petitioners' [Stroble's] arrest. (183)

Taking up first the issue of whether the confession was voluntary or coerced, Clark points out that Stroble "did object at the trial . . . to the introduction in evidence of a confession which he made after his arrival in the District Attorney's office" (186). After reviewing the record, however, he concludes that Stroble "from the time of his arrest until his trial . . . was anxious [eager] to confess to anybody who would listen—as much so after he had consulted with counsel as before" (191). Clark continues, "His willingness to confess to the doctors who examined him . . . in circumstances free of coercion suggest strongly" (191) that he wanted to cleanse himself of his guilt by confessing.

"We turn now," Clark writes, "to petitioner's [Stroble's] contention that the newspaper accounts of his arrest and confession were so inflammatory as to make a fair trial in the Los Angeles area impossible—even though a period of six weeks intervened between the day of his arrest and the beginning of his trial" (191). Clark says the question here is "whether newspaper accounts aroused such prejudice in the community that petitioner's [Stroble's] trial was [quoting from *Lisenba* v. *California* (1941)] 'fatally infected' with an absence of 'that fundamental fairness essential to the very concept of justice'" (191, 192).

Clark addresses this question first by reviewing the publicity given to this case. He notes that the full text of the confession was printed on the day it was read into the record at the preliminary hearing. He also points out that many stories were printed on the front page with "large headlines" (192) and that Stroble was called "'a werewolf,'" a "'fiend,'" and a "'sex-mad killer'" (192). Thereafter, however, the publicity "soon abated," and the "trial itself was reported by Los Angeles newspapers usually on inside pages" (193). From this review, Clark concludes, again quoting in reference to fairness from *Lisenba* v. *California* (1941), "We agree with the California Supreme Court that petitioner [Stroble] has failed to show that the newspaper accounts aroused against him such prejudice in the community as to 'necessarily prevent a fair trial'" (193).

A serious problem for Stroble arises from the fact that he did not ask for a change of venue to escape possible prejudicial effects of the publicity. Clark writes, "We think it significant that two deputy defenders who were vigorous in petitioner's [Stroble's] defense throughout the trial saw no occasion to seek a transfer of the action to another county on the ground that prejudicial newspaper accounts had made it impossible for petitioner [Stroble] to obtain a fair trial in the Superior Court of Los Angeles County" (194).

Although Stroble's attorneys claimed the publicity "'deprived [him] of the presumption of innocence,'" (194) the trial court asserted, "'There is nothing to show those jurors ever saw those papers or ever read those papers'" (194). Clark continues:

> Indeed, at no stage of the proceedings has petitioner [Stroble] offered so much as an affidavit to prove that any juror was in fact prejudiced by the newspaper stories. He asks the Court simply to read those stories and then to declare, over the contrary finding of two state courts, that they necessarily deprived him of due process. That we cannot do. (195)

Clark concludes his analysis of the extrajudicial publicity with these words:

> There is no affirmative showing that any community prejudice ever existed or in any way affected the deliberation of the jury. It is also significant that in this case the confession which was one of the most prominent features of the newspaper accounts was made voluntarily and was introduced in evidence at the trial itself. (195)

To Stroble's claim that he was denied effective counsel when he waived trial by jury on the issue of insanity, the Court says simply, "We find no substance in petitioner's [his] contention" (195). Clark adds, "Every psychiatrist who had testified, whether on behalf of petitioner [Stroble] or on behalf of the prosecution, had reached the same conclusion that petitioner [Stroble] was sane" (196).

In dismissing Stroble's assertion of an "unwarranted delay in arraignment," Clark writes, "Upon the facts of this case, we cannot hold that the illegal conduct of law enforcement officers in not taking petitioner [Stroble] promptly before a magistrate, coerced the confession he made . . . or in any other way deprived him of a fair and impartial trial" (197).

The last error asserted by Stroble is that his lawyer was not granted permission to consult with him during his interrogation by the district attorney. In reference to this assertion, the Court notes that counsel was sent by Stroble's son-in-law merely to inquire about his guilt. Since Stroble's attorney was not present at Stroble's request, there was no constitutional requirement that the interrogation be interrupted merely to satisfy the curiosity of a relative.

Ruling

Quoting from *Adams* v. *U.S.* (1942), Clark writes, "'It is not asking too much that the burden of showing unfairness be sustained by him who claims such injustice and seeks to have the result set aside'" (198). He continues, "The judgement of the Supreme Court of California is Affirmed" (198).

Justice Felix Frankfurter writes a dissenting opinion.

Frankfurter begins his analysis by pointing to the "misconduct" of the district attorney who "initiated the intrusions of the press into the process of the trial" (198). He writes, "To have the prosecutor himself feed the press with evidence that no self-restrained press ought to publish in anticipation of a trial, is to make the State itself . . . a conscious participant in trial by newspaper" (201).

Not impressed with the Court's assertion that the passage of time ameliorated the harmful effects of the extrajudicial publicity, Frankfurter writes:

Science with all its advances has not given us instruments for determining when the impact of such newspaper exploitation has spent itself or whether the powerful impression bound to be made by such inflaming articles as here preceded the trial can be dissipated in the mind of the average juror by the tame and often pedestrian proceedings in court. (201)

He concludes with an impassioned scolding:

To allow such use of the press by the prosecution as the California court here left undisciplined, implies either that the ascertainment of guilt cannot be left to the established processes of law or impatience with those calmer aspects of the judicial process which may not satisfy the natural, primitive, popular revulsion against horrible crime but do not vindicate the sober second thoughts of a community. (202)

Justice William O. Douglas writes a dissenting opinion.
Justice Hugo L. Black joins.

Douglas dissents for reasons unrelated to pretrial publicity. He asserts that any confession "obtained between the time of arrest and arraignment" is illegal (203). Allowing such confessions to stand, Douglas says, "breeds the third degree and the inquisition" (204). He points out that, in spite of repeated requests, Stroble's attorney was not allowed to see his client until after the confession was completed. In addition, he draws attention to the fact that the confession in the police car, the first of a series by Stroble, "was accompanied or preceded by blows and kicks of the police" (204).

Significance

It is significant that the Court said Stroble "failed to show that the newspaper accounts aroused against him such prejudice in the community as to necessarily prevent a fair trial." This statement implies he is required to show a causal relationship between extrajudicial publicity and a prejudiced jury. To make such a connection, the Court echoed words first written in reference to due process rights of "fundamental fairness." The Courts used a crucial phrase from *Lisenba* v. *California* (1941) in asserting that a defendant must demonstrate a jury was "fatally infected" with an unconstitutional prejudice in order to show a denial of due process rights to "that fundamental fairness essential to the very concept of justice" (*Lisenba* 237). Thus, Stroble could not merely assert the presence of community prejudice resulting from pretrial publicity, he must also present an affirmative showing. In short, the burden of showing unfairness must be sustained by one who claims to be the victim of an unfair trial and so seeks to have a verdict set aside.

In addition, one important way to demonstrate a belief in the harmful nature of the pretrial publicity, according to the Court, is to ask for a change of venue so that the trial can be held in a location untainted by prejudicial news articles. Significantly, Stroble failed to request such a change.

The Court also pointed out an important distinction that should be kept in mind when attempting to evaluate the harmful nature of extrajudicial publicity. If such information is presented in the trial, then the jury would be exposed to it anyway. Consequently, information printed in the press and introduced at trial is not nearly as harmful as information printed in the press but not introduced into evidence. This issue is also discussed at some length in *Murphy* v. *Florida* (1975) and *Patton* v. *Yount* (1984).

U.S. ex rel. Darcy v. Handy

United States of America, ex rel. David Darcy
v.
*Earl D. Handy, Warden of Bucks County Prison,
Dr. Fred S. Baldi, Warden of the Western State
Penitentiary, and Carl H. Fleckenstine, United States
Marshal for the Middle District of Pennsylvania*

Docket No. 1956-323
351 U.S. 454, 100 L.Ed. 1331, 76 S.Ct. 965 (1956)

Argued May 1 and 2, 1956. Decided June 11, 1956.

Background

By 1956, the Court had addressed for nearly a century the problems arising from extrajudicial publicity, with most of the attention focusing on pretrial news coverage, although some consideration had been given to publicity generated during a trial. This case raises a new question related to the conflict between the free press and a fair trial. Darcy claims that publicity, not about his own trial, but from a previous trial of two others convicted of committing the same crime that he is being tried for, unconstitutionally prejudiced his jury against him. The new question never before addressed by the Court, then, is this: Can publicity about the trial of one person prejudice jurors participating in the trial of another person?

Circumstances

At about 11:30 P.M. on December 22, 1947, David Darcy, 22, Harold Foster, 23, Harry Zeitz, 18, and Felix Capone, 16, arrived at the Feasterville Tavern located at the junction of Churchville-Newtown-Bustletown Roads, in the Village of Feasterville, Lower Southampton Township, near Doylestown, Bucks County, Pennsylvania. Darcy, Foster, and Zeitz, each armed with a revolver, entered the tavern while Capone served as a lookout. During the robbery Darcy fired two shots and engaged in a scuffle with Allen Hellerman and Edward Wunsch. Zeitz and Foster also used their guns during the scuffle. Hellerman fell to the floor, shot in the base of the neck and paralyzed in both lower legs. Two bullets struck Wunsch, one in the arm and one in the shoulder. The three youths then took money from the cash register and from eighteen patrons and fled.

Meanwhile, a woman escaped using a rear door and ran across the road to the Bucks Hotel, where she enlisted the help of the bartender and two other men. They all went outside as the robbers left; Zeitz fired a shot that hit William Kelly in the back of the head. Kelly died within two days.

A half hour later, the four robbed the proprietor and three or four patrons at the Deacon Inn near Penndel, eight miles from the Feasterville Tavern. When they returned to Philadelphia at 1:17 A.M. on December 23, they were arrested by the Philadelphia police.

Capone pleaded guilty; Foster and Zeitz were tried together before Judge Calvin S. Boyer in the Court of Oyer and Terminer of Bucks County. After their trial, which ran from May 24 to June 4, 1948, they were convicted of first-degree murder and sentenced to death. The next day a newspaper ran this quotation from the comments given by Judge Boyer to the jury:

> I don't see how you could, under the evidence, have reached any other verdict. Your verdict may have a very wholesome effect on other young men in all vicinities who may come to realize the seriousness of the folly in which so many young men indulge in these days. The only hope of stemming the tide of such crime by youth is to enforce the law which you have indicated by your decision. (458)

Darcy was then tried before Judge Hiram H. Keller beginning Monday, June 7, only three days after conviction of his companions. Judge Boyer was in attendance during much of the trial, sometimes sitting at the bench and at other times in the courtroom area reserved for attorneys and the press. Still, the Federal District Court asserted in this regard, " 'We find as a fact, that Judge Boyer did not at any time during the Darcy trial assist, attempt to assist, make any suggestion to or in any other manner aid the Commonwealth in the prosecution of the case against David Darcy' " (459). The jury found Darcy guilty on June 14 and recommended the death penalty.

The four leading newspapers of Bucks County in 1948 (then with a population of 107,715) are these: the *Daily Intelligencer* (circulation 5,329, published in Doylestown, the county seat, population 5,262); the *Daily Courier* (circulation 5,397, published in Bristol, population 11,895; it had a common co-owner with the *Intelligencer*); the *Enterprise* (a weekly with a circulation of 1,972, published in Newton, population 2,009); and the *Free Press* (a weekly with a circulation of 5,000, published in Quakertown, population 5,150).

Articles from all four newspapers characterized the defendants as "bandits," "thugs," "trigger happy youths," and "Philadelphians." The defense claimed an editorial "crusade" was started by the *Daily Intelligencer* to secure the electric chair for these urban outsiders who committed crimes in peace-loving, rural Bucks County. Darcy's lawyers said the most inflammatory editorial the *Daily Intelligencer* ran was headed "If Sob Sisters Lay Off," April 17, 1948. It read, in part, "Unfortunately . . . there still are Judges and Pardon Boards not yet convinced that thugs . . . should not be given an early opportunity to prey on the public. It seems to be time to stop making guinea pigs of the law-abiding members of society."

Upon appeal, Darcy said two actions denied him due process: His trial took place in an atmosphere of hysteria and prejudice brought about by a newspaper campaign to secure the death penalty, and that Judge Boyer who presided at Foster and Zeitz's trial, which had been held before his, prejudiced the jury against him.

Summary of the Court's Analysis

Justice Harold H. Burton writes for the Court.
Chief Justice Earl Warren and Justices Hugo Black, Stanley Reed,
Tom C. Clark, and Sherman Minton join.

Justice Burton says the Court grants certiorari "to review the charge . . . that he [Darcy] was denied due process" (460). Burton summarizes Darcy's charges as follows:

Petitioner's [Darcy's] charge is that (a) the news coverage of the robbery and of the proceedings prior to his trial including the Foster-Zeitz trial and Judge Boyer's reported remarks to the jury in that case, created such an atmosphere of hysteria and prejudice that it prevented him from having a fair trial, (b) notwithstanding that he was granted a severance, he was forced to go to trial within one week of the trial of his companions, Foster and Zeitz, and (c) in the light of (a) and (b) above, Judge Boyer's presence and participation in petitioner's [Darcy's] trial prevented him from being fairly tried since Judge Boyer, in effect, acted as an "overseer judge" and effectively guided and influenced petitioner's [Darcy's] jury. (461–462)

Before discussing the merits of Darcy's charges, Burton sets out two requirements Darcy must meet. The first requirement comes from *Adams* v. *U.S.* (1942). In *Adams,* the Court asserted these now famous and influential words: " 'It is not asking too much that the burden of showing essential unfairness be sustained by him who claims such injustice and seeks to have the result set aside, and that it be sustained not as a matter of speculation but as a demonstrable reality'" (462). The second—also well known—requirement was penned by Oliver Wendell Holmes, Jr., in *Holt* v. *U.S.* (1910). In *Holt*, Holmes stated, "'If the mere opportunity for prejudice or corruption is to raise a presumption that they exist, it will be hard to maintain jury trial under the conditions of the present day'" (462).

Burton notes immediately that Darcy fails to meet the second requirement. He writes, "We conclude that the most that has been shown is that, in certain respects, opportunity for prejudice existed" (462). Then Burton lists some of the protections that can be used to see that the opportunity for prejudice does not in fact result in prejudice. He mentions challenges of jurors during the *voir dire*, severance (separation) of trials of more than one defendant, and change of venue.

According to Burton, Darcy's failures to "use all of his peremptory challenges" and to "seek a continuance of the trial or a change of venue" are important (463). These failures, he asserts, in effect require the Court "to infer that the news coverage of the robbery and proceedings prior to petitioner's [Darcy's] trial . . . created such an atmosphere of prejudice and hysteria that it was impossible to draw a fair and impartial jury from the community or to hold a fair trial" (463). Burton says, however, there is "no justification in the record" to warrant the Court reading the news reports in order to discover if they "did create such an atmosphere that it infected the jurors and deprived petitioner [Darcy] of a fair trial on the evidence presented to them [the jurors]" (463).

Burton continues, "The Federal District Court . . . found, on the evidence before it, that petitioner's [Darcy's] trial was conducted in a calm judicial manner, without any disturbances, and that the news coverage was 'factual, with an occasional descriptive word or phrase, and on occasion, words of compassion or commendation'" (463). Moreover, Burton notes, Darcy used only ten of his twenty peremptory challenges, and "he made no motion for a continuance or a change of venue" (464). The justice concludes, "There is nothing in the record to show, as a 'demonstrable reality,' that petitioner [Darcy] was denied due process of law because of community hysteria and prejudice" (464).

In addition, Burton asserts, "Nor do we conclude that petitioner [Darcy] was prevented from obtaining a fair trial by reason of Judge Boyer's commendatory remarks to the Foster-Zeitz trial jury, reported in the local press two days before petitioner's [Darcy's] trial" (464). Referring again to Holmes's words in *Holt* v. *U.S.* (1910), Burton writes, "At most, petitioner [Darcy] has shown that this created a possible opportunity for prejudice" (464).

Next, Burton turns to Darcy's objections to the behavior of Judge Boyer, including the alleged passing of a note to the district attorney and the judge's remaining in court after he disposed of his miscellaneous business at the opening of the day. Regarding the passing of a note, Burton says the trier of fact here is the district court. That court found no note was passed, and this Court asserts it is "not justified in upsetting" its finding (465). Regarding the judge's presence in the courtroom, Burton notes that Darcy failed "to show that he [Darcy] was prejudiced in some way by the judge's presence" (466).

Third, Darcy's objection to Judge Boyer's comments during another case on June 11, 1956, is dismissed because "the remarks on June 11 could not have prejudiced the jury since that jury had no access to any sources of news that reported the incident" (466). His fourth objection—to Boyer's comments at the end of the Foster-Zeitz trial—is found to be without merit because Darcy's attorney "took no action to prevent . . . [it] from infecting" Darcy's trial (464). It may be the case, Burton says, that the attorney "did not deem it necessary to take any such action because the possibility of prejudice was too remote to justify it" (467), but the Court does not need to speculate about the attorney's reasons because Darcy "has not sustained the burden resting upon him to show that his trial was essentially unfair in a constitutional sense" (467).

Ruling

Burton writes, "The judgment of the Court of Appeals, therefore, is affirmed" (467).

Justice John M. Harlan writes a dissenting opinion.
Justices Felix Frankfurter and William O. Douglas join.

Harlan's dissent focuses on the conduct of Judge Boyer. He writes, "I consider that the jury must have been conscious of the unusual interest which Judge Boyer had in the case, and that it might well have been concluded that he felt the defendant should be dealt with severely" (469). The judge's actions, Harlan writes, "Require us to hold that the petitioner [Darcy] has been denied due process" (469). He concludes, "We should be especially scrupulous in seeing to it that the right to a fair trial has not been jeopardized by the conduct of a member of the judiciary" (469).

Significance

A question never before addressed by the Court is considered in this case: Can publicity about the trial of one person prejudice jurors participating in the trial of another person? Darcy claimed that the publicity from the trial of two others convicted of committing the same crime that he is being tried for unconstitutionally prejudiced his jury against him because his trial took place only a week after theirs. It is significant, first, that the Court said the burden rested on Darcy to show how the publicity from the previous trial unconstitutionally prejudiced the jury in his trial.

Relying on a well-known precedent, *Adams* v. *U.S.* (1942), the Court asserted, "The burden of showing essential unfairness [must] be sustained by him who claims such injustice and seeks to have the result set aside, and that it be sustained not as a matter of speculation but as a demonstrable reality" (462). To show unfairness "as a demonstrable reality," the Court added, means more than pointing out the fact that a mere opportunity for an unconstitutionally prejudiced jury existed—compare *Holt* v. *U.S.* (1910).

Second, the Court asserted that Darcy's failure to use legal remedies designed to ameliorate prejudice resulting from pretrial publicity makes it hard for the Court to accept his assertion that the publicity was in fact unconstitutional. The Court took note, for example, that Darcy did not use all his peremptory challenges, that he did not seek a continuance so that the time between the previous trial and his own was longer than a week, and he did not try to change the location of the trial to a place where news coverage of the previous trial was absent or considerably less intense. Instead, Darcy simply asked the Court to "infer that the news coverage of the robbery and proceedings prior" to his trial created an unconstitutionally prejudicial atmosphere. Darcy, in short, presented no evidence that the news stories fatally infected the jurors so that they could not base their verdict solely on the evidence introduced in court.

The significance of this case, then, is twofold. First, the Court reaffirmed its previous opinions that defendants must do more than merely assert that the possibility of prejudice exists from the presence of pretrial publicity. The burden to show that the publicity in fact denied a fair trial rests upon the defendants. Showing only that the possibility of prejudice existed is insufficient to prove a trial unfair. Second, defendants must take advantage of the various legal remedies designed to reduce the unfair influence of pretrial publicity if they want the Court to view favorably their assertions that the publicity is unconstitutional. Failure to seek ways for reducing the influence of pretrial publicity implies that the publicity is perceived, even by the defendants, to be incapable of infecting prospective jurors with unconstitutional prejudice. This is a theme the Court continually returns to in later decisions related to the conflict between a free press and a fair trial.

Marshall v. United States

Howard R. Marshall

v.

United States of America

Docket No. 1959-383

360 U.S. 310, 35 L.Ed.2d 1250, 79 S.Ct. 1171 (1959)

Argued March 25 and 26, 1959. Decided June 15, 1959.

Background

By 1959, no justice would argue against the proposition that an impartial jury is central to the concept of a fair trial. Indeed, when the middle of the twentieth century arrived, jurists had developed numerous complex rules governing the trial process so that jurors would not be exposed before or during a trial to prejudicial information. Some of these rules developed by the jurists were necessary because the First Amendment precludes courts from controlling information printed by the press. That is to say, trial judges were often faced with the difficult problem of what to do about the existence of clearly prejudicial information that could reach jurors from the pages of the press.

In this case, the very same information a judge ruled could not be introduced into evidence during a trial because it would prejudice the jurors nevertheless reached the jury when it was printed in a newspaper. Following the traditional practice of the time, the judge allowed the case to continue after he polled the members of the jury and received assurances from those who read the news story that they could still decide the case solely on the merits of the evidence introduced in court and that the news story did not prejudice them against the defendant.

The judge's action raises a question addressed for the first time by the Court. Are jurors just as likely to be prejudiced against a defendant by reading information in the press as they are if they hear that information in court? If the answer is no, then the threat to a fair trial from prejudicial news stories may not be as great as many jurists fear. If the answer is yes, then the threat from news stories to a fair trial may be so severe that it requires declaring a mistrial.

Circumstances

The seeds for this case were planted when Robert E. Keating, an undercover inspector for the U.S. Food and Drug Administration, met Howard R. Marshall at a mutual friend's house in Denver, Colorado, on April 18, 1956. Keating requested some pills to help him stay awake on a drive to Dallas, Texas, that evening. Marshall gave him a package with five tablets and two pills. Later Marshall gave Keating two vials containing fifty tablets and twenty-four capsules of a drug, which was eventually determined to be dextro-amphetamine sulfate. Marshall was convicted on two counts of violation of the Federal Drug and Cosmetic Act, 21 U.S.C.A. Section 301.

During Marshall's trial, two stories were published in the newspaper. Six of the jurors said they read one article, and two jurors said they read both. All of the jurors said the news reports would not affect their verdict.

One article said that Marshall had two previous felony convictions, that he had written and passed prescriptions for dangerous drugs, and that, while serving a forgery sentence in the Oklahoma State Penitentiary, he testified before a state legislative committee studying drug laws, telling the committee he practiced medicine with a $25 diploma received through the mail. It printed this startling note: "'Howard R. (Tobey) Marshall . . . acted as a physician and prescribed restricted drugs for Hank Williams before the country singer's death in December 1953'" (312).

The other article said Marshall had been arrested with his wife, who had been convicted on drug charges in the same court and sentenced to jail.

Since Marshall did not testify in his own defense, and so did not offer his character as a defense, much of the clearly prejudicial information printed in the newspaper as evidence was not admitted into the trial record. Indeed, the trial judge did not allow the members of the jury to hear it precisely because he thought it would unconstitutionally prejudice them against Marshall.

Summary of the Court's Analysis

Chief Justice Earl Warren and Justices Hugo L. Black,
Felix Frankfurter, William O. Douglas, Tom C. Clark,
John H. Harlan, William J. Brennan, Charles E. Whittaker,
and Potter Stewart concur.

In a *per curiam* opinion, the Court said it accepted this case for review "because of doubts whether exposure of some of the jurors to newspaper articles about petitioner [Marshall] was so prejudicial in the setting of the case as to warrant the exercise of our supervisory power to order a new trial" (310, 311).

The Court reviewed briefly the process the trial judge used to question jurors who read the prejudicial information he had not allowed to be entered into the trial record. It noted, "The trial judge on learning that these news accounts had reached the jurors summoned them into his chamber one by one and inquired if they had seen the articles" (312). Although seven jurors had seen at least one news story, "each . . . told the trial judge that he would not be influenced by the news articles, that he could decide the case only on the evidence of record, and that he felt no prejudice against petitioner [Marshall] as a result of the articles" (312). After "stating he felt there was no prejudice" against Marshall, the trial judge "denied the motion for mistrial" (312). Completing the review, the Court came to this conclusion:

> We have here the exposure of jurors to information of a character which the trial judge ruled was so prejudicial it could not be directly offered as evidence. The prejudice to the defendant is almost certain to be as great when that evidence reaches the jury through news accounts as when it is a part of the prosecution's evidence. It may indeed be greater for it is then not tempered by protective procedures. (312, 313)

Ruling

The Court states, "We think a new trial should be granted. Reversed" (313).

Justice Hugo L. Black dissents without comment.

Significance

An Act of the Territory of Utah passed in March 1884 played a major role in *Reynolds* v. *U.S.* (1878), a case that determined much of the pattern for determining juror prejudice. This law said that prospective jurors should not be disqualified after having read a news story about a case they may serve on if a trial judge believes their declaration that, in spite of having read such a news article, they believe they can judge the defendant impartially. Many other territories and states at that time had passed similar statutes, which are distinguished in no small part by the confidence they place in the abilities of jurors to remain impartial even after reading prejudicial news reports. These statutes are distinguished to no lesser degree by the similar confidence they place in trial judges to evaluate the assertions by prospective jurors of their own impartiality.

Perhaps nowhere is this confidence expressed more forcefully than in the words of Justice Oliver Wendell Holmes, Jr., in *Holt* v. *U.S.* (1910), who asserted jurors are able to ignore potentially prejudicial news reports because they are persons of "experience and common sense" (249). Referring to the inevitable existence of such news stories, he then penned these very well-known words: "If the *mere opportunity* [emphasis added] for prejudice or corruption is to raise a presumption that they exist, it will be hard to maintain jury trials under the conditions of the present day" (250).

Unlike Holmes, who expressed great confidence in the ability of jurors to ignore news reports, and unlike these nineteenth century legislators, who passed laws saying prospective jurors could not be declared unconstitutionally prejudiced if the court believes their assertion that they can evaluate a defendant impartially after they read a potentially prejudicial news story, the Court ruled here that the jurors' assertion of their own impartiality should be disregarded when information they read is inadmissible into the trial.

The Court ruled that information published in the newspaper can prejudice a jury as much as information introduced into court. Indeed, news articles may be more prejudicial, said the Court, because the information contained therein is not accompanied by safeguards attending the introduction of evidence into a trial. In a newspaper article, for example, there may be no comments from a judge to explain the significance of the evidence or to point out the purposes for which it should be considered.

This ruling serves notice, therefore, that, from this time forward, information a judge would consider prejudicial in a courtroom should also be considered prejudicial when it is read in a newspaper by members of a jury. Consequently, the impact of a newspaper article may be the same as that of introducing prejudicial information into a trial, including the possibility of declaring a mistrial. In addition, the Court served notice that a trial judge should not accept uncritically jurors' avowals that they can remain impartial after reading news reports about the case they are serving on when these reports contain information that the jurors would not otherwise be aware of because it is inadmissible into the trial.

Irvin v. Dowd

Leslie Irvin
v.
A. F. Dowd, Warden

Docket No. 1960-41

366 U.S. 717, 6 L.Ed.2d 751, 81 S.Ct. 1639 (1961)

Argued November 9, 1960. Decided June 5, 1961.

Background

Since government is prevented by the First Amendment from regulating the press, the courts have been forced to find other ways to avoid or to ameliorate conflicts between the free flow of information about a trial and a defendant's right to trial by an impartial jury. One of these methods is a change of venue. By holding the trial in a location where pretrial publicity is either absent or present at a level that poses no threat to unacceptably prejudicing prospective jurors, trial courts have been able to reduce, or in some cases nearly eliminate, the possibility of inadmissible evidence reaching a juror.

This method raises a number of important questions addressed here by the Court. Is it possible for pretrial publicity to be so intense and widespread that all prospective jurors in a given geographical area cannot be believed when asserting that they have remained impartial? When does exposure to pretrial publicity in the media ineluctably result in an opinion—of guilt or innocence—that is so imbedded in the mind that it renders jurors incapable of rendering a verdict solely on the basis of the evidence presented in the trial? How does a court determine the strength of pretrial opinions formed on the basis of information presented in the mass media?

Circumstances

A killing December 2, 1954, began a series of widely publicized unsolved murders in and around Vanderburgh and Gibson Counties, Indiana. After Leslie "Mad Dog" Irvin was arrested April 8, 1955, area newspapers, responding to a public relations release from the Evansville Police Department, said Irvin had confessed to the six crimes.

Joint news releases were issued from time to time by the prosecutor of Vanderburgh County and the Evansville chief of detectives. Among other things, they noted that Irvin was attempting to make a deal to plead guilty in exchange for a life sentence, but the prosecutor, refusing to compromise, would seek instead the death penalty. The Evansville *Courier* and Evansville *Press*, two daily newspapers of Gibson county, reached 95 percent of dwelling units of the mostly rural, agricultural county (population in 1955, 30,000).

During a radio interview by WJPS in Evansville, December 5, 1955, Paul Weaver, prosecuting attorney for Indiana, said he thought the widespread coverage given to the case by the newspapers and radio was the reason the judge was having trouble in getting a jury of people who were not already prejudiced against Irvin.

Irvin's attorneys asked for a change of venue on the basis of "widespread and inflammatory" prejudicial pretrial publicity. Since the trial was moved only a short distance to neighboring Gibson County, they asked for another change, which was denied because Indiana law allows only one. Later, two more change-of-venue motions and eight motions for continuances were filed. They were all denied.

Jury selection, begginning November 14, took four weeks. A total of 431 prospective jurors were questioned; 269 were challenged successfully for cause. Irvin exhausted all thirty peremptory challenges and challenged all twelve seated jurors for cause based upon unconstitutional prejudice.

On December 20 a jury found Irvin guilty of murdering Whitney Wesley Kerr, and on January 9, 1956, he was sentenced to death. He escaped January 18 from county jail.

After Irvin was captured February 17 in California, the Indiana Supreme Court affirmed his conviction and, following a series of appeals on technical points of law, the Seventh Circuit Court of Appeals eventually denied his request for a retrial.

Summary of the Court's Analysis

Justice Tom C. Clark writes for the Court.
Chief Justice Earl Warren and Justices William J. Brennan, Jr.,
Charles E. Whittaker, Potter Stewart, John M. Harlan,
Hugo L. Black, and William O. Douglas join.

Justice Clark begins the analysis by focusing first on change of venue: "At the outset we are met with the Indiana statute providing that only one change of venue shall be granted 'from the county' wherein the offense was committed" (720). Facing the issue directly, the Court quickly refuses to declare the Indiana law an unconstitutional violation of the right to due process. It reasons that, since the Indiana Supreme Court has held that the law allows a second change of venue for the purpose of obtaining an impartial jury, "the statute is not, on its face, subject to attack on due process ground" (721).

Clark then gives a cursory historical summary of the value of what he calls "the most priceless . . . [individual liberty] of trial by jury" (721). He ends the survey by asserting that an important message from *Reynolds* v. *U.S.* (1878) is, "The theory of the law is that a juror who has formed an opinion cannot be impartial" (722).

In contrast, Clark notes, "It is not required, however, that the jurors be totally ignorant of the facts and issues involved" (722). He supports this assertion with the message of *Spies* v. *Illinois* (1887):

> To hold that the mere existence of any preconceived notion as to the guilt or innocence of an accused, without more, is sufficient to rebut the presumption of a prospective juror's impartiality would be to establish an impossible standard. It is sufficient if the juror can lay aside his impression or opinion and render a verdict based on the evidence presented in court. (723)

He says the test stated in *Reynolds* is "'whether the nature and strength of the opinion formed are such as in law necessarily . . . raise the presumption of partiality'" (723). Thus, according to this test, in order to answer the question of whether or not Irvin received a fair trial, a court needs to determine if jurors' pretrial opinions are so deeply held that they would be unable to render a verdict solely on the basis of the evidence presented in court. Clark writes, "It was, therefore, the duty of the Court of Appeals to independently evaluate the voir dire testimony of the impaneled jurors" (723).

Clark notes that, in *Holt* v. *U.S.* (1910), the Court ruled that a "finding of impartiality should be set aside only where prejudice is 'manifest' [*Holt*, 248]" (724). The Indiana court said the jurors were indeed impartial under Indiana law because they told the trial judge they "could render an impartial verdict" (724). Calling this assertion by the jurors a "technical conception," Clark says the real point is the jurors' "state of mind" (724).

The Court here rejects the jurors' professions of impartiality because "the build-up of prejudice is clear and convincing" (715). Clark then reviews the nature of the publicity, noting, among other things, the following:

> [A] barrage of newspaper headlines, articles, cartoons and pictures was unleashed against him [Irvin] during the six or seven months preceding his trial. . . . In addition, the Evansville radio and TV stations . . . also carried extensive newscasts covering the same incidents. These stories revealed the details of his background, including a reference to crimes committed when a juvenile, his convictions for arson almost 20 years

previously, for burglary and by a court-martial on AWOL charges during the war. He was accused of being a parole violator. The headlines announced his police line-up identification, that he faced a lie-detector test, had been placed at the scene of the crime and that the six murders were solved but petitioner [Irvin] refused to confess. Finally, they announced his confession to the six murders. . . . Another [news story] characterized petitioner [Irvin] as remorseless and without conscience. . . . In many of the stories, petitioner [Irvin] was described as the "confessed slayer of six," a parole violator, and fraudulent-check artist. On the day before the trial the newspaper carried the story that Irvin had orally admitted the murder of Kerr. (725, 726)

Clark concludes, "The force of this continued adverse publicity caused a sustained excitement and fostered a strong prejudice among the people of Gibson County" (726).

Next, Clark turns to evidence of prejudice caused by this publicity. He writes, "'27 of the 35 prospective jurors questioned [on one Friday] were excused for holding biased pretrial opinions'" (726). He continues, "The panel consisted of 430 persons. The court itself excused 268 of those on challenges for cause as having fixed opinions as to the guilt of petitioner [Irvin]" (727). "370 prospective jurors or almost 90% of those examined on the point [of Irvin's guilt]," Clark writes, "entertained some opinion as to guilt—ranging in intensity from mere suspicion to absolute certainty" (727). Of the jurors "finally placed in the jury box," Clark observes, "Eight out of the 12 thought petitioner [Irvin] was guilty" (727).

From this survey Clark concludes, "With such an opinion permeating their minds, it would be difficult to say that each could exclude this preconception of guilt from his deliberations. The influence that lurks in an opinion once formed is so persistent that it unconsciously fights detachment from the mental processes of the average man" (727). He asserts, "We can only say that in the light of the circumstances here the finding of impartiality does not meet constitutional standards" (728).

Clark takes care to note, "No doubt each juror was sincere when he said that he would be fair and impartial," but he adds, "where so many, so many times, admitted prejudice, such a statement of impartiality can be given little weight" (728).

Ruling

Clark writes, "Petitioner's [Irvin's] detention and sentence of death . . . is in violation of the Constitution of the United States and he is therefore entitled to be freed therefrom" (728). He adds, "[Irvin] may be tried on this or another indictment" (728).

Justice Felix Frankfurter writes a concurring opinion.

Frankfurter takes the opportunity of this opinion to reproach the press. He writes:

> How can fallible men and women reach a disinterested verdict based exclusively on what they heard in court when, before they entered the jury box, their minds were saturated by press and radio for months preceding by matter designed to establish the guilt of the accused. A conviction so secured obviously constitutes a denial of due process of law in its most rudimentary conception. . . . This Court has not yet decided that the fair administration of criminal justice must be subordinated to another safeguard of our constitutional system—freedom of the press, properly conceived. (729, 730)

Significance

The significance of this case lies partially in the Court's assertion that appeals courts, when evaluating the prejudice of an entire jury, must review independently the *voir dire*. While the Court upheld the by now deeply embedded notion that a trial court's ruling on juror impartiality must not be overturned unless "manifestly" in error [*Holt* v. *U.S.* (1910)], it also asserted that massive extrajudicial publicity can undermine the credibility of jurors' assertions that they believe themselves to be impartial in spite of being exposed to pretrial publicity. Extending from *Marshall* v. *U.S.* (1959) a ruling directed at trial courts, the Court says here that appeals courts also must recognize that a simple declaration by members of the jury that they can render a verdict based solely on the evidence presented in court is in itself not necessarily sufficient to declare the jury impartial. If there is evidence of continued and massive pretrial publicity that has the potential of affecting the judgment of the entire jury panel, then appeals courts must take it into consideration and, on the basis of this evidence, may reject jurors' honestly held opinions that they are impartial.

The significance of this decision also lies partially in the Court's suggestion about how to respond to the test of juror impartiality stated in *Reynolds* v. *U.S.* (1878): "whether the nature and strength of the opinion formed are such as in law necessarily . . . raise the presumption of partiality." *Reynolds* states, on the one hand, that jurors who have formed an opinion about the guilt of the accused may be challenged. Consequently, the Court here suggested that jurors' declarations that they believe themselves to be impartial does not automatically make them so. Their assertions must be evaluated by the trial judge and their *voir dire* reviewed by the appeals courts.

On the other hand, *Reynolds* asserts that to qualify as unconstitutional, jurors' opinions of an accused's guilt "must be founded on some evidence, and be more than a mere impression" (155). Here the Court suggested that continued and massive pretrial publicity may very well constitute evidence that the judgment of the entire jury panel has been affected to the degree that the credibility of all jurors' honest assertions of impartiality is unconstitutionally undermined.

Beck v. Washington

David D. Beck

v.

Washington

Docket No. 1962-40
369 U.S. 541, 8 L.Ed.2d 98, 82 S.Ct. 955 (1962)

Argued November 14, 1961. Decided May 14, 1962.

Background

Coming in the middle of a series of four cases that are considered somewhat of a minor revolution in the Court's rulings related to pretrial publicity, this case seems a bit out of place. In many ways *Beck* appears more similar to three much earlier cases, two from the previous decade, than to the three most immediately before it and the one immediately after it.

The four chronologically closest cases all emphasize the dangers of pretrial publicity. *Marshall* v. *U.S.* (1959), for example, asserts that information published in the newspaper may be more prejudicial than information introduced into court because the process for printing a news article is not regulated by the same safeguards protecting the introduction of evidence into a trial. Consequently, the Court noted, the impact of publishing a newspaper article may result in a mistrial. In *Irvin* v. *Dowd* (1961) the Court ruled that a simple declaration by members of the jury that they can render a verdict based solely on the evidence presented in court is not sufficient to declare them impartial. It further stated that appeals courts, when evaluating the credibility of an entire jury, must take into consideration evidence of continued and massive pretrial publicity. In *Janko* v. *U.S.* (1961) the Court reversed without comment the conviction of Joseph W. Janko for income tax evasion after a newspaper article referred to him as a "former convict," who was found guilty in an earlier case on the same charge. Finally, in *Rideau* v. *Louisiana* (1963) the Court said the broadcast of a confession would result in a denial of the Fourteenth Amendment's right to due process because persons exposed to this publicity necessarily are rendered incapable of becoming impartial jurors.

The three earlier cases, in contrast, emphasize the burden of showing unfairness: *Adams* v. *U.S.* (1942), *Darcy* v. *Handy* (1956), and *Stroble* v. *California* (1952). This earlier series of cases stresses the requirement of showing unconstitutional jury prejudice as a "demonstrable reality" resulting from pretrial publicity, a burden Beck failed to uphold.

Circumstances

On February 26, 1957, the United States Senate Select Committee on Improper Activities in the Labor or Management Field (then known better as the McClellan Committee or the Senate Rackets Investigating Committee) began an investigation of labor unions and their officials. The publicity from the hearings for the most part concerned alleged misuse of Teamster Union funds by officers of the union.

Chief counsel for the committee was Robert F. Kennedy, who wrote of the incident in his book *The Enemy Within*.

In response to the hearings and resulting publicity, King County Superior Court Judge Lloyd Shorett convened May 20, 1957, a grand jury in King County, Seattle, Washington. The jury returned an indictment against Beck and his son July 12.

Beck's trial began December 2, and he was convicted December 14 of unlawfully appropriating for his own use the sum of $1,900 (representing the proceeds from the sale of a Teamster-owned automobile), which was received by his secretary and deposited to one of his personal bank accounts.

Although Beck asserted in appeal that all of the prospective jurors, including those selected to try his case, had read about him in newspapers or had seen the televised proceedings of his appearance before the Senate committee, the prosecution pointed out that Beck, after exhausting his thirty peremptory challenges, did not challenge for cause any of the twelve seated jurors.

Admitting that prior to this indictment Beck was subjected to much adverse publicity about the Senate hearings, the prosecution asserted that, in contrast, during the approximately five months from the date of the indictment in July to the date of the trial in December 1957, newspaper coverage was confined to factual reporting of events, such as pretrial legal maneuvers and press conferences, which, for the most part, were initiated by Beck himself. A large percentage of the other news items, according to the prosecution, were related to Beck's activities in the union. The prosecution also asserted that there was no attempt by the media to inflame the public against Beck or to try his case in public.

Nevertheless, Beck objected to the fact that the grand jurors were not admonished to base their deliberations solely upon evidence presented to them. Nor were they warned that radio, television, and newspaper reports were not evidence, that no inference of guilt should be drawn against a person who invokes the Fifth Amendment, and that their deliberations should be free from prejudice.

Summary of the Court's Analysis

Justice Tom C. Clark writes for the Court.
Justices John M. Harlan, William J. Brennan, Potter Stewart,
and Byron R. White join.

Three primary points are outlined in the opening section of Justice Clark's majority opinion. He writes:

> Petitioner David D. Beck contends that his conviction of grand larceny in the Superior Court of the State of Washington for King County is invalid under the Due Process and Equal Protection Clauses of the Fourteenth Amendment. This contention is based primarily on what is characterized as voluminous and continuous adverse publicity circulated by news media in the vicinity of Seattle, Washington, where he was indicted and tried. Specifically, he claims, *inter alia* [among other things], [1] that the grand jury was unfairly impaneled and instructed, [2] that the prosecutor acted improperly before the grand jury, and [3] that his motions for a change of venue [location of trial] and for continuances [postponements] were erroneously denied. (542)

Pretrial Publicity   The first issue Clark takes up is the adverse pretrial publicity. He begins by noting that Beck filed five motions objecting to this publicity, claiming it unconstitutionally prejudiced both the indicting grand jury and the trial jury. One motion sought to "quash [overthrow] the indictment," three sought trial delays from one month to an indefinite period, and one requested a change of trial location.

Next, Clark summarizes what he calls the "highlights" of the publicity. Most of the news accounts focused on Beck's taking the Fifth Amendment when he appeared before the United States Senate Select Committee on Improper Activities in the Labor or Management Field. Mention of Beck first occurred in March 1957, and he was indicted on July 12. On August 28, he was also indicted by a federal grand jury, this time for income tax evasion. His state trial began December 12, and he was found guilty December 14.

Objections to Grand Jury Proceedings   Beck bases his appeal, Clark writes, not on the contention that

> any particular grand juror was prejudiced or biased. Rather, he asserted that the judge impaneling the grand jury had breached [failed in] his duty to ascertain on voir dire whether any prospective juror had been influenced by the adverse publicity and that this error had been compounded by his failure to adequately instruct the grand jury concerning bias and prejudice. (545, 546)

The Court does not have to determine whether the due process clause of the Fourteenth Amendment requires the state to produce an unprejudiced grand jury, Clark asserts, because, according to the evidence, Beck's grand jury was in fact not biased.

Much of Clark's analysis focuses on the panel of twenty-three prospective jurors. He notes that, when asked "whether they were conscious of any prejudice or bias . . . , two admitted they were prejudiced by the publicity and were excused" (547). Another juror who was unsure was also excused. Three more were excused because they were "affiliated" with Beck's union. "The remaining seventeen," writes Clark, "swore that they would not 'present [any] person through envy, hatred or malice'" (547).

"It is true," Clark admits, "that the judge did not admonish the grand jurors to disregard or disbelieve news reports and publicity concerning petitioner [Beck]" (547). Nevertheless, the Court states, "We cannot say that the grand jury was biased" (548). "We therefore conclude," Clark writes, "that petitioner [Beck] has failed to show that the body which indicted him was biased or prejudiced against him" (549).

Having rejected Beck's due process objections, Clark moves to the three equal protection arguments. Beck's first claim is that "he is a member of a class (Teamsters) that was not accorded equal treatment in grand jury proceedings" (549). To this claim Clark responds, "The complete answer . . . is that references to the Teamsters were necessary in the voir dire to eliminate persons who might be prejudiced for or against petitioner [Beck] and in the instructions [to the jury] to explain the purpose and scope of this special body [the grand jury]" (549).

Beck's second argument is a bit ingenious. The Washington statute, the argument goes, "permitting persons in custody to challenge grand jurors . . . denied equal protection to persons not in custody who are investigated by grand jurors" (549). Here Beck loses on the technical issue of failing to present this point to the lower courts first. Beck's "formal attack at the trial court level," Clark writes, "did not even mention" (550) this issue. Moreover, Clark notes, "The failure to inject the equal protection contention into the case was carried forward to the proceedings before the Washington Supreme Court" (550). He concludes succinctly, "The argument cannot be entertained here under an unbroken line of precedent" (553). "Furthermore," Clark concludes his rejection of this point, "it was not within the scope of the questions to which the writ of certiorari in this case was specifically limited" (554).

The third equal protection claim asserts that the state of Washington denied Beck "the procedural safeguards the law affords others to insure an unbiased grand jury" (554). According to a footnote, Beck found two instances in which members of a Washington grand jury were questioned about their bias toward a defendant. Since the judge in Beck's case failed to ask the prospective jurors about their bias toward him, he says he was not given the same protection these other two defendants were given. Clark says that even if these two cases were to form a requirement that this particular procedural safeguard of asking jurors about their bias toward a defendant must be followed, failure to do so is simply a misapplication of the law. "Such misapplication cannot be shown to be an invidious discrimination," writes Clark, because "the Fourteenth Amendment does not 'assure uniformity of judicial decisions'" or "'immunity from judicial error'" [quoting from *Milwaukee Electric R. & Light Co.* v. *Wisconsin* (1920)] (554). Moreover, since the grand jury proceedings have been judged to be fair, to throw out a conviction based on a failure to follow this procedure would be "exalting form over substance," concludes Clark (555).

To Beck's contention that the prosecutor "improperly interrogated" a witness with "threats," Clark responds, "It appeared that they had no effect upon the witness whatsoever for he stuck to his story" (555).

Objections to the Trial Jury The Court notes that Beck objects not to the unconstitutional prejudice of an individual juror. Rather, writes Clark, "He argues that such a strong case of adverse publicity has been proved that any jury selected in Seattle at the time he was tried must be held to be presumptively biased and that the trial court's adverse rulings on his motions for a change of venue and for continuances were therefore in error" (555, 556).

Of the news coverage, Clark points out, "Even the occasional front-page items were straight news stories rather than invidious articles which would tend to arouse ill will and vindictiveness" (556). He concludes:

> Although most of the persons thus selected for the trial jury had been exposed to some of the publicity . . . , each indicated that he was not biased, that he had formed no opinion as to petitioner's [Beck's] guilt which would require evidence to remove, and that he would enter the trial with an open mind disregarding anything he had read on the case. We cannot say the pretrial publicity was so intensive and extensive or the examination of the entire panel revealed such prejudice that a court could not believe the answers of the jurors and would be compelled to find bias or preformed opinion as a matter of law. (557)

The fact that Beck "did not challenge for cause any of the jurors so selected," adds Clark, "is strong evidence that he was convinced the jurors were not biased and had not formed any opinions as to his guilt" (558).

Ruling

Clark quotes briefly from *Adams* v. *U.S.* (1942) a passage that is repeated in *Darcy* v. *Handy* (1956): "'It is not asking too much that the burden of showing essential unfairness be sustained by him who claims such injustice'" (559). He adds, "This burden has not been met. Affirmed" (559).

Justice Frankfurter took no part in the decision of this case.
Justice White took no part in the consideration or decision of this case.

Justice Hugo L. Black writes a dissenting opinion.
Chief Justice Earl Warren joins.

Black states the reason for his dissent at the outset: "I dissent from the Court's holding because I think that the failure of the Washington courts to follow their own state law by affirmative action to protect the petitioner [Beck] from being indicted by a biased and prejudiced grand jury was a denial to him of the equal protection of the laws guaranteed by the Fourteenth Amendment" (558).

He explains, "The question is . . . whether the judge who impaneled the grand jury took the precautions required by the statute and its controlling interpretation to insure a grand jury that would not be tainted by prejudice against Beck" (563). Black then answers his own question:

> The presiding judge failed to do what the state law required him to do—try to keep prejudiced persons off the grand jury. This failure was particularly serious here because of the extraordinary opportunity for prejudgment and prejudice created by the saturation of the Seattle area with publicity hostile and adverse to Beck in the months preceding and during the grand jury hearing. (563)

After reviewing highlights of the publicity, Black summarizes the responsibility it puts on the judge impanelling the grand jury: "The flood of intense public accusation of crime and breach of trust by prominent and highly placed persons, coupled with publicity resulting from Beck's refusal on ground of possible self-incrimination to answer questions before the Senate Committee as to the charges made imposed a very heavy duty on the presiding judge under Washington law to protect Beck from a biased and prejudiced grand jury" (564, 565).

"The judge failed," Blacks points out, "to ask a single juror a single question regarding whether he had read about . . . or discussed the charges against Beck. Moreover, he failed to ask a single juror who actually sat on the jury whether he was prejudiced against Beck or had already made up his mind about the many public charges" (565).

The instructions to the jury were also flawed according to Black. He writes, "Instead of instructing that the testimony and charges before the Senate Committee were not evidence before the grand jury and that it would be highly improper for the grand jury to consider them at all, the presiding judge called the jury's attention to the charges" (565). Such actions, Black asserts, are "a denial of equal protection of the law" (567).

The second reason Black gives for Beck's denial of equal protection is that the Washington law says only those persons in custody or on bail are entitled to an impartial grand jury, not those who are merely under investigation. He writes, "There can be no rational distinction between the need of the man who is not yet in custody and the need of the man who is in jail or on bail" (369).

Justice William O. Douglas writes a dissenting opinion.

Quoting from *Costello* v. *U.S.* (1956), Douglas notes early in his dissent, " 'The basic purpose of the English grand jury was to provide a fair method for instituting criminal proceedings against persons believed to have committed crimes' " (580). He adds, "One who reads this record is left with doubts of the most serious character that the procedure used in the selection of the grand jury was fair" (583).

In particular, Douglas objects to the judge's questions: "The judge was derelict in failing to ascertain whether the amount of adverse publicity petitioner [Beck] has received had prejudiced the jurors toward the case" (585–586).

Like Black, Douglas also objects to what he calls two classes of persons created by the law. He writes, "To grant that class [those persons in custody or out on bail] the right to challenge for prejudice and to deny it to those who are merely under investigation is to draw a line not warranted by the requirements of equal protection" (589).

Significance

In light of *Mu'Min* v. *Virginia* (1991), the *Beck* Court's ruling related to the instructions given a jury by a trial judge takes on significance. In *Beck* the Court ruled a judge is not required by the Sixth Amendment to admonish jurors to disregard or disbelieve news reports and publicity concerning a defendant. Indeed, unless shown otherwise by a defendant, the Court said it will assume a jury panel was not adversely biased or prejudiced. This opinion continues a series of similar rulings starting with *Adams* v. *U.S.* (1942) where the Court said the burden of showing an unfair trial must be sustained as a "demonstrable reality" by the person who claims an injustice and seeks to have the result set aside. In *Darcy* v. *Handy* (1956) the Court reaffirmed the *Adams* ruling when it asserted that the burden of proof rests on defendants to show as a "demonstrable reality" how pretrial publicity unconstitutionally prejudiced a jury and that, to make such a showing, defendants must do more than merely point out the fact that an opportunity for an unconstitutionally prejudiced jury existed. A decade before *Beck,* in *Stroble* v. *California*

(1952), the Court once again said persons who claim a trial is unfair must shoulder the burden of proof

The Court went on in *Beck* to say that, even if there does exist in Washington state law a requirement that this particular procedural safeguard of asking jurors about their bias toward a defendant must be followed, failure to do so is simply a misapplication of the law. Such a misapplication does not violate the Fourteenth Amendment because, according to the Court, the amendment does not "assure uniformity of judicial decisions" or "immunity from judicial error" (*Milwaukee Electric R. & Light Co.* v. *Wisconsin* [1920], 106).

All these rulings are important precedents that take center stage once again nearly thirty years after *Beck,* when Dawud Majid Mu'Min petitioned the Court to ask prospective jurors sixty-four questions he had prepared in an effort to discover their prejudice against him. In *Mu'Min* v. *Virginia* (1991), the Court strongly affirmed the essence of its ruling in *Beck* when it asserted that a trial judge's failure to ask questions that may be helpful in uncovering juror prejudice is not such a serious error that it reaches the level of being an unconstitutional fault. To be constitutionally compelled, the Court asserted, failure to ask questions must render the defendant's trial fundamentally unfair.

Another significant aspect related to the conflict between a free press and a fair trial is the Court's comments in *Beck* about news coverage. It noted, for example, that even front-page articles contained straight news stories rather than "invidious articles which would tend to arouse ill will and vindictiveness" (556). It also pointed out that most of the news accounts focused on Beck's taking the Fifth Amendment when he appeared before the Senate Select Committee on Improper Activities in the Labor or Management Field and that four months passed between these hearings and Beck's indictment and another five passed before his trial. These same two points about the content of the news stories and a time delay between most of the publicity and a trial were raised earlier in *Stroble* (1952) and repeated later in *Murphy* v. *Florida* (1975) and in *Patton* v. *Yount* (1984). Indeed, in *Sheppard* v. *Maxwell* (1966), the Court admonished the trial judge for not warning the press about the dangers of sensational coverage. In short, the Court is suggesting in all these cases that objective reporting of factual events is much less likely to threaten a fair trial than are subjective opinions and analyses.

Furthermore, the Court made significant comments in *Beck* about the veracity of jurors' assertions (1) that they are not biased; (2) that even though they admittedly had been exposed to some pretrial publicity, they said they formed no opinion about the defendant's guilt that would require evidence to remove; and (3) that they would enter the trial with an open mind disregarding anything they had read about the case. The Court said it would accept these assertions because the pretrial publicity was not intensive and the examination of the entire panel did not reveal widespread prejudice.

The Court's acceptance is particularly significant in light of its ruling in *Irvin* v. *Dowd* (1961) just one year earlier. In *Irvin*, the Court said if there is evidence of continued and massive pretrial publicity that has the potential of affecting the judgment of the entire jury panel, then, on the basis of this evidence, courts may reject jurors' honestly held opinions that they are impartial.

A final significant aspect of *Beck* traces its roots to *Hopt* v. *Utah* (1887) where the Court said that as long as there remained unused peremptory challenges, a verdict could not be changed on the basis of challenged jurors who were excused and did not sit in judgment. The Court reaffirmed this ruling in *Spies* v. *Illinois* (1887) when it ruled that a defendant is not injured if a court wrongly fails to dismiss a juror for cause when peremptory challenges remain unused. Although Beck exhausted all of his thirty peremptory challenges, he failed to challenge for cause any of the twelve seated jurors. Consequently, the Court said he accepted, in effect, the impartiality of these jurors.

Rideau v. Louisiana

Wilbert Rideau
v.
State of Louisiana

Docket No. 1963-630

373 U.S. 723, 10 L.Ed.2d 663, 83 S.Ct. 1417 (1963)

Argued April 29, 1963. Decided June 3, 1963.

Background

A constitutional question is raised in *Rideau* because a television station broadcast on three consecutive days a sheriff's interview that contained a confession of an arrested suspect. The question is whether these broadcasts make impossible the selection of an impartial jury in the geographical area of its viewers. The answer given by the Court is an unequivocal yes.

Circumstances

Nineteen-year-old William Rideau, at 6:55 P.M., on February 16, 1961, entered the Gulf National Bank at Lake Charles, Calcasieu Parish, Louisiana. At pistol point, he ordered three bank employees—Julia Ferguson, Dora McCain, and Jay Hickman—to fill a suitcase with money. He then forced them into Ferguson's car and had Ferguson drive them to an uninhabited area outside town. Once there, he pushed them out of the car, lined them up, and fired six shots. When Ferguson, who was still alive after the shooting, attempted to rise to her feet, Rideau stabbed her to death with his hunting knife.

Several hours later Rideau was apprehended, arrested, and confined to the Calcasieu Parish jail. Without benefit of counsel or being advised of his right to counsel, he made oral and written confessions that very night. The very next morning, a twenty-minute film with sound track was made of the sheriff of Calcasieu Parish interviewing Rideau in jail. During the interview, Rideau was "flanked by the sheriff and two state troopers," and he confessed to the crime, according to the Court, "in response to leading questions by the sheriff" (725).

The film was shown over a local television station on three occasions. According to rating charts provided by the program director of the station, about 24,000 persons were said to have viewed it February 17, 53,000 on February 18, and 29,000 on February 19. The 1960 census lists the population of Calcasieu Parish at 145,474 persons.

On March 3, Rideau was arraigned on counts of murder, kidnapping, and armed robbery. He pleaded guilty and at that point was given counsel who filed for change of venue. After the motion was denied at a hearing, trial was set for April 10.

Three members of the jury said they saw the television interview at least once. Two others held deputy sheriff commissions from the sheriff of Calcasieu Parish. Since the positions were honorary, the deputies received no pay, and they had never made an arrest. These jurors said the commission was used for their "convenience" (732) and that it "would not affect their ability to serve as jurors in any way" (733).

During the trial, the state offered into evidence both written and oral confessions. Rideau objected on grounds they were not voluntarily given because he had not been advised prior to his confessions of his right to counsel. Nevertheless, the court admitted them into evidence. A jury found Rideau guilty and sentenced him to death. The Supreme Court of Louisiana affirmed his conviction.

Summary of the Court's Analysis

Justice Potter Stewart writes for the Court.
Chief Justice Earl Warren and Justices Hugo L. Black,
William O. Douglas, William J. Brennan, Byron R. White,
and Arthur J. Goldberg join.

Justice Stewart states, "In a very real sense [the television interview] *was* [Stewart's emphasis] Rideau's trial—at which he pleaded guilty to murder" (726). He continues, "Any subsequent court proceedings in a community so pervasively exposed to such a spectacle could be but a hollow formality" (726).

Calling the event a "kangaroo court," Stewart asserts, "The people of Calcasieu Parish saw and heard, not once but three times, a 'trial' of Rideau in a jail, presided over by a sheriff, where there was no lawyer to advise Rideau of his right to stand mute" (727).

Stewart concludes, "But we do not hesitate to hold, without pausing to examine a particularized transcript of the voir dire examination of the members of the jury, that due process of law in this case required a trial before a jury drawn from a community of people who had not seen and heard Rideau's televised 'interview'" (727).

Ruling

Stewart writes:

For we hold that it was a denial of due process of law to refuse the request for a change of venue, after the people of Calcasieu Parish had been exposed repeatedly and in depth to the spectacle of Rideau personally confessing in detail to the crimes with which he was later to be charged. . . . Reversed. (726, 727)

Justice Tom C. Clark writes a dissenting opinion.
Justice John M. Harlan joins.

In contrast to the Court, Clark states, "I am unable to find any deprivation of due process under the Fourteenth Amendment" (728). He does concede, however, that, if this were a federal case, he "would vote to reverse the judgement before us" (729) under the Court's supervisory powers. For Clark, however, the sheriff's actions are not a fault of constitutional proportion.

Clark says the Court simply asserts, but does not document, a connection between the televised interview and an unfair trial. He writes, "Unless the adverse publicity is shown by the record to have fatally infected the trial, there is simply no basis for the Court's inference that the publicity, epitomized by the televised interview, . . . [made the] trial a meaningless formality" (729). He also notes that, although the broadcast interview was not admitted into evidence at the trial, the oral and written ones were.

As Clark sees it, the Court "must examine the publicity involved, the hearing on the motion for change of venue, and the record of the voir dire examination" (731). Concerning the publicity, Clark says the numbers presented by the program director "represent the typical number of viewers at the times when the interview was broadcast, as determined by a rating service which had conducted a sampling some months previous to the broadcasts" (731).

As for the three jurors who saw the broadcast, Clark states, "The record does not show that these three testified to holding opinions of petitioner's [Rideau's] guilt" (732). He continues, "They did testify, however, that they 'could lay aside any opinion, give the defendant the presumption of innocence as provided by law, base their decision solely upon the evidence'"(732).

Clark concludes, "It is an impossible standard to require that tribunal to be a laboratory, completely sterilized and freed from any external factors"

(733). He emphasizes the point that only the trial judge can observe the "demeanor" of jurors and so he is best qualified to judge impartiality. He ends his decision with a quote from *Adams* v. *U.S.* (1942), "'The burden of showing essential unfairness be sustained by him who claims such injustice and seeks to have the result set aside'" (733).

Significance

The Court said the broadcast of a confession raises a constitutional question because it would result in the denial of a right to a fair trial. Persons exposed to this publicity are rendered incapable of becoming impartial jurors. In fact, according to the Court, members of the audience became jurors when they saw the broadcast. These viewers, the Court asserts, convicted the accused on the basis of his televised confession.

In essence the Court applied its suggestions in *Irvin* v. *Dowd* (1961) for answering its test of juror impartiality first set forth in *Reynolds* v. *United States* (1878). The *Irvin* Court suggested that continued and massive pretrial publicity may constitute evidence that the judgment of the entire jury panel has been affected to the degree that the credibility of all jurors' honest assertions of impartiality is unconstitutionally undermined. Here the Court asserts that the broadcast of a confession represents just such evidence.

Clark, in dissent, says that, in order to prove denial of due process, the accused must show a connection between the broadcast and an unconstitutionally prejudiced community of prospective jurors.

Estes v. Texas

Billie Sol Estes

v.

State of Texas

Docket No. 1965-256

381 U.S. 532, 14 L.Ed.2d 543, 85 S.Ct. 1628 (1965)

Argued April 1, 1965. Decided June 7, 1965.

Background

The Court had ruled before on the televising of selected legal maneuvers related to a trial, but this is the first time it focused exclusively on the constitutional issue of televising a criminal trial.

The presence of modern mass media technology in the courtroom produced a reaction by the legal community as early as September 30, 1937, when the House of Delegates of the American Bar Association adopted the now-famous Canon 35. This Canon declares, "Proceedings in court should be conducted with fitting dignity and decorum," 62 A.B.A. Rep. 1134-35 (1937). In addition, it forbids the taking of photographs during sessions of the court on the theory that such an activity is "'calculated to detract from the essential dignity of the proceedings, degrade the court and create misconceptions with respect thereto in the mind of the public'" (596). Clearly, the concern in 1937 focused on the dignity of the court, not on the fairness of the trial.

Later, the vast publicity arising from the trial of Bruno Hauptmann, which was broadcast over radio, is credited with the condemnation, March 15, 1941, by the ABA's Committee on Professional Ethics of "direct radio broadcasting of court proceedings" (597).

Then in 1952 a special ABA committee on televising and broadcasting legislative and judicial proceedings condemned the practice of televising judicial proceedings. On February 5, the ABA House of Delegates adopted the following version of Canon 35, adding to the concern about dignity another concern, this one about detracting witnesses giving testimony:

> "The taking of photographs in the court room, during sessions of the
> court or recesses between sessions, and the broadcasting or televising of
> court proceedings detract from the essential dignity of the proceedings,

distract participants and witnesses in giving testimony, and create misconceptions with respect thereto in the mind of the public and should not be permitted." (600)

It is germane to note that a version of the Canon adopted after the Estes trial abandons the 1935 notion that photographs and broadcasting degrade the court; it focuses instead on the dangers to a fair trial.

Although nearly all states adopted Canon 35, Texas did not. Texas Judicial Canon 28 was adopted September 27, 1963. In a letter dated October 21, 1963, Judge Otis T. Dunagan (trial judge in the Estes case), secretary-treasurer of the Texas Judicial Section, transmitted a copy of the 1963 Cannon 28 to Texas judges (7 *South Texas Law Journal* [1964]: 212). Dunagan chose to follow Texas Canon 28 instead of ABA Canon 35. His decision is important primarily because Canon 28 of the Integrated State Bar of Texas allowed the trial judge in 1963 to decide whether or not court proceedings can be televised. It reads, in part, as follows:

> The taking of photographs in the court room, during sessions of the court or recesses between sessions, and the broadcasting or televising of court proceedings unless properly supervised and controlled, may detract from the essential dignity of the proceedings, distract participants and witnesses in giving testimony, and create misconceptions with respect thereto in the mind of the public. The supervision and control of such trial coverage shall be left to the trial judge who has the inherent power to exclude or control coverage in the proper case in the interest of justice.

Neither Canon is law.

It is worth noting that only noiseless, nonintrusive cameras were admitted into Estes's trial. Moreover, although Canon 28 disallowed floodlights and flashbulbs, modern technology since has rendered them unnecessary. In addition, no witness or juror requested not to be televised, and Estes did not take the stand. Still, the essential question faced by the Court was whether or not the televising of Estes's trial deprived him of his guarantee to due process. In other words, did the presence of television cameras make his trial a mere form, or was it still a valid process?

Circumstances

Born in 1925 on a farm near Clyde, Texas, Billie Sol Estes made his first financial deal as a high school student. He borrowed $3,500 from a local bank and purchased a railroad car-load of grain. He then sold the grain, one pickup-truck-full at a time at a lower-than-market price to nearby farmers.

After World War II, Estes bought empty military barracks for as little as $35 each, cut them apart, and sold the pieces as separate living units for as much as $4,000 each. In 1953 the Chamber of Commerce named him one of the ten most outstanding men in America.

Eventually Estes turned his attention to anhydrous ammonia, liquid fertilizer for cotton plants. He convinced farmers to take out in their own names mortgages for fertilizer tanks that Estes would give them the down payment for and then lease the tanks from them for the same monthly rate as the resulting mortgage payments. Estes, in turn, sold the mortgages to finance companies. More often than not, however, the tanks did not exist; in fact, he wrote 33,000 mortgages for only 1,800 tanks.

Strangely enough, the financial empire being assembled by Estes began to crumble only when he lost an election to the school board after a last-minute write-in candidate appeared. Estes blamed the Pecos *Independent & Enterprise*, a semiweekly newspaper founded in 1887. When he started his own opposition newspaper, the Pecos *Daily News*, the *Independent* began to investigate his fertilizer tank business.

Although the finance companies themselves continually were investigating Estes, he managed to fool them largely by changing or moving serial numbers on tanks. Armed with the information supplied by the newspaper, though, one investigator learned that Superior Manufacturing, Estes's supplier, could produce only 800 tanks a month working all three shifts at maximum capacity. Yet in January 1962, Estes wrote mortgages for 3,376 tanks in Reeves County alone. The finance companies turned him into the FBI. He was charged under Texas Penal Code (1925) Article 1545 with swindling, theft by false pretenses, and theft by a bailee.

Because of the widespread and intensive pretrial publicity, his trial was moved from Reeves County 500 miles away to Smith County. On September 24, 1962, the defense presented during a televised hearing two motions to the trial judge: One asked the court to ban television and news cameras from the trial and the other requested a continuance. The continuance was granted to October 22, but the judge refused to ban broadcasting and photographing.

According to the Court, the result of the electronic media at the hearing prevented "that judicial serenity and calm to which petitioner [Estes] was entitled" (356). Twelve cameramen moved about the courtroom, cables and wires were "snaked across" the floor, and three microphones were placed on the Judge's bench with "others beamed at the jury box and the counsel table" (356).

When the trial opened, however, changes had occurred. Most significant was a booth erected at the rear of the courtroom. It was painted the same color as the walls, and it had a small horizontal opening for four cameras: the three national networks and a local television station. Except for the opening and closing statements of the state and the giving of the jury's verdict, live broadcasting was prohibited. Videotaping was done without sound, and "cameras operated intermittently, recording various portions of the trial for broadcast on regularly scheduled newscasts later in the day and evening" (537).

In the District Court for the Seventh Judicial District of Texas at Tyler, Estes was convicted of swindling and sentenced to eight years in a penitentiary. He appealed the verdict, saying broadcasting his trial deprived him of his Fourteenth Amendment right to due process. Although the Texas Court of Criminal Appeals rejected his argument, the U.S. Supreme Court agreed with him and reversed his conviction.

Summary of the Court's Analysis

Justice Tom C. Clark writes for the Court.
Justices William O. Douglas and Arthur Goldberg join.

Justice Clark begins by asserting that live television coverage of a hearing in September contributed to the unconstitutional character of Estes's October trial. He writes, "The two-day hearing . . . emphasized the notorious character that the trial would take and, therefore, set it apart in the public mind as an extraordinary case" (538). He adds, "At the trial four of the jurors selected had seen and heard all or part of the broadcasts of the earlier proceedings" (538).

Clark then points out that the Sixth Amendment right to a public trial belongs to the accused, not to the public in general. He also asserts that forbidding television coverage does not favor the print media, nor does it discriminate against the electronic media. "The news reporter is not permitted to bring his typewriter or printing press" (540).

A major problem with broadcasting trials, Clark says, is that the rules developed over centuries to safeguard the integrity of a trial simply do not permit it. He writes, "We have always held that the atmosphere essential to the preservation of a fair trial—the most fundamental of all freedoms—must be maintained at all costs" (540).

Next, Clark lists the arguments—presented by the state—supporting the presence of television:

(1) "No prejudice has been shown by the petitioner [Estes] as resulting from the televising"
(2) "claims of 'distractions' during the trial due to the physical presence of television are wholly unfounded"
(3) "psychological considerations are for psychologists, not courts"

(4) "the public has a right to know what goes on in the courts"

(5) "the court has no power to 'suppress, edit, or censor events which transpire in proceedings before it'"

(6) "the televising of criminal trials would be enlightening to the public and would promote greater respect for the courts." (541)

The Court deals first with the assertion of the public's right to know. To this Clark responds, "Reporters of all media, including television are always present if they wish to be and are plainly free to report whatever occurs in open court through their respective media" (541, 542).

Next, he takes up the issue of "no isolatable prejudice." He writes, "A showing of actual prejudice is not a prerequisite to reversal" (542). He continues, "At times a procedure employed by the State involves such a probability that prejudice will result that it is deemed inherently lacking in due process" (542, 543). "Television in its present state and by its very nature, reaches into a variety of areas in which it may cause prejudice to an accused," Clark writes. "Still one cannot put his finger on its specific mischief and prove with particularity wherein he [Estes] was prejudiced" (544).

The fundamental problem, says Clark, is that television is "irrelevant" to the central objective of a trial: ascertaining the truth. He then enumerates some of the "numerous situations in which it might cause actual unfairness" (544, 545). The first is the impact upon jurors. He says it will affect the jurors' "attentiveness" and distract them from the business at hand. Moreover, "the televised jurors cannot help but feel the pressures of knowing that friends and neighbors have their eyes upon them" (546). Clark writes, "Not only will a juror's eyes be fixed on the camera, but also his mind will be preoccupied with the telecasting rather than with the testimony" (546). Finally, he says a new trial could be prejudiced by the televising of the original one having possible unconstitutional errors.

The second difficulty, according to Clark, is that "the quality of the testimony . . . will be impaired" because "witnesses" will know they are "being viewed by a vast audience" (547). He continues:

> Some may be demoralized and frightened, some cocky and given to overstatement; memories may falter, as with anyone speaking publicly, and accuracy of statement may be severely undermined. Embarrassment may impede the search for truth, as may a natural tendency for over dramatization. Indeed, the mere fact that the trial is to be televised might render witnesses reluctant to appear and thereby impede the trial as well as the discovery of the truth. (547)

The third set of difficulties is presented by the impact of television upon the judge, who, Clark says, should not have his "undivided attention" diverted by cameras. "Judges are human beings also," writes Clark, "and are subject to the same psychological reactions as laymen" (548). In addition,

Clark notes that, "where the judge is elected," "the telecasting of a trial becomes a political weapon" (548).

The impact upon the defendant forms the last issue. Television, Clark writes, "is a form of mental—if not physical—harassment, resembling a police lineup or the third degree" (549). He continues, "The inevitable close-ups of his [a defendant's] gestures and expressions during the ordeal of his trial might very well transgress his personal sensibilities, his dignity, and his ability to concentrate on the proceedings before him . . . dispassionately, freely, and without the distraction of wide public surveillance" (549).

Television, according to the Court, could also "deprive an accused of effective counsel" (549). Clark writes, "The distractions, intrusions into confidential attorney-client relationships and the temptation offered by television to play to the public audience might often have a direct effect . . . upon the lawyers" (549).

Before leaving this enumeration, Clark notes that "the necessity for sponsorships weighs heavily in favor of televising only notorious cases" (549). He also takes care to point out that these considerations are not "hypothetical" (550).

Ruling

Clark writes:

It is said that the ever-advancing techniques of public communication and the adjustment of the public to its presence may bring about a change in the effect of telecasting upon the fairness of criminal trials. Our judgment cannot be rested on the hypothesis of tomorrow but must take the facts as they are presented today.

The judgment is therefore reversed. (552)

Chief Justice Earl Warren writes a concurring opinion.
Justices William O. Douglas and Arthur J. Goldberg join.

Warren goes a step further than Clark when he writes unequivocally, "The televising of criminal trials is inherently a denial of due process" (552).

After reviewing at some length the events surrounding the use of television at the Estes hearing and trial, Warren turns to a cursory historical survey of the role of the jury. He ends by emphasizing that the Sixth and Fourteenth Amendments grant specific rights that are enjoyed in a particular location: a trial. Pointing out "the setting that the courtroom provides is itself an important element in the constitutional conception of trial," he asserts, "disorder can convert a trial into a ritual without meaning" (562). He adds, "The criminal trial under our Constitution has a clearly defined purpose, to provide a fair and reliable determination of guilt, and no procedure or occurrence which seriously threatens to divert it from that purpose can be tolerated" (564).

Warren bases his objection to the televising of trials on three grounds. He writes:

(1) that the televising of trials diverts the trial from its proper purpose in that it has an inevitable impact on all the trial participants; (2) that it gives the public the wrong impression about the purpose of trials, thereby detracting from the dignity of the court proceedings and lessening the reliability of trials; and (3) that it singles out certain defendants and subjects them to trials under prejudicial conditions not experienced by others. (656)

Warren continues, "Thus, the evil of televised trials . . . lies not in the noise and appearance of the cameras, but in the trial participants' awareness that they are being televised" (570). "The televising of trials would cause the public to equate the trial process with the forms of entertainment regularly seen on television," he writes, "and with the commercial objectives of the television industry" (571).

Turning to another argument, Warren asserts:

It is argued that television not only entertains but also educates the public. But the function of a trial is not to provide an educational experience; and there is a serious danger that any attempt to use a trial as an educational tool will both divert it from its proper purpose and lead to suspicions concerning the integrity of the trial process. (575)

Warren, like Clark, also rejects the state's argument that an isolated prejudice must be shown. Asserting there is an "inherent unfairness of television in the courtroom," (580) he writes, "The prejudice of television may be so subtle that it escapes the ordinary methods of proof" (578).

Like Clark, Warren says the right to a public trial "confers no special benefit on the press, the radio industry or the television industry" because it is the "accused's right" (583). He adds, "A trial is public, in the constitutional sense, when a courtroom has facilities for a reasonable number of the public to observe the proceedings" (584). "So long as the television industry . . . is free to send representatives to trials and to report on those trials to its viewers, there is no abridgment of the freedom of the press" (587).

He writes in summary, "On entering that hallowed sanctuary, where the lives, liberty and property of people are in jeopardy, television representatives have only the rights of the general public, namely to be present, to observe the proceedings, and thereafter, if they choose, to report them" (586).

Justice John M. Harlan writes a concurring opinion.

Unlike Warren, Harlan does not say that televising trials is inherently unconstitutional. Rather, he says, "There is no constitutional requirement that television be allowed in the courtroom" (587). Nevertheless, in this case, the process, for him, was unconstitutional. He writes, "The considerations against allowing television in the courtroom so far outweigh the countervailing factors advanced in its support as to require a holding that what was done in this case infringed the fundamental right to a fair trial" (587).

Harlan presents his view of the rationale for public trials when he writes, "Essentially, the public trial guarantee embodies a view of human nature . . . that judges, lawyers, witnesses, and jurors will perform their respective functions more responsibly in an open court than in secret proceedings" (588). Like Warren and Clark he asserts, "Thus, the right of a 'public trial' is not one belonging to the public, but one belonging to the accused" (588). Also like Warren and Clark, he concludes, "A reporter's constitutional rights are no greater than those of any other member of the public" (589).

Harlan shares a third conviction with Clark and Warren when he says it is not necessary to show an isolated prejudice produced by the presence of television in the courtroom. He writes, "Courtroom television introduces into the conduct of a criminal trial the element of professional 'showmanship,' an extraneous influence whose subtle capacities for serious mischief in a case of this sort will not be underestimated by a lawyer experienced in the elusive imponderables of the trial arena" (591).

Harlan says the presence of television in the courtroom increases the possibility "of a 'popular verdict' by subjecting the jurors to the view of a mass audience whose approach to the case has been conditioned by pretrial publicity [making] a bad situation [only] worse" (592). Like Warren, he rejects the argument that the educational function of televising trials is important, and he agrees with Clark that "we should not be deterred from making the constitutional judgment which this case demands by the prospect that the day may come when television will have become so commonplace an affair in the daily life of the average person as to dissipate all reasonable likelihood that its use in courtrooms may disparage the judicial process" (597).

Harlan says, "At the present juncture I can only conclude that televised trials, at least in cases like this one, possess such capabilities for interfering with the even course of the judicial process that they are constitutionally banned" (596).

Justice Potter Stewart writes a dissenting opinion.
Justices Hugo L. Black, William J. Brennan, Jr.,
and Byron R. White join.

Stewart begins, "The introduction of television into a courtroom, at least in the present state of the art, [is] an extremely unwise policy" (601). "But,"

he continues, "I am unable to escalate this personal view into a per se constitutional rule" (601, 602). He adds, "And I am unable to find . . . that the
circumstances attending this limited televising of the petitioner's [Estes's]
trial resulted in the denial of any right guaranteed to him by the United
States Constitution" (602).

Stewart sums up his position this way: "I would be wary of imposing any
per se rule which, in the light of future technology, might serve to stifle or
abridge true First Amendment rights" (604). He then reviews the events surrounding the trial, emphasizing the limited nature of the television presence.
Next, he rejects the pretrial publicity claims, saying they are not relevant since
the Court did not agree to review them when it granted certiorari.

Stewart presents a list prepared by the American Bar Association of the
dangers of televising criminal trials and then comments, "The plain fact of
the matter, however, is that none of these things happened in this case"
(613). He adds, "The trial itself was a most mundane affair, totally lacking
in the lurid and completely emotionless" (614). Stewart notes, "The transcript of the trial belies any notion that frequent interruptions and inconsistent rulings communicated to the jury any sense that the judge was unable
to concentrate on protecting the defendant and conduct the trial in a fair
manner" (614).

Finally, Stewart addresses a few of the arguments for banning television
from trials. He writes:

> The suggestion that there are limits upon the public's right to know
> what goes on in the courts causes me deep concern. The idea of impos-
> ing upon any medium of communications the burden of justifying its
> presence is contrary to where I had always thought the presumption
> must lie in the area of First Amendment freedoms. And the proposition
> that nonparticipants in a trial might get the "wrong impression" from
> unfettered reporting and commentary contains an invitation to censor-
> ship which I cannot accept. (615)

He concludes, "I cannot now hold that the Constitution absolutely bars
television cameras from every criminal courtroom, even if they have no
impact upon the jury, no effect upon any witness, and no influence upon the
conduct of the judge" (615).

Justice Byron R. White writes a dissenting opinion.
Justice William J. Brennan, Jr., joins.

White's single point is that the Court made a decision on the basis of
too little experience with television in the courtroom. He writes, "In my
view, the currently available materials assessing the effect of cameras in the
courtroom are too sparse and fragmentary to constitute the basis for a

constitutional judgment permanently barring any and all forms of television coverage" (616).

Significance

No one would question the assertion that this decision significantly reduced the televising of criminal trials for a few years. There is much disagreement, however, about whether or not the Court issued an absolute constitutional ban against cameras in the courtroom, disagreement reflected in the Court's eventual reconsideration of the effects of television, *Chandler* v. *Florida* (1981). Therefore, while the effect of the decision is clear, the meaning of it is not.

Perhaps observers should not be surprised that this meaning is unclear. In addition to the majority decision, two concurring and two dissenting opinions, for a total of five, were published. Moreover, the justices themselves admitted they were unable to put their finger precisely on the reasons television prevents a fair trial. At bottom, they asserted, among other things, that televising criminal trials is simply "inherently lacking in due process"; it is "irrelevant" to the central objective of a trial; and it "is a form of mental—if not physical—harassment" (549). The majority decision stated, "One cannot put his finger on its specific mischief and prove with particularity wherein he [Estes] was prejudiced" (554). One summary in particular highlights the essential problem the justices faced when banning television from the courtroom: "The prejudice of television may be so subtle that it escapes the ordinary methods of proof" (578).

For Warren, the problem takes on religious overtones. He says televising trials is "evil" simply because the trial participants are aware they are being televised. He calls the courtroom a "hallowed sanctuary" where television is irrelevant. Harlan's objection is more mundane; he sees "subtle capacities for serious mischief" in the "professional 'showmanship'" qualities of television. Yet, he terms the constitutional problems with televising criminal trials "elusive imponderables."

For the most part, the opinions supporting a ban focus on the psychological impact television has on the trial participants. These considerations consist primarily of heightened self-awareness, which could detract from the trial by leading on the one hand to excessive shyness or on the other to excessive showmanship.

One other part of the argument supporting the ban should not go unnoticed. At least two of the justices openly admitted that television technology could change so drastically that eventually it would no longer be a threat to a fair trial. The implication is that someday televising criminal trials would not be unconstitutional. Thus, many observers read this opinion as banning only a set of circumstances similar to those that occurred in the televising of the Estes trial, not absolutely banning the televising of all criminal trials for all time.

Arguments against the ban also deserve mention. White says this nation's experience with the effects of televising criminal trials is too meager to provide a valid guide to the Court. Stewart says he is concerned about arguments that imply limitations on a citizen's right to know what transpires in a criminal trial. He objects to placing upon a medium the burden of justifying its presence, and he fears that arguments against broadcasting will present the "wrong impression" of the Court's ruling as "an invitation to censorship."

Attorneys for the state of Texas admitted that the presence of spectators in a courtroom with eyes glued on witnesses during testimony undoubtedly provides distraction. In addition, for many defendants the presence of spectators clearly is embarrassing. The state argued, though, that if all distractions to witnesses and participants were to be removed in order to assure a fair trial, then public trials would be impossible. So long as trials are open to the public and the press, Texas asserted, there will be inevitable distractions.

Sheppard v. Maxwell

Samuel H. Sheppard

v.

E. L. Maxwell, Warden

Docket No. 1966-490

384 U.S. 333, 16 L.Ed.2d 600, 86 S.Ct. 1507 (1966)

Argued February 28, 1966. Decided June 6, 1966.

Background

By 1966, the Court had made it clear that pretrial and extra-trial publicity could indeed unconstitutionally prejudice jurors and so deprive a defendant from trial by an impartial jury. Never before, however, had it outlined more than a few isolated steps that could be taken by a trial court to reduce the effect upon jurors of information disseminated by the press.

Perhaps in part because the trial judge here claimed he could not control the press, the Court used this ruling to suggest a number of steps that he could have taken to regulate the press constitutionally. Indeed, *Sheppard* is considered a landmark case precisely because of its detailed prescriptions for ameliorating the deleterious effects on the fairness of a trial caused by pretrial and extra-trial publicity.

Some of the most important questions raised by this trial and its attendant publicity were posed by F. Lee Bailey in his brief asking the court to grant Sheppard a new trial. Of his eleven questions, the four below are the most relevant to this conflict.

> (1) Did the pretrial publicity in petitioner's [Sheppard's] case so prejudice the community that no fair and impartial jury could have been impanelled?
> (2) Did the trial judge fail to adequately protect the petit jury, once impanelled, from prejudicial extrinsic influence?
> (3) Did the trial judge fail to adequately interrogate the jurors when they had been exposed to prejudicial extrinsic matter through the news media during the trial?
> . . .
> (5) Did the trial judge deny petitioner a public trial by assigning nearly all the seats in the courtroom to newsmen?

Circumstances

Dr. Samuel H. Sheppard, an osteopathic neurosurgeon, was president of his class all three years at Cleveland Heights High School. As a senior he won an award as the school's most outstanding athlete. Sheppard first met his wife, Marilyn, at Roosevelt Jr. High School in Cleveland, and he married her in the summer of 1944 while still a student at the Osteopathic School of Physicians and Surgeons in Los Angeles. He says in his autobiography, *Endure and Conquer* (Cleveland: World Publishing, 1966) that her attitude towards sex changed after she experienced difficulty delivering their son, Sam Jr.

Upon completing his residency in neurosurgery at the Los Angeles County Hospital, he returned to Cleveland in 1951 to join his father and brother at the osteopathic hospital founded by his father. He was appointed chief surgeon in charge of the emergency room. As police surgeon of Bay Village and Westlake, he became close friends with the village's part-time mayor and nearby neighbor, J. Spencer Houk.

Don and Nancy Ahern, also neighbors of the Sheppards, were visiting the evening Marilyn Sheppard was murdered. Sam said in his autobiography that he fell asleep on the couch before they left at about 12:30 A.M. on July 4, 1954. He said Marilyn unsuccessfully tried to wake him when she went to bed shortly thereafter.

Sheppard said in court testimony that he awoke on the living room couch, probably sometime between 3 and 4 A.M., after hearing his wife cry out. When he got to the bedroom, he saw a white "form" that he struggled with until he was "struck on the back of the neck and rendered unconscious" (336). When he regained consciousness, he saw the "form" running out the door. He gave chase, wrestled with it a second time, and, after being put in some sort of strangle hold, again lost consciousness. Upon awakening with half of his body in the surf, he returned to the house and called Spencer Houk, who, after coming over with his wife, called the police. Dr. Samuel Gerber, the Cuyahoga County Coroner, who was also an attorney, said Marilyn Sheppard was struck 35 times with a blunt instrument, and, although she suffered several skull fractures, her skull was not crushed. On July 30, Sheppard was arrested on the charge of murder in the first degree.

Sheppard called the events that followed his arrest an "assault" by the press; the Court called it a "Roman Circus." According to the Court, "Dr. Gerber, the Coroner, is reported—and it is undenied—to have told his men, 'Well it is evident the doctor did this, so let's go get the confession out of him'" (337). The publicity in the media, especially in the Cleveland *Press*, began immediately. An inquest was held by the coroner in a school gymnasium with "a swarm of reporters and photographers" (339) in attendance. The Court noted, "When Sheppard's chief council attempted to place some documents in the record, he was forcibly ejected from the room by the Coroner, who received cheers, hugs, and kisses from ladies in the audience" (340).

The Court said, "Throughout this period the newspapers emphasized evidence that tended to incriminate Sheppard and pointed out discrepancies in his statements to authorities" (340). The Court also commented in a footnote, "A number of articles calculated to evoke sympathy for Sheppard were printed, such as letters Sheppard wrote to his son while in jail" (340). After a July 28 Cleveland *Press* editorial (entitled "Quit Stalling—Bring Him In") "'demanded that Sheppard be taken to police headquarters,'" he was arrested at 10:00 P.M. and charged with murder.

In addition, the Court took note of the fact that the trial began "two weeks before the November general election at which the chief prosecutor was a candidate for common pleas judge, and the trial judge, Judge Edward Blythin, a former mayor of Cleveland, was a candidate to succeed himself" (342). After the case was over, Judge Blythin was reelected in a landslide, and prosecutor John Mahon won election to the bench of the Court of Common Pleas. Moreover, the Cleveland newspapers published the names and addresses of the veniremen, who then received anonymous letters and telephone calls about the case.

Members of the press were given seats on all the newly erected benches in the courtroom except for one reserved for Sheppard's family, and one television station was allowed to broadcast from a room next to the jury room. According to the Court, "The daily record of the proceedings was made available to the newspapers and the testimony of each witness was printed verbatim in the local editions, along with objections of counsel, and rulings by the judge" (344). Finally, the Court noted, "Every juror, except one, testified at voir dire to reading about the case in the Cleveland papers or to having heard broadcasts about it" (345).

The Court listed nine examples of what it called "flagrant episodes" of "intense publicity" (345). Among the episodes are these. Radio station WHK broadcast a live debate in which it was "asserted that Sheppard conceded his guilt by hiring a prominent criminal lawyer" (346). When Sheppard's counsel complained, the trial judge said, "'WHK doesn't have much coverage'" (346). Hundreds of reporters watched the jury visit the scene of the murder. Walter Winchell said in a television and radio broadcast, "Carole Beasley [at the time under arrest in New York for armed robbery] . . . had stated that, as Sheppard's mistress, she had borne him a child" (348). In addition, the judge told well-known newspaper gossip columnist Dorothy Kilgallen Kollimar that Sam was guilty and the case was open and shut. Many citizens were suspicious of Sheppard after they learned he had a sexual relationship with Susan Hayes, a medical technician at Bay View Hospital.

Two jurors testified that they heard the Winchell story, but said it would not influence their verdict. Eleven said they saw or heard pretrial publicity, and thirteen of the sixty-four prospective jurors where dismissed for the cause of prejudice. Sheppard was convicted of second-degree murder on December 21, 1954.

After conviction, Sheppard began what turned out to be a fairly complicated series of appeals that included a refusal by the Supreme Court on November 11, 1956, to hear his case. After William J. Corrigan, his highly competent attorney, died in 1961, F. Lee Bailey, then 33, took over. Although he had no way of knowing it, Sheppard's luck began to change when Ariane Tebbejohannus read about his case in the waiting room of her dentist in Dusseldorf, Germany, in December 1954. Nearly ten years later, on July 22, 1964, Sheppard and Tebbejohannus were married with F. Lee Bailey as best man.

The marriage took place after Federal Judge Carl A. Weinman ruled on a habeas corpus petition by Bailey on July 15, 1964, ordering Sam released on $10,000 bond and giving the government sixty days to retry him. E. L. Maxwell, warden of the Ohio State Penitentiary at Columbus, appealed the district court's order that he set Sheppard free. By a divided vote, the Court of Appeals for the Sixth Circuit reversed Weinman's ruling, but the U.S. Supreme Court upheld him. Finally, on November 16, 1966, a second jury declared Samuel H. Sheppard not guilty.

Summary of the Court's Analysis

Justice Tom C. Clark writes for the Court.
Chief Justice Earl Warren and Justices William O. Douglas,
John M. Harlan, William J. Brennan, Jr., Byron R. White,
Potter Stewart, and Abe Fortas join.

Justice Clark says the essential question is "whether Sheppard was deprived of a fair trial in his state conviction for the second-degree murder of his wife because of the trial judge's failure to protect Sheppard sufficiently from the massive, pervasive and prejudicial publicity that attended his prosecution" (335). He then answers his own question, "We have concluded that Sheppard did not receive a fair trial consistent with the Due Process Clause of the Fourteenth Amendment" (335).

Clark begins his analysis by affirming the importance of a free press to a fair trial. He writes:

> A responsible press has always been regarded as the handmaiden of effective judicial administration, especially in the criminal field. The Press does not simply publish information about trials but guards against the miscarriage of justice by subjecting the police, prosecutors, and judicial processes to extensive public scrutiny and criticism. (350)

As a result, Clark says, the Court has "been unwilling to place any direct limitations on the freedom" (350) of the press to report news from the courthouse. Nevertheless, Clark asserts, "The jury's verdict [must] be based on evidence received in open court, not from outside sources" (351).

Here the jurors were not shielded from "outside sources." Clark writes, "The Sheppard jurors were subjected to newspaper, radio and television coverage of the trial while not taking part in the proceedings" (353). Moreover, the judge only "suggested" and "requested" the jurors not "expose themselves to comment upon the case" (353). In addition, the Court says, "The jurors were thrust into the role of celebrities by the judge's failure to insulate them from reporters and photographers" (353).

Clark concludes, "While we cannot say that Sheppard was denied due process by the judge's refusal to take precautions against the influence of pretrial publicity alone, the court's later rulings must be considered against the setting in which the trial was held" (354, 355). Saying that "bedlam reigned" at the trial, the Court found "the arrangements made by the judge with the news media caused Sheppard to be deprived" (355) of a "calm" and serene trial. Clark says the judge "lost his ability to supervise" the courtroom because he "assigned almost all of the available seats" (355) to the news media. The "absolute free reign" given to the "throng of newsmen" resulted, says Clark, in a "total lack of consideration for the privacy of the jury" (355).

Clark continues, "Nor is there doubt that this deluge of publicity reached at least some of the jury" (357). He writes, "On the only occasion that the jury was queried, two jurors admitted in open court to hearing the highly inflammatory charge that a prison inmate claimed Sheppard as the father of her illegitimate child" (357). He concludes, "In these circumstances, we can assume that some of the material reached members of the jury" (357).

The Court then presents a list of suggestions outlining procedures that the trial judge could have used to guarantee Sheppard a fair trial. The main problem with the judge's approach to publicity, according to Clark, is that, "since he viewed the news media as his target, the judge never considered other means . . . to protect the jury from outside influence" (358).

Saying the trial took place in a "carnival atmosphere," Clark asserts that many problems could have been avoided if the judge simply had been more aware that "the courtroom and courthouse premises are subject to the control of the court" (358). The first thing the Court suggests he could have done was, at the first sign that the presence of reporters would disrupt the trial, limit their number. In addition, "The judge should have more closely regulated the conduct of newsmen in the courtroom" (358).

"Secondly," Clark writes, "the court should have insulated the witnesses" (359). The witnesses, he notes, had "the full verbatim testimony available to them in the press" (359). "Thirdly," Clark continues, "the court should have made some effort to control the release of leads, information, and gossip to the press by police officers, witnesses, and the counsel for both sides" (359).

In addition, "the judge should have at least warned the newspapers to check the accuracy of their accounts" (360), and he should have "sought to alleviate this problem [of inaccurate news reports] by imposing control over statements made to the news media by counsel, witnesses, and especially the Coroner and police officers" (360). Clark adds, "More specifically, the trial court might well have proscribed extrajudicial statements by any lawyer, party, witness, or court official which divulged prejudicial matters, such as the refusal of Sheppard to submit to interrogation or to take any lie detector tests; . . . the identity of prospective witnesses or their probable testimony; [or] any belief in guilt or innocence" (361).

Taking another tack, Clark writes, "The court could also have requested the appropriate city and county officials to promulgate a regulation with respect to dissemination of information about the case by their employees" (362). Furthermore, the court could have pointed out to "reporters who wrote or broadcast prejudicial stories" the "impropriety of publishing material not introduced in the proceedings" (362).

To make sure "the accused receives a trial by an impartial jury free from outside influences," Clark says "the judge should continue a case until the threat [of prejudicial pretrial publicity] abates, or transfer it to another county not so permeated with publicity" (363). Another action would be "sequestration of the jury" or even ordering a new trial if the fairness of the present one is threatened.

Clark summarizes the Court's strong opinions about a judge's control of the courtroom when he writes, "The courts must take such steps by rule and regulation that will protect their processes from prejudicial outside interferences" (363). He adds, "Information affecting the fairness of a criminal trial is not only subject to regulation, but is highly censurable and worthy of disciplinary measures" (363).

Ruling

Clark writes:

Since the state trial judge did not fulfill his duty to protect Sheppard from the inherently prejudicial publicity which saturated the community and to control disruptive influences in the courtroom, we must reverse the denial of the habeas petition. The case is remanded to the District Court with instructions to issue the writ and order that Sheppard be released from custody unless the State puts him to charges again within a reasonable time. (363)

Justice Hugo L. Black dissents without writing an opinion.

Significance

This case is significant because, for the first time, the Court outlined a number of steps trial courts can take to protect jurors from prejudicial publicity originating outside the courtroom. It should be noted, however, that the Court was not prepared to assert flatly that Sheppard was denied due process solely on the basis of the pretrial publicity. The trial was ruled unfair only when the massive pretrial publicity was added to the judge's failure to control the flow of information from the courtroom after the trial began.

Perhaps in response to a dissenting opinion by Justice Tom C. Clark in *Rideau* v. *Louisiana* (1963), the Court said it was not necessary to show that the jurors were aware of the extrajudicial publicity. There, Clark asserted that, in order to prove denial of due process, the accused must show a connection between the broadcast of his confession and an unconstitutionally prejudiced community of prospective jurors. Here, the Court said that because the pretrial publicity was so pervasive, one could assume the members of the jury were exposed to it.

Most important, trial judges must be aware, according to the Court, that the courtroom and courthouse premises are subject to the control of the court. Not only is information affecting the fairness of a trial subject to regulation, but it is also "highly censurable and worthy of disciplinary measures" (363). The trial judge would have been more likely to take charge of the publicity flow, says the Court, had he been aware that the media constitute only one aspect of the dissemination process. Judges can regulate the release of some forms of information, and they can warn the media about the impropriety of printing information outside the court's control.

Here is a summary of the actions the Court said the trial judge could have taken to guarantee a fair trial by an impartial jury:

(1) The number of journalists admitted into the court could be limited.

(2) The behavior of journalists in court can be regulated.

(3) Witnesses can be insulated from extrajudicial information.

(4) The judge can control the release of information to the press by police officers, witnesses, and the counsel for both sides. In particular the judge can order these persons not to discuss such topics as the refusal of a defendant to submit to interrogation to take any lie detector tests; the identity of prospective witnesses or their probable testimony; any belief in guilt or innocence.

(5) The judge can warn reporters to check the accuracy of their news stories.

(6) The court could also point out the impropriety of publishing material not introduced in the proceedings to reporters who, in spite of warnings, wrote or broadcast prejudicial stories.

(7) The judge can request the appropriate city and county officials to issue regulations governing the dissemination by their employees of information about the case.

(8) A case can be continued until the threat of prejudicial pretrial publicity abates or dies out.

(9) The trial can be moved to another county where the publicity level is acceptable.

(10) The jury can be sequestered, where the inflow of information can be more easily regulated.

(11) If all else fails, then a new trial can be ordered when it appears that the fairness of the present one is threatened. (358–363)

Unconstitutional prejudicial publicity that results from not following these eleven steps were outlined in an amicus curiae brief by the American Civil Liberties Union. They are helpful in understanding the categories of extra-trial publicity that could be harmful to a fair trial:

(1) Publicity relating to the strength of the state's case or the guilt of the accused, procured or cooperated in by the state law enforcement authorities.

(2) Publicity relating to testimony of witnesses not offered at trial by the prosecution.

(3) Publicity relating to evidence which would have been inadmissible if offered at trial.

(4) Publicity which made celebrities of the trial jurors.

(5) Publicity charging guilt or attacking the character of the accused.

Murphy v. Florida

Jack Roland Murphy

v.

State of Florida

Docket No. 74-5116

421 U.S. 794, 44 L.Ed.2d 589, 95 S.Ct. 2031 (1975)

Argued April 15, 1975. Decided June 16, 1975.

Background

In four previous cases the Court reversed convictions because of massive pretrial publicity that it said perforce made impossible an impartial jury. See *Irvin* v. *Dowd* (1961), *Rideau* v. *Louisiana* (1963), *Estes* v. *Texas* (1965), and *Sheppard* v. *Maxwell* (1966). It is not surprising, therefore, that Murphy, a criminal of some national notoriety, would assert that he too did not receive a fair trial because of the abundance of prejudicial pretrial publicity surrounding his trial.

In effect, Murphy was asserting he was such an infamous criminal that he could never receive a fair trial because the whole country was already unconstitutionally prejudiced against him. The Court foils his attempt, however, by drawing a line between how much pretrial publicity is unconstitutionally harmful and how much is not. This question is taken up again by the Court in *Mu'Min* v. *Virginia* (1991).

Circumstances

A former child prodigy who played violin with the Pittsburgh Symphony Orchestra, Jack Roland Murphy first attracted nationwide publicity for his role in the 1964 theft of the Star of India, a 565-carat sapphire housed in the New York Museum of Natural History. Because of his splashy lifestyle, he continued to interest reporters who dubbed him "Murph the Surf." He served two years for the theft.

On January 28, 1968, Murphy, wearing a pair of sheer black panties as a mask, and three others were arrested for a daring daylight robbery attempt at the Pine Tree Drive house of wealthy Miami Beach resident Mrs. Olive

Wofford. They forced her to open a safe by threatening to torture her eight-year-old niece with boiling water. When she complied, a silent alarm was triggered, bringing two police officers within sixty seconds. Although Murphy fled through a glass door, slashing his face and knee, he was apprehended immediately.

Before Murphy could be tried, he was arrested and indicted in May 1968 for the double murder of two young female secretaries, Terry Rae Kent Frank and Annalie Mohn. When the bodies of the bikini-clad women surfaced in a creek named after bootleggers who had used it decades earlier, the press dubbed the crimes the "Whiskey Creek Murders." The two murdered women had been involved in a securities theft investigation in which Murphy was also implicated. On August 14, 1968, Murphy and three others were indicted for conspiring to transport a half-million stolen securities in interstate commerce from Los Angeles, California, to Miami Beach, Florida. Murphy went to trial for the murder of Terry Rae Frank and was found guilty on March 1, 1969. In August, 1969, the Wofford robbery case was re-filed.

Prior to the trial for the Miami Beach robberies, Murphy filed a change-of-venue motion based on publicity from his past criminal life, including the New York sapphire theft and the "Whisky Creek Murders." When seventy-eight jurors were questioned about the robbery charge, twenty "were excused by the court as having prejudged" him (796). From this panel, though, six jurors (enough for trial in Florida) and two alternates were picked, none of whom were acceptable to Murphy. Jury selection began July 27, 1970, and ended August 10. Most jurors knew he had been found guilty in the Whiskey Creek Murders, the Star of India theft, and the 100-carat DeLong Ruby theft. All knew he was a convicted felon who was serving time for murder and who had served time for jewel theft, and all said their knowledge came from the mass media.

Judge Joe Eaton wrote the following in a statement related to a motion for a change of venue filed on August 10, 1970:

> It is simply foolhardy to come down here asking folks if they know anything about Mr. Murphy. . . . I went over between Punta Gorda and Arcadia last weekend, halfway up the Peace River in the woods, and I mean really in the woods, and an old gentleman that used to be a fishing guide came up there in his boat, and I had not run into anybody up there in the last three times I have been there, that is how wild it is; but he says, "Hey Judge, did you hear about Murph the Surf?"

Murphy did not take the stand in his own behalf and offered no evidence. He also declined to cross-examine any witnesses because he did not accept the jury panel. After his plea of insanity was rejected, he was found guilty and sentenced to life for breaking and entering a dwelling with intent to commit armed robbery. A judge warned that Murphy should never be released into "the free world with a law-abiding society."

After his conviction, Murphy filed a habeas corpus petition saying a refusal to change venue and the prejudiced jurors denied him a fair trial. The United States District Court for the Southern District of Florida rejected the petition as did the United States Court of Appeals for the Fifth Circuit. He was released in 1986 at age 49 after serving seventeen years.

Summary of the Court's Analysis

Justice Thurgood Marshall writes for the Court.
Justices William O. Douglas, Potter Stewart, Byron R. White,
Harry A. Blackmun, Lewis F. Powell, and William H. Rehnquist join.

Justice Thurgood Marshall focuses quickly on the primary issue. He writes, "The question presented by this case is whether the petitioner [Murphy] was denied a fair trial because members of the jury had learned from news accounts about a prior felony conviction or certain facts about the crime with which he was charged" (795).

To answer this question, Marshall first addresses the applicability of *Marshall* v. *U.S.* (1959) to state criminal proceedings. In *Marshall,* the Court ruled that information published in the newspaper is capable of prejudicing a jury at least as much as is information introduced into court because news stories are not accompanied by safeguards attending the introduction of evidence into a trial.

The first point *Marshall* raises here is that the *Marshall* case originated in the federal courts and so the decision there was based not on constitutional grounds, but on the Court's supervisory power over the lower federal courts. Murphy says, nevertheless, four other cases, taken together, establish a constitutional rule "that persons who have learned from news sources of a defendant's prior criminal record are presumed to be prejudiced" (798). (See *Irvin* v. *Dowd* [1961], *Rideau* v. *Louisiana* [1963], *Estes* v. *Texas* [1965], and *Sheppard* v. *Maxwell* [1966].) Marshall responds, "They [these four cases] cannot be made to stand for the proposition that juror exposure to information about a state defendant's prior convictions or to news accounts of the crime with which he is charged *alone* [emphasis added] presumptively deprives the defendant of due process" (799). To determine if the trial was not "fundamentally fair," Marshall points out, the Court must look at "the totality of circumstances" (799).

"Qualified jurors need not, however, be totally ignorant of the facts and issues involved" (800), Marshall writes as he begins his examination of "the totality of circumstances." He continues, "At the same time, the juror's assurances that he is equal to this task cannot be dispositive of the accused rights" (800). In short, the defendant must prove that opinions held by jurors are in fact prejudicial.

Marshall then looks at the transcript of the *voir dire* in an attempt to find unconstitutional prejudice. He finds "a vague recollection of the robbery . . . and some knowledge of petitioner's [Murphy's] past crimes, but none betrayed any belief in the relevance of petitioner's [Murphy's] past to the present case" (800). Marshall admits, "One juror conceded that his prior impression of petitioner [Murphy] would dispose him to convict" (801), but the Court must also consider "the leading nature of counsel's questions and the juror's other testimony indicating that he had no deep impression of petitioner [Murphy] at all" (802).

The Court went on to say, though, that, even if Murphy cannot prove the existence of prejudice in individual jurors, he can still obtain a reversal of his conviction if he can show that "the general atmosphere in the community or courtroom is sufficiently inflammatory" (802). Here Marshall notes the publicity "appears almost entirely during the period between December 1976 and January 1969 . . . seven months before the jury in this case was selected" (802). In addition, the news stories were "largely factual in nature" (802). If the community prejudice was "deeply hostile to the accused," then individual protestations of impartiality by jurors could be "drawn into question" because "they may unwittingly have been influenced by it" (803). In this case, though, Marshall says the publicity "by no means suggests a community with sentiment so poisoned against petitioner as to impeach the indifference of jurors who displayed no animus of their own" (803).

Ruling

Marshall writes, "Petitioner [Murphy] has failed to show that the setting of the trial was inherently prejudicial or that the jury selection process of which he complains permits an inference of actual prejudice. The judgment of the Court of Appeals must therefore be Affirmed" (803).

Chief Justice Warren E. Burger writes a concurring opinion.

Justice Burger begins by scolding the lower court. He writes, "The trial judge was woefully remiss in failing to insulate prospective jurors from the bizarre media coverage of this case and in not taking steps to prevent pretrial discussion of the case among them" (803, 804).

If this were a federal case, then he says he would "not hesitate to reverse petitioner's [Murphy's] conviction in the exercise of our supervisory powers" (803), but since it is a state case, he does not vote to reverse because "the circumstances of petitioner's [Murphy's] trial did not rise to the level of a violation of the Due Process clause of the Fourteenth Amendment" (804).

Justice William J. Brennan, Jr., writes a dissenting opinion.

Brennan would reverse the conviction because "the trial court made no attempt to prevent discussion of the case or petitioner's [Murphy's] previous criminal exploits among the prospective jurors, and one juror freely admitted that he was predisposed to [convict] petitioner [Murphy]" (804).

Brennan does not agree that the bias of one juror who knew of Murphy's previous crimes "can be overlooked simply because the juror's response was occasioned by 'a leading or a hypothetical question'" (805). He also notes that another juror, who called Murphy a "'menace'" (805), said that "it would be difficult, during deliberations, to put out of his mind that petitioner [Murphy] was a convicted criminal" (805). A third juror, who knew Murphy was a convicted murderer, said that, even though she had no fixed opinion, "the fact that petitioner [Murphy] was a convicted criminal would probably influence her verdict" (806). Yet another juror said he heard a venireman say Murphy was "'thoroughly rotten'" (807).

Brennan writes, "It is of no moment that several jurors ultimately testified that they would try to exclude from their deliberations their knowledge of petitioner's [Murphy's] past misdeed and of his community reputation" (807). "The attitude of the entire venire toward Murphy," writes Brennan, "was infected with the taint of the view that he was a 'criminal' guilty of notorious offenses" (808). Thus, a change of venue, according to Brennan, was necessary for a fair trial.

Significance

This case is significant first because it relates concepts in *Marshall* v. *U.S.* (1959), which affected only federal courts under the Court's supervisory powers, to state courts, which are subject only to selective aspects of the Fourteenth Amendment. In *Marshall,* the Court ruled that information published in the newspaper is capable of prejudicing a jury in a federal court at least as much as is information introduced into that court because news stories are not accompanied by safeguards attending the introduction of evidence into a trial.

In *Murphy,* though, the Court refused to establish a constitutional rule asserting that jurors with some extrajudicial knowledge of a defendant's prior criminal record are necessarily incapable of being impartial. To show a level of unconstitutional fault, defendants, says the Court, must do at least one of two things. First, they must show unconstitutional prejudice of an individual juror resulting from pretrial publicity. Second, they must show that the attitude of the community at large was so hostile that it inherently prevented a fair trial by an impartial jury.

In regards to an individual juror, the Court reaffirmed its long-standing notion (see, for example, *Reynolds* v. *U.S.,* 1887) that a mere assertion of impartiality is not sufficient to declare a prospective juror free of unconstitutional prejudice. The defendant has the right to challenge this assertion and to demonstrate the existence of a deeply held prejudice that should not be overlooked. Moreover, the appeals court can also examine the *voir dire* to look for evidence indicating the strength of an opinion formed on extrajudicial evidence.

Showing the presence of a "general atmosphere" that is sufficiently "inflammatory" to make any jury in a given geographical area unconstitutionally prejudiced against a defendant is the second way the Court said Murphy could seek a reversal of his conviction. In this trial, for example, most of the publicity appeared seven months before the jury was selected, and the news stories were declared by the Court to be largely factual in nature. Thus, the publicity attending Murphy's trial here was felt by the Court to be insufficiently indicative of a community possessing sentiments so poisoned against a defendant as to call into question the validity of an individual juror's assertion of impartiality.

Murphy's downfall was his failure to present evidence for either requirement. In fact, the Court, in its independent investigation of the record, also could find none.

It could be said, then, that the primary significance of this case is the importance of presenting sufficient evidence supporting at least one of two assertions: (1) that an individual juror or (2) that the jury as a whole is unconstitutionally prejudiced against a defendant.

Burger's concurring opinion should not be ignored. He said the errors of the trial judge would be sufficient to overturn a federal conviction as part of the Court's supervisory powers over lower federal courts, but the errors were not sufficient to raise constitutional questions.

Nebraska Press Association v. Stuart

Nebraska Press Association, et al.
v.
Hugh Stuart, Judge,
District Court of Lincoln County, Nebraska, et al.

Docket No. 75-817
427 U.S. 539, 49 L.Ed.2d 683, 96 S.Ct. 2791 (1976)

Argued April 19, 1976. Decided June 30, 1976.

Background

Sheppard v. *Maxwell* (1966) is thought by many observers to have made the courts a bit more sensitive to the importance of an impartial jury and to its role in guaranteeing this Sixth Amendment right. It is not surprising, therefore, that a judge eventually would attempt to protect persons accused of a crime from potentially prejudicial pretrial publicity simply by forbidding the publishing of information contrary to the interests of a defendant.

The essential question raised by this form of prior restraint is (assuming such a curb on the press is efficacious; that is, that this curb would actually guarantee an impartial jury) whether or not it is necessary to protect a defendant's right to a fair trial. Could other measures—in particular, measures not restricting First Amendment rights—be used to decrease the possibility of a jury prejudiced against a defendant?

Another important aspect of this case is the defense's argument that, since a criminal trial does not begin until the time a jury of the prescribed number is sworn and ready to hear the evidence, news stories printed prior to this point represent pretrial publicity. (The Court ruled in *Wade* v. *Hunter* [1949] that for purposes of double jeopardy a trial begins when the first witness is sworn, but in *Downum* v. *U.S.* [1963] it ruled a trial begins when the jurors are sworn.) Although the Court declines in *Nebraska* to address the question of deciding exactly at what point for First Amendment purposes a trial starts, eventually it will be unable to avoid the issue because the tactic tried here (of denying the mass media access to information) will be extended over time to include what are often termed pretrial procedures.

Moreover, since much of the Court's attention in the past had been directed toward the damage imposed by the publication of a confession, it is not surprising that the damage to a fair trial caused by knowledge of a confession received much attention in this case. The basic question here can be stated as follows: Does publication of a confession necessarily increase significantly the possibility that prospective jurors may be prejudiced unconstitutionally against a defendant?

Circumstances

Edwin Charles Simants was arrested around 8 A.M., Sunday, October 19, 1975, and arraigned soon thereafter for the murder the night before of six members of the Henry Kellie family of Sutherland, Nebraska, a village of 850 persons in West Central Nebraska. Those murdered were Henry Kellie, 66; his wife, Marie, 57; his son, David, 32; David's two children, Daniel, 5, and Deanne, 6; and the elder Kellie's granddaughter, Florence Kay, 10. Medical testimony indicated that there was at least one attempt at penetration of the 10-year-old girl and that the attempted commission of three sexual assaults on female victims could have occurred after death.

The community was immediately alerted by a break-in news announcement on television. Soon thereafter a dance was closed, several bars were shut down, and at least one family left town as rumors spread that a sniper was loose and that the authorities had been ordered to shoot on sight. When news of Simants's arrest was broadcast over radio and television, the tension of the night before was relieved.

Kelly Armstrong, reporter for the Associated Press in Omaha, Nebraska, attended Simants's late Sunday morning arraignment in the Lincoln County Court with Judge Ronald A. Ruff presiding. Lincoln County Attorney Milton Larson asked that part of the arraignment be closed on the grounds that an open hearing could be prejudicial to Simants. Armstrong was required to leave the courtroom for five or ten minutes.

While Armstrong was absent, Dr. Miles Foster testified that all of the victims had been shot in the head. Two were shot twice, the other four once, by .22 or .25 caliber bullets. Powder burns on two victims indicated they were shot from one-and-one-half to two inches away. James Robert Boggs, 13-year-old nephew of Erwin Simants, testified that on Saturday night, October 18, Simants got a .22 caliber automatic rifle from the bedroom of Boggs's parents. He left for about fifteen minutes, came back, cleaned the rifle, and told Boggs he had shot the Kellies.

In other testimony, Amos Simants, Erwin's father, said his son came to their home at about 9 P.M., telling them he beat the Kellies to death. The father did not believe Erwin, so he went to see for himself. He called an ambulance when he saw dead bodies.

Gordon D. Gilster, the Lincoln County sheriff, testified he arrested Simants at Boggs's home at about 8 A.M. that morning. Although only five bodies were found immediately, June Lindstrom, an ambulance driver, said David Kellie, who was still alive when she arrived, had been rushed to the Great Plains Medical Center at North Platte (the county seat holding 9,000 of the 21,000 residents of Lincoln County) and died in the emergency room.

On Wednesday morning, October 22, Armstrong attended the preliminary hearing and was given a copy of what has come to be known as a "gag" order because Judge Ruff told reporters they not only could not report any testimony given at the hearing but they could not report the existence of the order itself.

Armstrong said she already knew all the testimony of ambulance driver Lindstrom because she had interviewed this driver earlier and the Associated Press had published the information before the preliminary hearing started. Other members of the media arrived in Sutherland by 11:30 P.M., Sunday, including an NBC helicopter from Denver, Colorado.

According to Justice William J. Brennan, Jr., in his concurring opinion, "During the period from October 19 until the first restrictive order was entered three days later, representatives of the press made accurate factual reports of the events that transpired, including reports of incriminating statements made by Simants to various relatives" (574). Because of the continued "widespread news coverage," the county attorney for Lincoln County and Simants's attorney three days later "joined in asking the County Court to enter a restrictive order" (542) barring the press from reporting certain information. After hearing oral argument, receiving no evidence, and without the presence of the press or attorneys for the press, the county judge entered the order October 22.

The order prohibited the attorneys from releasing information to the journalists and "required members of the press to observe the Nebraska Bar-Press Guidelines" (542). This action began a complicated series of requests by the media to a number of courts and justices, asking that this order and the others that eventually replaced it be stayed or vacated. The most significant are highlighted here.

District Judge Stuart agreed to intervene, and "on October 27, entered his own restrictive order" (543). He justified it with the rationale that "'there is a clear and present danger that pre-trial publicity could impinge upon the defendant's right to a fair trial'" (543). The order, which expired when a jury was impaneled, "specifically prohibited petitioners from reporting five subjects" (543): (1) "the existence of contents of a confession," (2) statements Simants made to other persons, (3) "the contents of a note he wrote the night of the crime," (4) some medical testimony, and (5) "the identity of the victims of the alleged sexual assault and the nature of the assault" (543, 544). In addition, the order "also prohibited reporting the exact nature of the restrictive order itself" (544).

Justice Harry A. Blackmun granted a partial stay of Judge Stuart's order on November 20, saying "Each passing day constituted an irreparable infringement on First Amendment values" (580). He objected to imposing the Nebraska Bar-Press Guidelines because they were voluntary and "'not intended to be mandatory'" and because they were "'sufficiently riddled with vague and indefinite admonitions' . . . that they did 'not provide the substance of a permissible court order in the First Amendment area'" (580). He also stayed the portions that prohibited "reporting of the details of the crimes, the identities of the victims, and the pathologist's testimony at the preliminary hearing . . . because . . . such 'facts in themselves do not implicate'" the defendant (580). Because he felt that some forms of prior restraint are indeed justifiable, however, Blackmun did not stay that portion forbidding publication of the confession; nor did he stay the portion forbidding publication of the order itself.

On December 1, the Nebraska Supreme Court eventually issued a *per curiam* opinion modifying Judge Stuart's order. The court prohibited the reporting of three items: (1) any confessions made to police, (2) any confessions made to others, and (3) "other facts 'strongly implicative' of the accused" (545). Justice Brennan's opinion contains a lengthy history of attempts by the media to stay or vacate these orders.

Summary of the Court's Analysis

Chief Justice Warren E. Burger writes for the Court.
Justices William H. Rehnquist and Harry A. Blackmun join.

The first question addressed by the Court is jurisdiction because, by the time this case is taken up, the order had expired (January 7, 1976). Article III, Section 2 of the Constitution limits the Court's authority to only those cases and controversies that still actually exist. The Court asserts, quoting in part from *Southern Pacific Terminal Co.* v. *ICC* (1911), that an issue is not moot, however, if "the underling dispute between the parties is one 'capable of repetition, yet evading review'" (546). This case fits that situation, Burger says, for two reasons. First, Simants's conviction could be reversed and a new trial ordered. Second, "the Nebraska Supreme Court's decision authorizes prosecutors to seek restrictive orders in appropriate [future] cases" (546, 547). So, Burger concludes, "If we decline to address the issue . . . , the dispute will evade review" (547).

Burger then presents an historical review of some conflicts between the First and Sixth Amendments, noting that only in rare cases are the conflicts serious. At the end of the review he writes, "Taken together, these cases demonstrate that pretrial publicity—even pervasive, adverse publicity—does not inevitably lead to an unfair trial" (554). Juries, he notes, are capable of putting pretrial publicity in proper perspective. Moreover, a trial judge can take measures "to mitigate the effects of pretrial publicity" (555). He asserts, on the one hand, that "the state trial judge in the case before us acted responsibly, out of a legitimate concern, in an effort to protect the defendant's right to a fair trial" (555) and, on the other hand, that the question to be decided is whether "the means employed were foreclosed by another provision of the Constitution" (556).

In *Near* v. *Minnesota* (1931) the Court noted that the First Amendment affords special protection against prior restraint. Burger writes, "Prior restraints on speech and publication are the most serious and the least tolerable infringement on First Amendment rights" (559). He adds, "If it can be said that a threat of criminal or civil sanctions after publication 'chills' speech, prior restraint 'freezes' it at least for the time" (559). In addition, he notes, "Protection against prior restraint should have particular force as applied to reporting of criminal proceedings" (559).

As for the media, Burger asserts, "The extraordinary protections afforded by the First Amendment carry with them something of a fiduciary duty to exercise the protected rights responsibly" (560). He adds, "It is not asking too much to suggest that those who exercise First Amendment rights in newspapers or broadcasting enterprises direct some effort to protect the rights of an accused to a fair trial by unbiased jurors" (560).

To rule on the case in question, though, the Court turns to the record. Burger writes, "We must examine the evidence before the trial judge when the order was entered to determine (a) the nature and extent of pretrial news coverage; (b) whether other measures would be likely to mitigate the effects of unrestrained pretrial publicity; and (c) how effectively a restraining order would operate to prevent the threatened danger" (562). The purpose of all this, he says, is to "consider whether the record supports the entry of a prior restraint on publication, one of the most extraordinary remedies known to our jurisprudence" (562).

First, Burger says the trial judge "was justified in concluding that there would be intense and pervasive pretrial publicity" (562). He was also acting reasonably to believe "that publicity might impair the defendant's right to a fair trial" (563). Burger notes, "His conclusion as to the impact of such publicity on prospective jurors," however, "was of necessity speculative dealing as he was with factors unknown and unknowable" (563).

Indeed, Burger observes that the trial judge "made no express findings" related to alternate measures not threatening First Amendment rights. He then suggests a few, adding, "Pretrial publicity, even if pervasive and concentrated, cannot be regarded as leading automatically and in every kind of criminal case to an unfair trial" (566).

Another "feature of this case leads" the Court to believe the restrictive order is "not supportable" (567). Burger writes, quoting in part from *Sheppard* (1966), "To the extent that this order prohibited the reporting of evidence adduced at the open preliminary hearing, it plainly violated settled principles: 'there is nothing that proscribes the press from reporting events that transpire in the courtroom'" (568). In addition, Burger says the part of the order "regarding 'implicative' information is too vague and too broad to survive the scrutiny we have given to restraints on First Amendment rights" (568).

In summary, Burger writes, "It is not clear that further publicity, unchecked, would so distort the views of potential jurors that 12 could not be found who would, under proper instructions, fulfill their sworn duty to render a just verdict exclusively on the evidence presented in open court" (569). The trial judge, he notes, simply was unable to meet "the heavy burden of demonstrating, in advance of trial, that without prior restraint a fair trial will be denied" (569).

Nevertheless, Burger does take care to point out, "However difficult it may be, we need not rule out the possibility of showing the kind of threat to fair trial rights that would possess the requisite degree of certainty to justify restraint" (569, 570). He notes also, "This Court has frequently denied that First Amendment rights are absolute and has consistently rejected the proposition that a prior restraint can never be employed" (570). In short, he observes, "We reaffirm that the guarantees of freedom of expression are not an absolute prohibition under all circumstances, but the barriers to prior restraint remain high and the presumption against its use continues intact" (570).

Ruling

Burger writes:

We hold that, with respect to the order entered in this case . . . the barriers [against prior restraint] have not been overcome; to the extent that this order restrained publication of such material [reports or comments on judicial proceedings] it is clearly invalid. To the extent that it prohibited publication based on information gained from other sources, we conclude that the heavy burden imposed as a condition to securing a prior restraint was not met and the judgment of the Nebraska Supreme Court is therefore reversed. (570)

Justice Byron R. White writes a concurring opinion.

White writes separately to record his "grave doubt" that "orders with respect to the press such as were entered in this case would ever be justifiable" (570). He also notes that it may become necessary "at some point [to] announce a more general rule and avoid the interminable litigation that our failure to do so would necessarily entail" (571).

Justice Lewis F. Powell, Jr., writes a concurring opinion.

Powell says he writes "to emphasize the unique burden that rests upon the party . . . who undertakes to show the necessity for prior restraint on pretrial publicity" (571). He then outlines three requisite conditions: (1) "a clear threat to the fairness of a trial"; (2) the "threat is posed by the actual publicity to be restrained"; and (3) "no less restrictive alternatives are available" (571).

Justice William J. Brennan, Jr., writes a concurring opinion.
Justices Potter Stewart and Thurgood Marshall join.

Brennan asserts that, although "the right to a fair trial by a jury of one's peers is unquestionably one of the most precious and sacred safeguards enshrined in the Bill of Rights," he "would hold . . . that resort to prior restraint on the freedom of the press is a constitutionally impermissible method for enforcing that right" (572). There is "a broad spectrum of devices" available, says Brennan, that do not threaten "the equally fundamental and salutary constitutional mandate that discussion of public affairs in a free society" be open (573).

The next section of Brennan's opinion contains a history of the media's attempts to stay or vacate restraining orders. He then asserts, "No one can seriously doubt, however, that unmediated prejudicial pretrial publicity may destroy the fairness of a criminal trial" (587). Nevertheless, he affirms his conviction: "There can be no prohibition on the publication by the press of any information pertaining to pending judicial proceedings or the operation of the criminal justice system, no matter how shabby the means by which the information is obtained" (588). "An accused's rights to a fair trial," Brennan says, "may be adequately assured through methods that do not infringe First Amendment values" (588).

Brennan reviews *Near* in an attempt to see if there are any categories of speech that can be subjected constitutionally to prior restraint. *Near,* he says, lists three, two of which—obscenity and incitement to violence—were later ruled by the court as speech "not encompassed by the First Amendment" (590). He continues, "Thus, only the third category in *Near* contemplated the possibility that speech meriting and entitled to constitutional protection might nevertheless be suppressed before publication in the interests of some overriding countervailing interest" (591). He calls this the "military security" exception and notes that it "has only been adverted to in dictum and has never served as the basis for actually upholding a prior restraint" (591).

The central question now becomes for Brennan whether this military security exception can offer guidelines for proposing other exceptions. The most important lesson to be learned from this exception, he says, quoting in part from *Southeastern Promotions, Ltd.* v. *Conrad* (1975), is that "the purpose for which a prior restraint is sought to be imposed 'must fit within one of the narrowly defined exceptions to the prohibition against prior restraints'" (592). In addition, he asserts, even these narrow exceptions can be justified only when "'*direct, immediate, and irreparable damage* [Brennan's emphasis] to our Nation" (593) will result.

The problem with Stuart's arguments, according to Brennan, is that they "urge . . . the creation of a new, potentially pervasive exception to this settled rule of virtually blanket prohibition of prior restraints" (594). He adds, "There are compelling reasons for not carving out a new exception to the rule against prior censorship of publication" (594, 595). He now begins to elaborate on these reasons.

First, Brennan writes, "Much of the information that the Nebraska courts enjoined petitioners [press association] from publishing was already in the public domain, having been revealed in open court proceedings or through public documents" (595, 596). He asserts, "It should be clear that no injunction against the reporting of such information can be permissible" (598).

The "rule against prior restraint" holds firm for Brennan "even if [the information is] derived from non-public sources and regardless of the means employed by the press in its acquisition" (599). The main problem with a restraining order, he says, is that its effects "must inherently remain speculative" (599). Giving a long list of difficulties with such orders, Brennan writes:

> A judge importuned to issue a prior restraint in the pretrial context will be unable to predict the manner in which the potentially prejudicial information would be published, the frequency with which it would be repeated or the emphasis it would be given, the context in which or purpose for which it would be reported, the scope of the audience that would be exposed to the information, or the impact, evaluated in terms of current standards for assessing juror impartiality, the information would have on that audience. (600)

He concludes, "These considerations would render speculative the prospective impact on a fair trial of reporting even an alleged confession or other information 'strongly implicative' of the accused" (600).

In addition, Brennan says that "there are adequate devices for screening from jury duty those individuals who have in fact been exposed to prejudicial pretrial publicity" (601). In particular, he says, "The trial judge should employ the voir dire to probe fully into the effect of publicity" (602).

Brennan says "practical reasons" also exist for rejecting the proposed exception to the constitutional prohibition against prior restraint. "Judges

would be forced to evaluate," he writes, "whether the public interests in receiving the information outweighed the speculative impact on Sixth Amendment rights" (607). Such actions, he continues, "will thus inevitably interject
judges at all levels into censorship roles that are simply inappropriate and
impermissible under the First Amendment" (607). Moreover, "judges . . .
might in some cases be determining the propriety of publishing information
that reflects on their competence, integrity, or general performance on the
bench" (607).

Procedural matters would produce another set of difficulties, Brennan
says. For example, the temptation to overuse these orders could "entail the
possibility of restraint proceedings collateral to every criminal case before
the courts" (608). These hearings could cause a "significant financial drain
on the media" and appeals could delay resolution to the point where the
"judicial proceeding could itself destroy the contemporary news value of the
information" (609).

Brennan says it is not necessary to choose between the First and the
Sixth Amendments. He writes, "For although there may in some instances
be tension between uninhibited and robust reporting by the press and fair
trials for criminal defendants, judges possess adequate tools short of injunc-
tions against reporting for relieving that tension" (612). Furthermore, he
says, "And the necessary impact of reporting even confessions can never be
so direct, immediate, and irreparable that I would give credence to any
notion that prior restraints may be imposed on that rationale" (612).

In short, Brennan asserts, "The decision of what, when, and how to
publish is for editors, not judges" (613).

Justice John Paul Stevens writes a concurring opinion.

Stevens says he tends to agree with Brennan, but he is not yet ready
to say that prior restraint is wrong "no matter how shabby or illegal the
means by which the information is obtained, no matter how serious an intru-
sion on privacy might be involved, no matter how demonstrably false the
information might be, no matter how prejudicial it might be to the interests
of innocent persons, and no matter how perverse the motivation for publishing is" (617).

Significance

Without question this case is significant because of the limitations imposed on a judge's ability to issue prior restraining orders. Although the
Court refused to declare all such orders unconstitutional, it did set at least
three conditions that a judge would have to satisfy before issuance.

To meet what the Court called "the heavy burden of demonstrating, in advance of trial, that without prior restraint a fair trial will be denied," a trial court must (1) examine the nature and extent of pretrial news coverage, (2) determine whether measures other than prior restraint would be likely to mitigate the effects of unrestrained pretrial publicity, and (3) show how effectively a restraining order would prevent the threatened danger.

When examining pretrial publicity, trial judges, said the Court, should determine, first, whether it "would be intense and pervasive." Then the judge should consider whether "that publicity might impair the defendant's right to a fair trial," including the "speculative" task of evaluating "the impact of such publicity on prospective jurors."

When investigating the possibility of whether measures other than prior restraint would be likely to mitigate the effects of unrestrained pretrial publicity, a trial judge, said Burger, should produce "express findings" because "pretrial publicity, even if pervasive and concentrated, cannot be regarded as leading automatically and in every kind of criminal case to an unfair trial."

Determining how effective a restraining order will be, said the Court, is "difficult" because trial judges are forced "to predict what information will in fact undermine the impartiality of jurors" and to draft "an order that will effectively keep prejudicial information from prospective jurors." Moreover, an order of prior restraint must be narrow, achieving a minimal breadth no greater than what is necessary to assure a fair trial.

The Court also said that reporting information from public records, such as Court proceedings, have a special protection from prior restraints. Here the Court reaffirmed its ruling in *Cox* v. *Cohn* (1975) that the press cannot be forbidden to report "events that transpire in the courtroom." Nor should what might not inaccurately be termed the negative significance of this ruling be overlooked. By making it extremely difficult to issue a constitutionally adequate order of prior restraint, the Court turned the attention of trial judges to access. These judges reasoned that if they could not control the media's dissemination of prejudicial information, then why not simply prevent reporters from getting the information in the first place?

Gannett v. DePasquale

Gannett Co., Inc.
v.
Daniel A. DePasquale, et al.

Docket No. 77-1301

433 U.S. 368, 61 L.Ed.2d 608, 99 S.Ct. 2898 (1979)

Argued November 7, 1978. Decided July 2, 1979.

Background

After *Nebraska Press Association* v. *Stuart* (1976), trial courts were aware of the severe limitations imposed upon their authority to forbid the press from publishing information that might be prejudicial to a defendant. It is not surprising, therefore, that another tactic for guaranteeing an impartial jury emerged. If it was going to be extremely difficult to prevent the media from disseminating potentially prejudicial information, then why not simply prevent them from getting the information in the first place? The media cannot disseminate information they do not have.

Denying the press access to information available in trials or closely related pretrial hearings, however, raises First, Sixth, and, in the case of a state court, Fourteenth Amendment questions. One question is whether the Sixth Amendment right to a public trial includes public access to related pretrial maneuvers. Another is whether this right is limited only to the accused or whether it includes the general citizenry. Does the accused's right to a public trial mean that defendants can compel a closed trial? A fourth question is whether the First Amendment guarantees public access to trials, and, if so, a fifth question arises over whether the Fourteenth Amendment extends such a right of access to criminal trials in state courts.

Since the *Gannett* Court ruled the Sixth Amendment right to a public trial is personal to the accused and so does not include the general citizenry, and since it refused to consider First Amendment rights of public access to criminal trials, it saw no need to address the issue of what, if any, closely related pretrial maneuvers were included in the definition of a trial; the Court held that "members of the public have no constitutional right under the Sixth and Fourteenth Amendments to attend criminal trials" (391). Nevertheless, the Court also denied defendants a right to compel a private trial because it said common law recognizes strong societal interests in public trials.

In short, the Court said that, even if the media do have some—as yet not clearly articulated—First Amendment rights of access to criminal trials, Judge DePasquale did not trespass on them. Instead, the judge simply ruled against media access because he felt it "was outweighed by the defendant's right to a fair trial" (393).

Circumstances

The origin of events leading up to the pretrial hearing in Seneca County can be traced to a fishing trip on one of New York's scenic finger lakes. Off-duty Brighton police officer Wayne F. Clapp, 42, of Henrietta, N.Y., a suburb of Rochester, apparently was shot and killed with his own gun on July 16, 1976, while fishing with two recent male acquaintances in Seneca Lake, about forty miles from Rochester, the Gannett corporate headquarters. His body was never found, but it was believed to have been weighted with an anchor and thrown into the lake.

Eventually, Michigan police apprehended his two companions and a female after recognizing a truck described in an interstate bulletin. Kyle Edwin Greathouse, then 16, from San Antonio, Texas, and David Rae Jones, then 21, from North Carolina, subsequently were arraigned before a Seneca County Magistrate on charges of second-degree murder and, along with Marilea Dienglewicz, also 16 at the time and also from San Antonio, on charges of second degree-grand larceny. All three were indicted on August 2 by a grand jury in Seneca County.

Attorneys for the trio were given a ninety-day period in which to file pretrial motions. One of these motions was a request to suppress a gun and certain statements—including confessions—made to the police. The suppression hearing was held November 5 before Judge Daniel A. DePasquale. According to the Court, the following events then took place:

> Defense attorneys [Thomas L. Jones for Greathouse and Stuart O. Miller for Jones] argued that the unabated buildup of adverse publicity had jeopardized the ability of the defendants to receive a fair trial. They thus requested that the public and the press be excluded from the hearing. The District Attorney [Walter J. Ward] did not oppose the motion. Although Carol Ritter, a [Gannett] reporter [correspondent for the *Democrat and Chronicle* and the *Times Union*] . . . was present in the courtroom, no objection was made at the time of the closure motion. The trial judge [DePasquale] granted the motion. (375)

The next day, after consulting with Gannett attorneys, Ritter wrote DePasquale a letter saying she had a right to cover this hearing and requesting to see the transcript. DePasquale said the suppression hearing was over, reserved his decision on the transcript, but scheduled another hearing to consider a motion to set aside his order excluding the press. At the conclusion of the second hearing the judge said a defendant's right to a fair trial outweighed a right of the press to cover the suppression hearing.

Gannett then challenged the judge's order on First, Sixth, and Fourteenth Amendment grounds before the Supreme Court of the State of New York, Appellate Division, Fourth Department. That Court ruled on December 17 that the judge's order overlooked the public's interest in a public hearing and constituted unlawful prior restraint and so vacated the order. The New York Court of Appeals said the case was technically moot (by then the two men had pleaded guilty to lesser charges and a transcript of the hearing was made available to the press), but it retained jurisdiction to consider the merits of the case. This appeals court said that the presumption of open public trials is overcome by the danger to fair trials and upheld the original exclusionary order.

Summary of the Court's Analysis

Justice Potter Stewart writes for the Court.
Chief Justice Warren E. Burger and Justices Lewis F. Powell, Jr.,
William H. Rehnquist, and John Paul Stevens join.

Justice Stewart takes up first the question of mootness. Citing *Nebraska Press Association* v. *Stuart* (1976), and quoting from *Weinstein* v. *Bradford* (1975), he notes that the two conditions for overcoming technical mootness are present here: "'(1) the challenged action was in duration too short to be fully litigated prior to its cessation or expiration, and (2) there was a reasonable expectation that the same complaining party would be subjected to the same action again'" (377). As a consequence, Stewart turns to the merits of the case.

Stewart begins his analysis with the assertion that "[a]dverse publicity can endanger the ability of a defendant to receive a fair trial" (378). Moreover, a trial judge may take measures to protect an accused's right to a fair trial "even when they are not strictly and inescapably necessary" (378). These dangers are "particularly acute," he continues, at a pretrial suppression hearing.

Since Stewart feels the "overriding purpose" of the Sixth Amendment's protections is to protect the "accused from prosecutorial and judicial abuses" (379), he says those rights—including the right to a public trial—belong solely to the accused. He writes, "The Constitution nowhere mentions any right of access to a criminal trial on the part of the public; its guarantee . . . is personal to the accused" (379, 380). In *Re William Oliver* (1948) and

Estes v. *Texas* (1965), according to Stewart, "recognize that the constitutional guarantee of a public trial is for the benefit of the defendant. There is not the slightest suggestion in either case that there is any correlative right in members of the public to insist upon a public trial" (381).

Stewart then denies that the Sixth Amendment guarantees defendants a right "to compel a private trial" (382), and he recognizes "strong societal interests in public trials" (383). He writes, "Openness in court proceedings may improve the quality of testimony, induce unknown witnesses to come forward with relevant testimony, cause all trial participants to perform their duties more conscientiously, and generally give the public an opportunity to observe the judicial system" (383).

Nevertheless, admitting a public interest, Stewart continues, "is a far cry . . . from the creation of a constitutional right" (383). Although defendants cannot "wave a jury trial without the consent of the prosecutor and judge," he says, they do not need additional permission from the public. Stewart says the public's interest is "fully protected by the participants" in "our adversary system of criminal justice" (384).

History, Stewart asserts, "ultimately demonstrates no more than the existence of a common-law rule of open civil and criminal proceedings" (384). To him, even if that common-law notion were reflected in the Sixth Amendment—and he feels it is not—it does not grant "the public any right to attend pretrial proceedings" (387). "Closed pretrial proceedings," he writes, "have been a familiar part of the judicial landscape" in "both Britain and America" (390). He concludes, "We hold that members of the public have no constitutional right under the Sixth and Fourteenth Amendments to attend criminal trials" (391).

Having disposed of the Sixth Amendment arguments for media access to criminal trials, Stewart moves to the First and Fourteenth Amendments. Even if the media do have some rights here, he asserts, the trial judge did not trespass on them. Although the reporter present did not object to closure, Judge DePasquale scheduled a hearing where media arguments for access could be heard. DePasquale, says Stewart, simply ruled against access because he felt it "was outweighed by the defendant's right to a fair trial" (393). Stewart also notes that the order was "temporary," expiring once the danger of a fair trial was over, and he points out that a transcript was prepared and made available to the press after the men pleaded guilty.

Ruling

Stewart writes, "We hold that the Constitution provides no such right [of access by the public or the media to pretrial proceedings]. Accordingly, the judgement of the New York Court of Appeals is affirmed" (394).

Chief Justice Warren E. Burger writes a concurring opinion.

First, Burger reaffirms Stewart's assertion that granting a public "interest" in open trials "does not create a constitutional right" (394). Second, he says pretrial proceedings were never considered to be as public as a trial. Indeed, participants were aware of "the untoward effects that could result from the publication of information before . . . a person was bound over for trial" (394, 395). He writes, "It has never occurred to anyone, so far as I am aware, that a pretrial deposition or pretrial interrogatories were other than wholly private to the litigants" (396).

Justice Lewis F. Powell, Jr., writes a concurring opinion.

Since the Court "reserved" the question of a First Amendment right to attend criminal trials, Powell writes to address it. He notes, "I would hold explicitly that petitioner's [Gannett's] reporter had an interest protected by the First and Fourteenth Amendment in being present at the pretrial suppression hearing" (397). This right, though, is not absolute, according to Powell. "It is limited," he writes, "both by the constitutional right of defendants to a fair trial . . . and by the needs of government to obtain just convictions and to preserve the confidentiality of sensitive information and the identity of informants" (398).

"It is all the more important, therefore," he writes, "that this Court identify for the guidance of trial courts the constitutional standard by which they are to judge whether closure is justified, and the minimal procedure by which this standard is to be applied" (398). "The question for the trial court," he concludes, "in considering a motion to close a pretrial suppression hearing is whether a fair trial for the defendant is likely to be jeopardized by publicity, if members of the press and the public are present and free to report prejudicial evidence that will not be presented to the jury" (400).

Before issuing an order excluding the public, a trial court, according to Powell, "should consider whether there are alternative means reasonably available by which the fairness of the trial might be preserved without interfering substantially with the public's interest in prompt access to information concerning the administration of justice" (400). In addition, he feels the public and the press "have the right to demand that it [an exclusionary order] extend no farther than is likely to achieve these goals [a fair trial]" (400). Moreover, he says "representatives" of the public and the press "must be given an opportunity to be heard on the question of their exclusion . . . at the time the motion for closure is made" (401).

Powell places on the defense some of the responsibility for closing hearings when he asserts, "It is the defendant's responsibility as the moving party to make some showing that the fairness of his trial likely will be prejudiced by public access to the proceedings" (401). If the state joins the motion to close, then it must "show that public access would interfere with its interests in fair proceedings or preserving the confidentiality of sensitive information" (401). In contrast, the press and the public "have the responsibility of showing to the court's satisfaction that alternative procedures are available that would eliminate the dangers shown by the defendant and the State" (401).

According to Powell, the trial judge "fully comported with that required by the Constitution" (403) and "the substantive standard applied was essentially correct" (403). He sees no error.

Justice William H. Rehnquist writes a concurring opinion.

Rehnquist too wishes to address the First as well as the Sixth Amendment issues. He writes, "But the Court's [words] . . . should not be interpreted to mean that under the Sixth Amendment a trial court can close a pretrial hearing or trial only when there is a danger that prejudicial publicity will harm the defendant" (403, 404). He adds, "The trial court is not required by the Sixth Amendment to advance any reason whatsoever for declining to open a pretrial hearing or trial to the public" (404).

Concerning the First Amendment, Rehnquist writes, "Lower courts should not assume that after today's decision they must adhere to the procedures employed by the trial court in this case or to those advanced by Mr. Justice Powell in his separate opinion in order to avoid running afoul of the First Amendment" (405). He adds, "They remain . . . free to determine for themselves the question whether to open or close the proceeding" (405).

Justice Harry A. Blackmun writes an opinion concurring in part and dissenting in part. Justices William J. Brennan, Jr., Byron R. White, and Thurgood Marshall join.

Blackmun agrees with the Court that the question before them is not moot, but he dissents from the rest of the opinion. He also does not accept the Court's statement of the question at issue or the Court's concern over the harmful effects of the publicity in this case.

Concerning the publicity, Blackmun writes, "I fear that the Court surrenders to the temptation to overstate and overcolor the actual nature of the pre-August 7, 1976, publicity" (406). Because of this temptation, the Court promulgates what Blackmun calls "an inflexible per se rule" that "if the defense and the prosecution merely agree to have the public excluded from a suppression hearing, and the trial judge does not resist . . . closure shall take place" (406).

Blackmun describes the Gannett coverage as "placid, routine, and innocuous" (407) as well as fairly infrequent. He feels neither the trial court nor the attorneys involved showed the publicity was either "unabated" or "adverse" (409).

It is particularly important to note that, unlike Powell, Blackmun does not "find any First Amendment right of access to judicial or other governmental proceedings" (411). Consequently, he looks at the Sixth. He writes, "The requirement that a trial of a criminal case be public embodies our belief that secret judicial proceedings would be a menace to liberty" (412). He says an open trial "ensures that not only judges but all participants in the criminal justice system are subjected to public scrutiny as they conduct the public's business of prosecuting crime" (412).

Noting that the "literal terms" of the Sixth Amendment grants rights only to an accused, Blackmun, nevertheless, asserts that the Court has recognized it "may implicate interests beyond those of the accused" (415). He points out, for example, that the Court rejected the idea that a defendant "had an absolute right" to reject a jury trial. After reviewing a general history and three cases in particular (*Singer* v. *U.S.* [1965], *Barker* v. *Wingo* [1972], and *Faretta* v. *California* [1975]), he asserts that "the accused may [not] compel a private proceeding simply by waiving that right [to a public trial]" (418). Instead, "any such right to compel a private proceeding must have some independent basis in the Sixth Amendment" (418), and Blackmun now looks at this basis. He examines English common law heritage first, particularly Hale and Blackstone. From the review he concludes, "There is strong evidence that the public trial . . . widely was perceived as serving important social interests, relating to the integrity of the trial process, that exist apart from, and conceivable in opposition to, the interests of the individual defendant" (423).

Next, Blackmun looks to our American experience. He writes:

> I consequently find no evidence in the development of the public-trial concept in the American Colonies and in the adoption of the Sixth Amendment to indicate that there was any recognition in this country, and more than in England, of a right to a private proceeding or a power to compel a private trial arising out of the ability to waive the grant of a public one. (427)

As a result of his historical forays, Blackmun asserts, "I also find that, because there is a societal interest in the public trial that exists separately from, at times in opposition to, the interests of the accused, . . . a court may give effect to an accused's attempt to waive his public right only in certain circumstances" (428).

Blackmun outlines society's interests, some of which do not coincide with the defendant's interests, in a public trial. He notes first, "The defendant himself may benefit from the partiality of a corrupt, biased, or incompetent judge" (428). Likewise, public trials "enable the public to scrutinize the performance of police and prosecutors in the conduct of public judicial business" (428). He adds, "An interest on the part of the prosecution in hiding police or prosecutorial misconduct or ineptitude may coincide with the defendant's desire to keep the proceedings private, with the result that the public interest is sacrificed from both sides" (428).

The "educative" role of judicial proceedings is also important to Blackmun. He notes that victims and their families "have an interest in observing the course of a prosecution" (428). The public may also wish to observe proceedings because "judges, prosecutors, and police officials often are elected" (428). After another extensive review of historical background and of societal benefits, Blackmun writes:

> I therefore conclude that the Due Process Clause of the Fourteenth Amendment, insofar as it incorporates the public-trial provision of the Sixth Amendment, prohibits the States from excluding the public from a proceeding within the ambit of the Sixth Amendment's guarantee without affording full and fair consideration to the public's interests in maintaining an open proceeding. (432, 433)

Before looking at what consideration must be given to the public, Blackmun considers whether pretrial proceedings have the same presumption of openness as do trials. He begins by asserting, "First, the suppression hearing resembles and relates to the full trial in almost every particular" (434). He adds, "Moreover, the pretrial suppression hearing often is critical, and it may be decisive, in the prosecution of a criminal case" (434). In addition, he notes, "The suppression hearing often is the only judicial proceeding of substantial importance that takes place during a criminal prosecution" (434). Finally, he observes that a motion to suppress "typically involves, as in this case, allegations of misconduct by police and prosecution that raise constitutional issues" (435). He then writes:

> These factors lead me to conclude that a pretrial suppression hearing is the close equivalent of the trial on the merits for purposes of applying the public-trial provision of the Sixth Amendment.
>   Accordingly, I conclude that the Sixth and Fourteenth Amendments prohibit a State from conducting a pretrial suppression hearing in private, even at the request of the accused, unless full and fair consideration is first given to the public's interest, protected by the Amendments, in open trials. (436)

He notes that the pretrial hearings referred to by the Court are not suppression hearings, but hearings to bind a defendant over for trial, and these latter kind are "not close equivalents of the trial form itself" (437).

Since extrajudicial publicity may "harm irreparably, under certain circumstances, the ability of a defendant to obtain a fair trial" (439), Blackmun concludes the Sixth Amendment "does not require that all proceedings be held in open court when to do so would deprive a defendant of a fair trial"

(439). The rights granted to the public by the Sixth Amendment, Blackmun asserts, are not absolute. The judge, for example, may "exclude unruly spectators" (439). Nevertheless, Blackmun feels, "The public's interest in maintaining open courts requires that any exception to the rule [of public trials] be narrowly drawn" (440). Therefore, Blackmun says the accused must "establish that it [closure] is strictly and inescapably necessary in order to protect the fair-trial guarantee" (441).

Blackmun now proceeds to outline the requirements for seeking to close a pretrial hearing. He begins, "The accused who seeks closure should establish . . . at a minimum the following. First, he should provide an adequate basis to support the probability that irreparable damage to his fair trial will result from conducting the proceeding in public" (441). This showing, Blackmun continues, requires evidence of an "impact on the jury pool," including "information relating to the size of the pool, the extent of the media coverage . . . , and the ease with which change of venire can be accomplished" (441).

"Second," Blackmun writes, "the accused should show a substantial probability that alternatives to closure will not protect adequately his right to a fair trial" (441). Among the alternatives Blackmun lists these: "continuance, severance, change of venue, change of venire, voir dire, peremptory challenges, sequestration, and admonition of the jury" (441).

"Third, the accused should demonstrate that there is a substantial probability that closure will be effective in protecting against the perceived harm" (442), Blackmun asserts, continuing, "The trial court should begin with the assumption that the Sixth Amendment requires that a pretrial suppression hearing be conducted in open court unless a defendant carries his burden to demonstrate a strict and inescapable necessity for closure" (443). In contrast, "the public need demonstrate no threshold of respectability in order to attend" (443).

Blackmun also takes care to note, "A high level of publicity is not necessarily inconsistent with the ability of the defendant to obtain a fair trial where the publicity has been largely factual in nature" (443). He adds, "To some extent the harm that the defendant fears from publicity is speculative" (444).

If closure is granted, then Blackmun feels it "should be temporary in that the court should ensure that an accurate record is made of those proceedings held in camera and that the public is permitted proper access to the record as soon as the threat to the defendant's fair-trial right has passed" (445). He continues, "As a final safeguard, I would conclude that any person removed from a court should be given a reasonable opportunity to state his objections prior to the effectiveness of the order" (445, 446).

Turning to the case at hand, Blackmun writes, "There was no factual basis upon which the court could conclude that a substantial probability existed that an open proceeding would result in harm to the defendant's rights to a fair trial" (447). He notes, "The stories were largely factual in nature. The reporting was restrained and free from editorializing or sensationalism" (447). He also points out, "The only fact not known to petitioner [Gannett] prior to the suppression hearing was the content of the confessions" (448).

From this Blackmun concludes, "It is thus not at all likely that the openness of the suppression hearing would have resulted in the divulgence of additional information that would have made it more probable that Greathouse and Jones would be denied a fair trial" (448).

Blackmun closes his opinion with a list of four ways that open proceedings are, in the words of Jeremy Bentham, " 'the soul of justice' " (448). For one thing, they "protect against judicial, prosecutorial, and police abuse" (448). Second, they "provide a means for citizens to obtain information about the criminal justice system and the performance of public officials" (448). Third, they "safeguard the integrity of the courts" (448). Fourth, "publicity is essential to the preservation of public confidence in the rule of law and in the operation of courts" (448).

Significance

The Court issued an unequivocal holding: The public and so too the media have no Sixth Amendment right of access to trials or to pretrial proceedings. Although the Court recognized no absolute First Amendment right of access either, it did admit there is a common law and First Amendment interest in a public trial.

The significance of concurring and dissenting opinions in this case should not be ignored. On the one hand, Justice Rehnquist asserts that the Court can close pretrial hearings without being required to do as little as stating on the record its reasons. On the other, Justice Blackmun lists a series of specific steps that a trial court should be required to take before closure. In addition, Blackmun bases his argument on the Sixth Amendment, whereas Powell bases a case for access on the First. Within a year, the Court, in *Richmond Newspapers* v. *Virginia* (1980), accepts much of Powell's argument and with it his assertion that the First, not the Sixth, Amendment is the one most relevant to the issue of public access to hearings and trials.

In August 1978—while this appeal was still in process—the American Bar Association adopted a new Criminal Justice Standard, Section 8-3.2. The new standard provided that pretrial proceedings were to be held in camera only after two showings. The first showing is that dissemination of information from a public proceeding would create a clear and present danger to the fairness of a trial. The second is that the prejudicial effect of disseminating this information cannot be avoided by reasonable means other than closing the hearing to the public and the press.

It is interesting to note, as well, that several alternative methods to closure presented by Gannett's attorneys were accepted by Blackmun in his dissenting opinion, and some eventually were adopted to various degrees by the Court in future rulings. Eight of them are as follows:

1. Granting continuance to allow time for pretrial publicity to die down

2. Severance; that is, separating the issues so that an entire pretrial hearing does not have to be changed to protect the fairness of a trial

3. Change of venue to a location where prospective jurors have not heard any pretrial publicity

4. Change of venire by selecting jurors who are not from the area where the pretrial publicity was so intense

5. Intensive *voir dire* in an attempt to discover whether publicity about pre-trial hearings had much impact on the attitudes of prospective jurors about a defendant's guilt

6. Additional peremptory challenges that would allow more opportunity for the defense to dismiss jurors exposed to pretrial publicity

7. Sequestration of witnesses and jurors so that they would not be exposed to mass media coverage during a trial

8. Admonitory instructions to the jury, warning them about the dangers of not deciding guilty based only on information presented in court

Richmond Newspapers, Inc. v. Virginia

Richmond Newspapers, Inc., et al.
v.
Commonwealth of Virginia

Docket No. 79-243
448 U.S. 555, 65 L.Ed.2d 973, 100 S.Ct. 2814 (1980)
Argued February 19, 1980. Decided July 2, 1980.

Background

After *Gannett* v. *DePasquale* (1979) the Court was eager to look again very soon at the issue of public access to criminal trials in order to address other important aspects of the conflict between a free press and a fair trial. Although *Gannett* was concerned with pretrial proceedings, this case focuses on the trial itself and so once again is deferred the question of at what point for First Amendment purposes a trial begins.

The right to attend a criminal trial is founded upon the First, Ninth, and, for state courts, Fourteenth Amendments. The essential question asked by the Court is this: Do the First, Sixth, and Fourteenth Amendments to the Constitution, singly or in combination, give members of the public a right of access to criminal trials even if this right is not asserted by the participants in the litigation? While the Court found such an implicit right in the First Amendment's explicit right of a free press, it also carefully pointed out that this access is not absolute. Indeed, only two years later, in *Globe* v. *Superior Court* (1982), the Court set forth conditions for closing to the public certain parts of a criminal trial.

Circumstances

The partially clothed body with multiple stab wounds of Lillian Emma Keller, manager of the Holly Court Motel, Ashland, Virginia, was found in her apartment at about 6 P.M., December 2, 1975. The apartment adjoined the front office and another apartment occupied by Howard Franklin Bittorf, the brother-in-law of John Paul Stevenson, a resident of Baltimore, Maryland. Stevenson was charged with the murder. The police found Stevenson's wallet on the floor in Bittorf's apartment, a bloodstained knife and towel, but no fingerprints.

On December 5, 1975, a police officer went to the Baltimore address printed on Stevenson's driver's license, which was taken from his wallet, and asked Mrs. Stevenson for the clothes her husband was wearing when he arrived home from Ashland. Among other things, she gave the officer a bloodstained knit-type pullover shirt. Tests revealed later that the blood sample was ABO, the same type as the victim's. Only 4.7 percent of the population has this blood type.

On March 16, 1976, a Commonwealth of Virginia grand jury for Hanover County indicted John Paul Stevenson for the murder of Lillian Emma Keller, and on July 16 a Hanover County Circuit Court jury convicted him of second-degree murder. Then, on October 7, 1977, the Virginia Supreme Court reversed Stevenson's conviction. That court said the action of Mrs. Stevenson giving the police officer her husband's shirt was a nonverbal communication for the purpose of showing that the shirt belonged to Stevenson and was worn by him on the day of the murder. Consequently, the officer's testimony relating to the shirt was inadmissible as evidence because it violated the hearsay rule. In addition, the results of any scientific tests conducted on the shirt were introduced without proper foundation, and so they too were inadmissible.

Stevenson's second trial, on May 30, 1978, was declared a mistrial after a member of the jury asked to be excused due to a nervous condition and no alternate was available. A few days later, on June 6, 1978, Stevenson's third trial also ended in a mistrial, this time because a prospective juror told other prospective jurors about newspaper accounts of Stevenson's previous trials.

The fourth trial began September 11, 1978. By oral order the Honorable Richard H. C. Taylor granted Stevenson's motion to close the entire trial to press and public. Timothy B. Wheeler and Kevin McCarthy, reporters for the Richmond *News Leader* and the Richmond *Times-Dispatch,* who along with the prosecution did not object to closure, were ejected.

Later that day, however, Richmond Newspapers asked for a hearing at which it could move to vacate the closure order. The newspaper company argued that the judge did not present any evidence supporting closure and that he did not consider other, less drastic, measures to protect Stevenson's right to a fair trial. Stevenson argued that the media threatened his right to his fourth attempt at a fair trial.

After the motion to vacate was denied, Hanover County Circuit Court proceeded in secrecy with the trial of Stevenson. In the absence of the public and the mass media, the judge quickly excused the jury, took under advisement Stevenson's motion that a mistrial be declared, upheld his motion to rule out the shirt as evidence, and then declared Stevenson not guilty.

On November 8, 1978, the newspaper filed with the Virginia Supreme Court petitions appealing the Hanover County Circuit Court's closure and writs ensuring access to trial to all future criminal trials in Hanover County Circuit Court. After the Virginia Supreme Court refused the petition for appeal and dismissed the request for writs, the newspaper appealed to the United States Supreme Court. Subsequently, the Supreme Court granted certiorari, but asserted it had no jurisdiction for an appeal because the validity of the Virginia Code was not explicitly challenged.

Summary of the Court's Analysis

Chief Justice Warren E. Burger writes for the Court.
Justice Byron R. White and John Paul Stevens join.

Chief Justice Burger begins by noting, "The narrow question presented in this case is whether the right of the public and press to attend criminal trials is guaranteed under the United States Constitution" (558). He continues, "The precise issue presented here has not previously been before this court for decision" (563, 564). "For the first time," Burger writes, "the Court is asked to decide whether a criminal trial itself may be closed to the public upon the unopposed request of a defendant, without any demonstration that closure is required to protect the defendant's superior right to a fair trial, or that some other overriding consideration requires closure" (564).

After a selective review of English and American history, Burger writes, "We have found nothing to suggest that the presumptive openness of the trial . . . was not also an attribute of the judicial system of colonial America" (567). He continues, "The historical evidence demonstrates conclusively that at the time when our organic laws were adopted, criminal trials both here and in England had long been presumptively open" (569).

Burger then cites historical support for open trials. First, he says there has long been "widespread acknowledgement . . . that public trials had significant community therapeutic values" (570). He writes, "People sensed from experience and observation that, especially in the administration of criminal justice, the means used to achieve justice must have the support derived from public acceptance of both the process and its results" (571).

A second purpose is termed "prophylactic" (571). Burger writes, "Without an awareness that society's responses to criminal conduct are underway, natural human reactions of outrage and protest are frustrated and may manifest themselves in some form of vengeful 'self-help,' as indeed they did regularly in the activities of vigilante 'committees' on our frontiers" (571).

The media have a special role to play today in this regard. Burger writes, "Instead of acquiring information about trials by firsthand observation or by word of mouth from those who attended, people now acquire it chiefly through the print and electronic media. In a sense, this validates the media claim of functioning as surrogates for the public" (572, 573).

After completing his review, Burger writes, "We are bound to conclude that a presumption of openness inheres in the very nature of a criminal trial under our system of justice" (573). "There remains the question," he continues, "whether, absent an explicit provision, the Constitution affords protection against exclusion of the public from criminal trials" (575).

To answer this question, Burger looks to the First Amendment. He writes, "The First Amendment can be read as protecting the right of everyone to attend trials so as to give meaning to those explicit guarantees" (575). He continues. "What this means in the context of trials is that the First Amendment guarantees of speech and press, standing alone, prohibit government from summarily closing courtroom doors which had long been open to the public at the time that Amendment was adopted" (576). He adds, "The explicit, guaranteed rights to speak and to publish concerning what takes place at a trial would lose much meaning if access to observe the trial could, as it was here, be foreclosed arbitrarily" (576, 577).

Burger makes note of other reasons for supporting public trials. The First Amendment right of assembly relates to trials in part because, he writes, "people assemble in public places not only to speak or to take action, but also to listen, observe, and learn" (578). Moreover, the presence of the public and the media "enhance the integrity and quality of what takes place" (578).

The Constitution, especially the Ninth Amendment, also guards "certain unarticulated rights," Burger asserts, such as the right to be presumed innocent and the right to be judged by a standard of proof beyond a reasonable doubt. Burger writes, "We hold that the right to attend criminal trials is implicit in the guarantees of the First Amendment" (580).

Turning to the closure order that spawned this suit, Burger makes the following observations, "The trial judge made no findings to support closure; no inquiry was made as to whether alternative solutions would have met the need to ensure fairness; there was no recognition of any right under the Constitution for the public or press to attend the trial" (580, 581). Burger says "tested" alternatives to closure do exist, even if they "admittedly present difficulties for trial courts" (581).

Ruling

Burger writes, "Absent an overriding interest articulated in findings, the trial of a criminal case must be open to the public. Accordingly, the judgment under review is reversed" (581).

Justice Byron R. White writes a concurring opinion.

White says it would not have been necessary to find a First Amendment right to attend public trials if the Court had recognized such a Sixth Amendment right in *Gannett.*

Justice John Paul Stevens writes a concurring opinion.

Calling this a "watershed" case, Stevens writes, "Never before has it [the Court] squarely held that the acquisition of newsworthy matter is entitled to any constitutional protection whatsoever" (582). He continues, "For the first time, the Court unequivocally holds that an arbitrary interference with access to important information is an abridgement of freedoms of speech and of the press protected by the First Amendment" (583). "I agree," Stevens concludes, "that the First Amendment protects the public and the press from abridgement of their rights of access to information about the operation of their government, including the Judicial Branch" (584).

Justice William J. Brennan, Jr., writes a concurring opinion.
Justice Thurgood Marshall joins.

Brennan begins by noting that the First Amendment through the Fourteenth does mean that "without more, agreement of the trial judge and the parties cannot constitutionally close a trial to the public" (585). Commenting upon prior cases, he writes, "Read with care and in context, our decisions must therefore be understood as holding only that any privilege of access to governmental information is subject to a degree of restraint dictated by the nature of the information and contervailing interests in security or confidentiality" (587). In short, Brennan says the right of public access to a criminal trial is not absolute. Two considerations, among others, that limit this right are security and confidentiality.

In addition to presenting the guarantees of free expression, the First Amendment also plays "a structural role" "in securing and fostering our republican system of self-government" (587), according to Brennan. Public debate has an "antecedent assumption" that, to be valuable, "must be informed" (587). He writes, "An assertion of the prerogative to gather information must accordingly be assayed by considering the information sought and the opposing interests invaded" (588). To guide a discussion of these interests, Brennan proposes two "helpful principles."

"First," he writes, "the case for a right of access has special force when drawn from an enduring and vital tradition of public entree to particular proceedings or information" (589). "Secondly," he continues, "the value of access must be measured in specifics" (589). To measure the specifics in this case, Brennan looks to the history of the notion of a public trial. He concludes, "As a matter of law and virtually immemorial custom, public trials have been the essentially unwavering rule in ancestral England and in our own Nation" (593).

Brennan moves now to the specific purposes "advanced" by publicity. He writes, "Open trials play a fundamental role in furthering the efforts of our judicial system to assure the criminal defendant a fair and accurate adjudication of guilt or innocence" (593). In addition, in order for courts in an open society to work, citizens "must share the conviction that they are governed equitably" (595). In this regard, Brennan writes, "Open trials assure the public that procedural rights are respected, and that justice is afforded equally" (595).

A trial for Brennan is "a genuine governmental proceeding" (596), which means that its conduct is "pre-eminently a matter of public interest" (596). Public trials also act as an important check on judicial power. "Finally," Brennan writes, "a trial aims at true and accurate factfinding" (596). Witnesses, he asserts, may find it easier to lie in private than in public.

He closes his opinion by noting that the Court does not need to address the question of "what countervailing interests might be sufficiently compelling to reverse this presumption of openness" because the Virginia Code, in his opinion, "violates the First and Fourteenth Amendments" (589).

Justice Potter Stewart writes a concurring opinion.

Stewart asserts, "The First and Fourteenth Amendments clearly give the press and the public a right of access to trials themselves, civil as well as criminal" (599). He warns, though, "But this does not mean that the First Amendment right of members of the public and representatives of the press to attend civil and criminal trials is absolute" (600). Instead, he writes, "A trial judge [may] impose reasonable limitations upon the unrestricted occupation of a courtroom by representatives of the press and members of the public" (600).

Justice Harry A. Blackmun writes a concurring opinion.

Blackmun writes, "I remain convinced that the right to a public trial is to be found where the Constitution explicitly placed it—in the Sixth Amendment" (603). But because of the Court's ruling here, he writes, "I am driven to conclude, as a secondary position, that the First Amendment must provide some measure of protection for public access to the trial" (604).

Justice William H. Rehnquist writes a dissenting opinion.

Rehnquist writes:

I do not believe that either the First or Sixth Amendment, as made applicable to the States by the Fourteenth, requires that a State's reasons for denying public access to a trial, where both the prosecuting attorney and the defendant have consented to an order of closure approved by the judge, are subject to any additional constitutional review at our hands. And I most certainly do not believe that the Ninth Amendment confers upon us any such power to review orders of state trial judges closing trials in such situations. (605)

The issue here is not whether the "right" to freedom of the press conferred by the First Amendment to the Constitution overrides the defendant's "right" to a fair trial conferred by other Amendments to the Constitution; it is instead whether any provision in the Constitution may fairly be read to prohibit what the trial judge in the Virginia state court system did in this case. (606)

Significance

The clear significance of this case is an assertion that the First Amendment confers a limited or qualified right to the public (and so the media) to attend criminal trials. In addition, the Court reaffirmed its denial of a Sixth Amendment right to attend trials, continuing to feel, as it did the year before in *Gannett*, that the Sixth Amendment right to a public trial is personal to the accused.

The Court's view here of the First Amendment is avowedly based on common law presumptions of open trials at the time the amendment was adopted. This historically based presumption of openness meant to the Court that the First Amendment guarantee of a free press prohibits government from summarily closing courtrooms that had long been open to the public at the time this amendment was adopted. The Court reasoned that the explicit right to publish what takes place at a trial would lose much meaning if access to observe the trial could be denied arbitrarily. Thus, there is recognized in the First Amendment an implicit right to attend criminal trials.

This implicit right of access, however, is limited. While failing to stipulate precisely what actions a trial court should follow to close constitutionally a trial, or at least parts of it, the Court did note that the trial judge here failed to take two steps. Burger took care to point out, first, that the trial judge neither made nor articulated any findings supporting closure. Second, he failed to inquire about the possibility of alternative solutions that would have ensured a fair trial without threatening the First Amendment.

Clearly, significance arises from these conditions. Trial courts wishing to close parts of trials or pretrial maneuvers, the Court asserts, should make findings supporting closure only after investigating alternative solutions that could ensure a fair trial without at the same time threatening the First Amendment.

Chandler v. Florida

Noel Chandler and Robert Granger
v.
State of Florida

Docket No. 79-1260

449 U.S. 560, 66 L.Ed.2d 740, 101 S.Ct. 802 (1981)

Argued November 12, 1980. Decided January 26, 1981.

Background

Several years after *Estes* v. *Texas* (1965), the American Bar Association reaffirmed in 1972 its ban on television in the courtroom when it replaced Canon 35 of the Canons of Judicial Ethics—adopted in 1937—with Canon 3A(7) of the Code of Judicial Conduct. Then when an ABA committee on Fair-Trial-Free Press in 1978 proposed revising the new canon to allow television in the courtroom, the ABA House of Delegates (officially voting February 12, 1979), rejected the proposal.

Another group looked differently, however, upon the presence of cameras in the courtroom. The Court notes:

> In 1978, based upon its own study of the matter, the Conference of State Chief Justices, by a vote of 44 to 1, approved a resolution to allow the highest court of each state to promulgate standards and guidelines regulating radio, television, and other photographic coverage of court proceedings. (564)

So, although the Florida legislature adopted the substance of Canon 3A(7) in 1975, the Florida Supreme Court in 1976 "announced an experimental program for televising one civil and one criminal trial" (564) with the consent of all relevant parties. When such consent could not be obtained, that court "established a new one-year pilot program during which the electronic media were permitted to cover all judicial proceedings in Florida . . . subject to detailed standards with respect to technology and the conduct of operators" (564, 565). After the program concluded, the Florida Supreme Court "promulgated a revised Canon 3A(7)" (566) allowing carefully regulated televising of criminal trials.

And so the first case to reach the Court originated in Florida where television cameras were allowed to record a criminal trial.

Circumstances

Noel Chandler and Robert Granger, Miami Beach police officers, were charged July 1, 1977, with conspiracy to commit a felony, burglary, grand larceny, and possession of burglary tools, arising out of an early morning May 23 breaking and entering into Picciolo's Restaurant, a well-known South Miami Beach dining establishment.

According to the Court, "The State's principal witness was John Sion, an amateur [ham] radio operator who, by chance, had overheard and recorded conversations between the appellants [Chandler and Granger] over their police walkie-talkie radios during the burglary" (567). "These novel factors," according to the Court, "attracted the attention of the media" (567).

July 5, 1977, is the date the Florida courts embarked on a one-year experimental program authorizing electronic media and still photographic coverage of all criminal and civil trials regardless of a defendant's objections. This rule was promulgated by the Florida Supreme Court, pursuant to its general supervisory power under Article V, Section 2 of the Florida Constitution (1972), which authorizes that court to enact rules of procedure regulating the proceedings in all Florida courts. Only four days before the experiment was to begin, officers Chandler and Granger were arrested.

On July 21 the two officers filed a motion to declare unconstitutional the experimental rule, but on July 27 the trial court denied the motion. The jurors impaneled said the presence of television cameras would not affect their decision. One camera recorded the events of a single afternoon as well as the closing arguments. Eventually, a total of two minutes and fifty-five seconds were broadcast. The two policemen were found guilty on all four counts and sentenced to seven years in prison and five years probation. They appealed, saying the mere fact of television coverage denied them a fair trial.

The Florida Court of Appeals affirmed the convictions as did the District Court of Appeals, and the Florida Supreme Court refused review.

Summary of the Court's Analysis

Chief Justice Warren E. Burger writes for the Court.
Justices William J. Brennan, Jr., Thurgood Marshall, Harry A. Blackmun,
Lewis F. Powell, Jr., and William H. Rehnquist join.

Burger sets forth the general issue in these words: "The question is whether . . . a state may provide for radio, television, and still photographic coverage of a criminal trial for public broadcast, notwithstanding the objection of the accused" (562). He begins, "At the outset, it is important to note that . . . the Florida Supreme Court pointedly rejected any state or federal constitutional right of access on the part . . . of the broadcast media to televise or electronically record and thereafter disseminate court proceedings" (569).

The first specific issue to be faced is whether *Estes* announced a per se constitutional rule asserting that "the televising of criminal trials is inherently a denial of due process" (570). The answer to this question, Burger says, hinges upon the opinion of Harlan, who joined the *Estes* plurality to create a majority decision only on a very limited basis. The essential problem, writes Burger, is this: "Parsing the six opinions in *Estes*, one is left with a sense of doubt as to precisely how much of Justice Clark's [plurality] opinion was joined in, and supported by, Justice Harlan" (572). Burger does say, though, that it appears Harlan had a narrower view of the decision than did Clark and that Harlan limited his decision to cases similar to *Estes*. Consequently, Burger writes, "We conclude that Estes is not to be read as announcing a constitutional rule barring still photographic, radio, and television coverage in all cases and under all circumstances. It does not stand as an absolute ban on state experimentation with an evolving technology" (573, 574).

Burger then asserts that a request to institute such a per se rule would be approached by the Court as a "matter of first impression" (574). Burger begins these first impressions by reaffirming the dangers inherent in televising criminal trials. These dangers, he points out, are not unlike the dangers of newspaper coverage. He writes, "The risk of juror prejudice is present in any publication of a trial, but the appropriate safeguard against such prejudice is the defendant's right to demonstrate that the media's coverage of his case— be it print or broadcast—compromised the ability of the *particular* [emphasis added] jury that heard the case to adjudicate fairly" (575).

In considering the psychological impact of televising criminal trials, Burger takes note of the changes in television technology since 1962, when Estes was tried. He also takes care to point out the safeguards built into the Florida program. In particular, he notes that the "objections of the accused to coverage [should] be heard and considered on the record by the trial court" (577). This action, he notes, "allows the trial court to define the steps necessary to minimize or eliminate the risks of prejudice to the accused" (577). "The record" of this case, however, writes Burger, "does not indicate that appellants [Chandler and Granger] requested an evidentiary hearing to show adverse impact or injury. Nor does the record reveal anything more than generalized allegations of prejudice" (577). He adds, "To demonstrate prejudice in a specific case a defendant must show something more than juror awareness that the trial is such as to attract the attention of broadcasters" (581).

One important difficulty with promulgating a per se constitutional rule banning the televising of criminal trials, writes Burger, is that "no one had been able to present empirical data sufficient to establish that the mere presence of the broadcast media inherently has an adverse effect" on the trial (579). Likewise, the problems of television networks selecting only sensational trials and of the existence of an entertainment milieu, says Burger, "Must also await the continuing experimentation" (581).

Finally, Burger takes care to point out that this case does not have any of the characteristics of the " 'Roman circus' or 'Yankee Stadium' atmosphere, as in *Estes*" (582).

Ruling

Burger writes, "In this setting, because this Court has no supervisory authority over state courts, our review is confined to whether there is a constitutional violation. We hold that the Constitution does not prohibit a state from experimenting with the program authorized by revised Canon 3A(7). Affirmed" (582, 583).

Justice Potter Stewart writes a concurring opinion.

Stewart refuses to join the majority because he "does not think the convictions in the case can be affirmed without overruling *Estes* v. *Texas*" (583). He writes, "I believe now, as I believed in dissent then, that *Estes* announced a per se rule that . . . 'prohibits cameras from a state courtroom whenever a criminal trial is in progress' "(583). He adds, "I would flatly overrule it" (583).

Stewart continues, "The restrictions on television in the *Estes* trial were not significantly different from those in the trial of these appellants [Chandler and Granger]" (583). He says the "constitutional violation" in *Estes* did not "stem from physical disruption that might one day disappear with technological advances" (584). Instead, the violation, he feels, was perceived to lie "in the mere presence of cameras . . . [having] an effect on the trial participants prejudicial to the accused" (594).

Stewart says that Harlan's opinion is not so narrowly tailored as Burger asserted, and he notes in closing that Harlan said his limitation to cases similar to *Estes* "may not be meaningful" (585).

Justice Byron R. White writes a concurring opinion.

White feels the *Estes* decision can be read either way, that is, as setting forth and as not setting forth a per se constitutional rule banning the presence of television cameras in a criminal trial. In any case, he writes, "Whether the decision in *Estes* is read broadly or narrowly, I agree with Justice Stewart that it should be overruled" (587).

White then reaffirms his *Estes* position: "Absent some showing of prejudice to the defense, I remain convinced that a conviction obtained in a state court should not be overturned simply because a trial judge refused to exclude television cameras and all or part of the trial was televised to the public" (587, 588).

Turning to the case at hand, White asserts, "Although the Court's opinion today contends that it is consistent with *Estes*, I believe that it effectively eviscerates *Estes*" (588). He continues, "The majority [here] indicates that not even the narrow reading of *Estes* will any longer be authoritative" (588). In short, White feels the Court in this case reduces "*Estes* to an admonition to proceed with some caution" (588). To this admonition he responds, "I agree that those risks are real and should not be permitted to develop into the reality of an unfair trial" (589).

Significance

This case gains significance from the Court's refusal to promulgate a per se constitutional rule against the presence of television cameras in a criminal trial. It should be noted, though, that the Court also did not assert a constitutional right to televise criminal trials live or even on tape. In brief, this ruling simply allows continuation of state experiments with televising criminal trials. Moreover, all of the justices remained convinced that, because televising criminal trials indeed does pose a number of significant dangers to fairness, trial courts should allow defendants to present showings that the presence of television cameras can indeed preclude fairness in their particular trials.

The controversy over the meaning of the *Estes* trial is also significant. Since the Court refused to overturn *Estes* on the basis that it was unnecessary because that case did not establish a per se constitutional rule, then it is possible, in spite of White's assurances to the contrary, that a state trial court could still use *Estes* to ban the televising of a trial perceived to be similar to *Estes*. White's opinion that *Estes* has been "eviscerated" has had the effect, however, of discouraging such an action.

Globe Newspaper Co. v. Superior Court

Globe Newspaper Company
v.
Superior Court for the County of Norfolk

Docket No. 81-611
457 U.S. 596, 73 L.Ed.2d 248, 102 S.Ct. 2613 (1982)

Argued March 29, 1982. Decided June 23, 1982.

Background

Section 16A, Chapter 278, of Massachusetts General Laws reads in part as follows:

> "At the trial of a complaint or indictment for rape, incest, carnal abuse or other crime involving sex, where a minor under eighteen years of age is the person upon, with or against whom the crime is alleged to have been committed, . . . the presiding justice shall exclude the general public from the court room." (598)

The constitutionality of this section depends to a considerable degree upon its scope. A too-broad law, for example, could be thought to infringe upon First Amendment rights articulated in *Richmond Newspapers* v. *Virginia* (1980). Since *Richmond* recognized a limited or qualified First Amendment right of the public to attend criminal trials, the Court looked at the Massachusetts statute to determine if it put forth a special interest that, because of its strong importance in a narrow area, would justify overriding in particular circumstances the public's right to attend a trial.

The Massachusetts Supreme Judicial Court asserted there did exist in the statute a sufficiently narrow interest so important that it constitutionally justified overriding the public's interest in attending a trial. This court construed the law to require the exclusion of the press and public from the courtroom during the testimony of a minor victim of a sexual crime even over the opposition of the defendant, and even in the absence of a request for exclusion by the prosecution or the victim. The question the Court sought to answer, therefore, is whether this law as interpreted by the Massachusetts court is constitutional. In other words, does a statute requiring closure of criminal trials during testimony of a minor victim of a sexual crime transgress implicit First Amendment guarantees of access?

The Globe Newspapers Company was one of three wholly owned subsidiaries of Affiliated Publications: the other two being Affiliated Broadcasting, Inc., which had twelve radio stations in 1979, and Affiliated Cable, which owned 45 percent of McCaw Communications Companies. The Globe itself had then four subsidiaries: Community Newsdealers; Suburban News Agency; the Globe Pequot Press, Inc.; and Wilson-Tinsdale Company.

Circumstances

After a trial entirely closed to the public, a Norfolk Superior Court jury on Thursday, May, 10, 1979, found Wellesley, Massachusetts, tennis pro Albert T. Aladjem, Jr., 33, innocent of charges that he raped three teenage girls—two 16, one 17—the previous September. The three high school juniors said a masked assailant assaulted them on September 23, 1978, at gunpoint in a wooded area near Dana Hall High School in Wellesley, as they returned to their dormitories after a dance. They testified that, although the mask covered the assailant's mouth and nose, it slipped during the assault and exposed his face. When one of the girls was shown Aladjem's photograph after the attack, she said it could not be him because she knew him, but she changed her testimony at trial.

Three witnesses corroborated Aladjem's testimony that he was at a restaurant in neighboring Wayland when the three girls were raped. In addition, Aladjem, who testified at length, accounted for all his time surrounding the rape.

During hearings on preliminary motions on April 19, 1979, a judge of the Superior Court for the County of Norfolk, who was sitting in Dedham, a town about fifteen miles southwest of Boston, closed his courtroom by hanging a sign stamped "closed" on the door. Court personnel were ordered to turn the public away. The Globe Newspaper Company asked the court to revoke the order, but the judge denied the request and ordered the public and the press out of the courtroom during the trial.

The girls did not object to press attendance at trial so long as no one printed their names, photographs, or other personal data that might identify them. They were concerned primarily that their grandparents not find out about the rapes.

A single justice of the Supreme Judicial Court of Massachusetts at a hearing on April 26 said the Globe Company had no First Amendment right to attend the trial and denied its request for injunctive relief. On May 17 the Globe filed its notice of appeal to the Supreme Judicial Court for the Commonwealth, but on February 26, 1980, the Supreme Judicial Court dismissed the Globe's appeal. This court did agree with the newspaper, however, that

Section 16A does not require the trial court to exclude the press from the entire trial; instead this section requires the court to be closed only during the testimony of victims not yet 18 years of age.

Following the *Richmond* decision (1980) by the Court, the Globe appealed, and the Court vacated the judgment of the Supreme Judicial Court of Massachusetts and remanded the case for further consideration consistent with *Richmond.* The Massachusetts court, noting that, in contrast to most criminal trials, trials of sexual offenders are often closed, again dismissed the Globe's appeal. Globe appealed a second time to the Court.

One noteworthy sidelight is that the chairperson of the jury was Dorothy J. Newell, a *Patriot Ledger* news executive. The day after the trial was over, she printed her account of it in the May 11 city edition of the Quincy *Patriot Ledger.*

Summary of the Court's Analysis

Justice William J. Brennan, Jr., writes for the Court.
Justices Byron R. White, Thrugood Marshall, Harry A. Blackmun,
and Lewis F. Powell, Jr., join.

The Court reverses the Supreme Judicial Court of Massachusetts and holds "that the mandatory closure rule contained in Section 16A violates the First Amendment" (602).

Dealing first with the issue of jurisdiction, Brennan refers to *Nebraska* v. *Stuart* (1976) and observes that this case, like *Nebraska,* although moot on the face of it according to Article III, Section 2, of the Constitution, nevertheless, is capable of repetition, yet evading review (603)—see *Weinstein* v. *Bradford* (1975), *Sosna* v. *Iowa* (1975), and *Gannett* v. *DePasquale* (1979). Therefore, the Court accepts jurisdiction.

Brennan points out that the Court recognized in *Richmond* for the first time an implicit, limited public First Amendment right of access to criminal trials. He notes that two "features of the criminal justice system" (605) justify in particular this right of access. He writes, "First, the criminal trial historically has been open to the press and general public" (605).

The second feature is divided into four parts. That press and public attendance at open trials (1) "enhances the quality" and (2) "safeguards the integrity of the fact finding process" (606). In addition, (3) public respect is heightened by the appearance of fairness, and (4) the public can participate through attendance as a check on the judicial process. Brennan summarizes, "The institutional value of the open criminal trial is recognized in both logic and experience" (606).

"The circumstances under which the press and public can be barred from a criminal trial are limited" (606), writes Brennan, and the justification must be "a weighty one" (606). He adds, "It must be shown that the denial is necessitated by a compelling governmental interest, and is narrowly tailored to serve that interest" (607). There are two questions to be answered by the Court: What is the "compelling governmental interest" asserted by Massachusetts? and Is the Massachusetts statute drawn narrowly enough so that it supports only that specific "compelling" interest, but no other interests that would be insufficiently compelling?

Brennan says the state's interests can be reduced to two areas: "[1] The protection of minor victims of sex crimes from further trauma and embarrassment; and [2] the encouragement of such victims to come forward and testify in a truthful and credible manner" (607). "The first interest," writes Brennan, "is a compelling one" (607). Yet it does not require a closed trial because, he writes, "the circumstances of the particular case may affect the significance of the interest" (608). In other words, Brennan asserts that, depending on the circumstances, sometimes the state's interest in protecting from trauma and embarrassment minors who are victims of sex crimes may be sufficient to close a trial (or part of one), and other times it may not be.

A case-by-case evaluation, Brennan says, is a better solution than required closure. "Factors to be weighed are the minor victim's age, psychological maturity and understanding, the nature of the crime, the desires of the victim, and the interests of parents and relatives" (608). He notes that Section 16A "requires closure even if the victim does not seek the exclusion of the press and general public, and would not suffer injury by their presence" (608).

Thus, according to the Court, one fatal flaw in Section 16A is that it "cannot be viewed as a narrowly tailored means of accommodating the State's asserted interest" (609). In contrast, a case-by-case evaluation, says Brennan, "ensures that the constitutional right of press and public to gain access to criminal trials will not be restricted except where necessary to protect the State's interest" (609).

The problem with the state's second interest, as Brennan sees it, is that no empirical support is presented to support the claim that automatic closure will encourage "minor victims of sex crimes to come forward and provide accurate testimony" (609). He also feels this claim "is open to serious question as a matter of logic and common sense" because "the press is not denied access to the transcript, court personnel, or any other possible source that could provide an account of the minor victim's testimony" (610). Moreover, even if the section were effective in preventing the press from gaining access to the victim's testimony, Brennan writes, "[I]t is doubtful that the interest would be sufficient to overcome the constitutional attack" (610). If Section 16A were declared constitutional, he warns, then a host of other closure laws may be proposed based on an attempt to encourage statements from witnesses reluctant to testify in public.

Ruling

Brennan writes, "We hold that Section 16A, as construed by the Massachusetts Supreme Judicial Court, violates the First Amendment to the Constitution. Accordingly, the judgment of the Massachusetts Supreme Judicial Court is reversed" (610, 611).

Justice Sandra Day O'Connor writes a concurring opinion.

Justice O'Connor writes, "I interpret neither *Richmond Newspapers* nor the Court's decision today to carry any implications outside the context of criminal trials" (611). In other words, O'Connor says it is her opinion that the *Richmond* case and this one do not apply also to other legal procedures, such as civil trials.

Chief Justice Warren E. Burger writes a dissenting opinion.
Justice William H. Rehnquist joins.

Chief Justice Burger notes that, even though our society goes "to great length to protect minors *charged* [his emphasis] with crime," the Court's decision "holds unconstitutional a state statute designed to protect . . . the minor *victims* [his emphasis]" (612).

Burger objects to what he feels is the Court's interpretation of *Richmond,* an interpretation wrongfully extending the right of public access to "all aspects of all criminal trials under all circumstances" (612). In opposition to the traditional notion of presumptively open criminal trials Burger, places a "long history of exclusion of the public from trials involving sexual assaults, particularly those against minors" (614).

Burger gives what he feels is the actual rationale for Section 16A:

> The purpose of the Commonwealth in enacting Section 16A was to give assurance to parents and minors that they would have this moderate and limited protection from the trauma, embarrassment, and humiliation of having to reveal the intimate details of a sexual assault in front of a large group of unfamiliar spectators—and perhaps a television audience—and to lower the barriers to the reporting of such crimes which might come from the victim's dread of public testimony. (615)

Thus, for Burger, the avowed purpose of this Massachusetts law is not "to deny the press or public access to information" (616), even though such denial may in fact be an inescapable result of enforcing Section 16A. The question presented by this statute, as he sees it, is as follows: "Whether the interests of the Commonwealth override the very limited incidental effects of the law on First Amendment rights" (616). He writes, "Our obligation in this case is to balance the competing interests; the interests of the media for instant access against the interest of the State in protecting child rape victims from the trauma of public testimony" (616).

Burger terms the impact on the First Amendment "minimal" and the state's interest "in protecting child victims" "overriding" (616). Since the press has access to testimony through transcripts, Burger asserts that the only First Amendment interest that may be limited by closure is the value of simply being present in the courtroom. In opposition to this interest of public presence he places the state's "interest in protecting the victimized child [which] is a compelling interest" (616) that meets the test of *Richmond*.

Burger distinguishes his views from the Court's this way:

> The Court apparently believes that the statute does not prevent any significant trauma, embarrassment, or humiliation on the part of the victim simply because the press is not prevented from discovering and publicizing both the identity of the victim and the substance of the victim's testimony. Section 16A is intended not to preserve confidentiality, but to prevent the risk of severe psychological damage caused by having to relate the details of the crime in front of a crowd which inevitably will include voyeuristic strangers. (618)

The problem with the case-by-case approach, according to Burger, is that it does not offer enough assurance of protection from public testimony. He writes, "The mere possibility of public testimony may cause parents and children to decide not to report these heinous crimes" (619).

Burger ends his dissent by observing, "The Massachusetts statute has a relatively minor incidental impact on First Amendment rights and gives effect to the overriding state interest in protecting child rape victims" (619, 620).

Justice John Paul Stevens writes a dissenting opinion.

Justice Stevens's dissent focuses first on the issue of the Court's jurisdiction. He points out that, unlike the laws reviewed in *Richmond* (1980), *Gannett* (1979), and *Nebraska* (1976), state law in this case "was materially changed after the trial court's order had expired by its own terms" (620). He views the Massachusetts Supreme Judicial Court's ruling to be a substantive change in the law applied by the trial judge. For him, therefore, the case is moot because, he writes, quoting from *Gannett*, "There . . . is no possibility "'that the same complaining party will be subject to the same action again'" (620).

Stevens also objects to the nature of the Court's remedy. He writes, "The Court holds only that if ever such an [closure] order is entered, it must be supported by adequate findings" (622). Yet, the remedy for inadequate findings, he asserts, is not a reversal of a closure order but "a remand for fact finding" (622). He concludes, "The infeasibility of this course of action —since no such order was entered in this case and since the order that was entered has expired—further demonstrates that the Court's comment on the First Amendment issues implicated by the Massachusetts statute is advisory, hypothetical, and, at best, premature" (622). In short, Stevens appears to be asserting that, because the whole issue is now moot, the Court's ruling is not binding.

Significance

Although the Court did assert that statutes requiring unconditional closure of criminal trials in a given situation are unconstitutional, the media were granted only half a loaf by this ruling. Then, too, the Court did not rule that criminal trials must be public from opening to closing arguments. Instead, it ruled that at times a courtroom may be closed and that at other times it may not. The determination of whether or not to close a portion of a criminal trial, moreover, should be decided on a case-by-case basis.

For a statute requiring closure in a given situation to pass the test of constitutionality, it must first set forth a "compelling governmental interest" in closure. Second, the statute must be narrow enough so that it supports only that particular and specific "compelling" interest. The state's interest in protecting from trauma and embarrassment minors who are victims of sex crimes is not a compelling enough reason, says the Court, to require closure in all cases during the time a minor is testifying. At times this interest may be compelling enough to close part of a trial and at other times it may not.

The Court asserted that a constitutional statute should allow a trial judge who would be considering motions for closure to reflect upon items such as the victim's age, psychological maturity, and understanding of the event; the nature of the crime; the desires of the victim; and the interests of parents and relatives.

Moreover, a law requiring closure would prevent the public from attending a trial (or part of one) even if victims do not want the public excluded. Victims may feel that the public should hear what they have to say about the sex crime they suffered. Thus, the law in this situation would work against, not for, the wishes of the victim and so against the Commonwealth's own interest to support the victim's desires.

In dissent Burger says that an automatic closure order is not unconstitutional (1) if it sets forth a compelling reason and (2) if it produces only a minor or incidental limitation on the implicit First Amendment rights to attend trials. To Burger, protection from the trauma, embarrassment, and humiliation of having to reveal the intimate details of a sexual assault in front of a large group of unfamiliar spectators is indeed a compelling reason. He also believes that closing a courtroom to the public during the testimony of a minor who is a victim of a sex crime produces only a slight limitation of First Amendment rights.

Press-Enterprise Co. v. Superior Court

Press-Enterprise Company
v.
Superior Court of California, Riverside County

Docket No. 82-556
464 U.S. 501, 78 L.Ed.2d 629, 104 S.Ct. 819 (1984)
Argued October 12, 1983. Decided January 18, 1984.

Background

Although *Richmond Newspapers, Inc.* v. *Virginia* (1980) ruled that the public, and so the press, did indeed hold a First Amendment right to attend criminal trials, a California judge later excluded the press from much of the time devoted to questioning prospective jurors in a criminal trial. In addition, the judge then refused to release the transcript of this *voir dire*.

These actions raise some important questions related to defining the chronological boundaries of a trial. When does a trial begin? Does it begin when a fully constituted jury enters the courtroom to hear testimony or when the first prospective juror is asked a question? Does it begin at another point between these two events? Are the often-numerous pretrial proceedings in actuality part of the trial itself? Answers to these questions are important considerations when determining how much access the press has to a trial. The Court ruled in *Wade* v. *Hunter* (1949) that for purposes of double jeopardy, a trial begins when the first witness is sworn, and in *Downum* v. *U.S.* (1963) it ruled the trial begins when the jurors are sworn. Nevertheless, these two cases, the Court said in a footnote, are not directly relevant to defining the extent of First Amendment interests in open trials.

Another set of questions is raised by the conflict between an asserted right of privacy for jurors on the one hand and the right of the public to know what transpires in open court on the other. The Press-Enterprise Company argued that, if a juror's right of privacy actually exists and if the state has a legitimate concern to protect that interest, then any rule or procedure, according to *Globe Newspaper Co.* v. *Superior Court* (1982), must be "narrowly tailored" to serve that interest. In other words, the entire questioning of prospective jurors does not have to be closed in order to preserve the privacy of answers to questions about a particularly sensitive issue, such as attitudes toward the death penalty. The company also asserted that closing the *voir dire* and then preventing the transcript from ever being released creates a dangerous atmosphere that encourages perjury and other misconduct; those few persons who are inclined to lie, it argued, will be more likely to do so when there is no fear of being discovered.

The trial judge asserted, in contrast, that it could be potentially more disturbing and work a greater hardship on the jury system if prospective jurors gave testimony about their most intimate and personal lives with the belief that their responses were being held in confidence, and then later discovered that feelings and experiences they would never have otherwise revealed had been exposed because the transcripts were made public.

Circumstances

The Honorable J. William Mortland in the fall of 1981 denied reporters from the Press-Enterprise Company permission to attend and observe the questioning of prospective jurors. Mortland was judge of the Riverside, California, Superior Court, and the Press-Enterprise Company published in Riverside two newspapers, the *Morning Press Enterprise* and the *Evening Press Enterprise*.

On October 19, 1981, the newspaper presented oral and written motions to open to the press and the public the *voir dire* of prospective jurors for the trial of Albert Greenwood Brown, Jr., 26, who had a prior conviction of forcible rape on an adolescent girl, and who was currently accused of the rape and murder of a 15-year-old girl on her way to school. The state opposed the motion, asserting that open questioning of veniremen would threaten a fair trial.

After hearing arguments, Judge Mortland ruled the press could attend only the "general voir dire," lasting about three days. The "individual voir dire" lasted nearly six weeks. The court said questioning of jurors about their attitudes toward the death sentence—sometimes referred to by the macabre phrase "the death-qualifying of jurors"—would be done individually outside the presence of the public.

Once the jury was selected, the company on December 30 asked the court to release a transcript of the questioning. Both Brown's attorneys and the state objected, saying the transcript would violate the jurors' right to privacy. The court refused to release the transcript, saying, "'I just think there is [*sic*] certain areas that the right of privacy should prevail and a right to a fair trial should prevail and the right of the people to know, I think, should have some limitations'" (504).

On February 23, 1982, Judge Mortland refused a second request for the transcript after Brown had been tried, convicted, and sentenced to death. He said, "'The jurors were questioned in private relating to past experiences, and while most of the information is dull and boring, some of the jurors had some special experiences in sensitive areas'" (540).

The California Court of Appeals denied a request to order the release of the transcript, and the California Supreme Court refused a request for a hearing on the order.

Eventually, three orders by Judge Mortland were submitted to the Court for review: the initial order closing the "death-qualifying" of prospective jurors, the second order sealing the transcript of the questioning, and the permanent order sealing the transcript.

Summary of the Court's Analysis

Chief Justice Warren E. Burger writes for the Court.
Justices William J. Brennan, Jr., Byron R. White,
Harry A. Blackmun, Lewis F. Powell, Jr., William H. Rehnquist,
John Paul Stevens, and Sandra Day O'Connor join.

Chief Justice Burger says the court "granted certiorari to decide whether the guarantees of open public proceedings in criminal trials cover proceedings for the voir dire examination of potential jurors" (503). The question before the Court, in other words, is whether or not the Bill of Rights guarantees the press and the public the right to sit in a courtroom while prospective jurors are being examined. To answer the question, Burger says it is important to note, "The process of juror selection is itself a matter of importance, not simply to the adversaries but to the criminal justice system" (505). In this regard, he asserts, "A review of the historical evidence . . . reveals that . . . the process of selection of jurors has presumptively been a public process with exceptions only for good cause shown" (505).

Burger gives an important rationale for open trials when he writes, "This open process gave assurance to those not attending trials that others were able to observe the proceedings and enhance public confidence" (507). Indeed, one very important aspect of this rationale is that open trials guarantee that "standards of fairness are being observed" (508). Burger writes, "The sure knowledge that *anyone* [Burger's emphasis] is free to attend gives assurance that established procedures are being followed and that deviations will become known. Openness thus enhances both the basic fairness of the criminal trial and the appearance of fairness so essential to public confidence in the system" (508).

Another important benefit of open trials (also noted in *Richmond Newspapers, Inc.* v. *Virginia* [1980]) is their "'therapeutic value'" (508). Burger writes, "Public proceedings vindicate the concerns of the victims and the community in knowing that offenders are being brought to account for their criminal conduct by jurors fairly and openly selected" (509).

As valuable as open proceedings are and even though their openness is presumed, Burger says they can, at times, be closed for good reasons. He writes:

> The presumption of openness may be overcome only by an overriding interest based on findings that closure is essential to preserve higher values and is narrowly tailored to serve that interest. The interest is to be articulated along with findings specific enough that a reviewing court can determine whether the closure order was properly entered. (510)

Having reviewed the relevant historical materials and analyzed their significance, Burger turns to the case at hand: "The superior court asserted two interests in support of its closure order and orders denying a transcript: the right of the defendant to a fair trial, and the right to privacy of the prospective jurors" (510). According to Burger, the court failed to support the asserted interests with specific findings. In addition, Burger writes, the court "failed to consider whether alternatives were available to protect the interests of the prospective jurors that the trial court's orders sought to guard" (511). He concludes, "Absent consideration of alternatives to closure, the trial court could not constitutionally close the voir dire" (511).

One thing the judge could have done, Burger says, is allow those jurors concerned about privacy to "request an opportunity to present the problem to the judge in camera but with counsel present and on the record" (512). In fact, "valid privacy interests," Burger writes, "may rise to a level that part of the transcript should be sealed, or the name of a juror withheld" (512).

Ruling

Burger writes, "The trial judge provided no explanation why his broad order denying access to information at the voir dire was not limited to information that was actually sensitive and deserving of privacy protection" (513). He concludes, "Thus not only was there a failure to articulate findings with the required specificity, but there was also a failure to consider alternatives to closure and to total suppression of the transcript. The judgement of the Court of Appeals is vacated, and the case is remanded for proceedings not inconsistent with this opinion" (513).

Justice Harry A. Blackmun writes a concurring opinion.

Blackmun asserts, "I write separately to emphasize my understanding that the Court does not decide, nor does this case require it to address, the asserted 'right to privacy of the prospective jurors'" (513, 514). Blackmun is concerned that such a right could "unnecessarily complicate the lives of trial judges attempting to conduct a voir dire proceeding" (515).

The jurors' right to privacy, Blackmun asserts, can be protected by the interests of the defendant and the state which seek their full cooperation. Thus, there is no need at present, as he views it, to determine if a juror has a right to privacy.

Justice John Paul Stevens writes a concurring opinion.

Stevens says the right to a fair trial is so important that a claim to a right of access to the trial must be based on an assertion that access contributes to fairness, which is the case here. He writes, "Public access cannot help but improve public understanding of the voir dire process" (518). Thus, the right of access does have limits. These limits, he says, must be determined by examination of the jurors to evaluate the importance of privacy claims.

In this case, though, Stevens asserts, "The trial court applied an impermissible broad rule of secrecy" (520).

Justice Thurgood Marshall writes a concurring opinion.

Marshall writes separately "to stress that the constitutional rights of the public and press to access to all aspects of criminal trials are not diminished in cases in which 'deeply personal matters' are likely to be elicited in voir dire proceedings'" (520). He proposes, therefore, the following requirement: "Prior to issuing a closure order, a trial court should be obliged to show that the order in question constitutes *the least restrictive means available* [Marshall's emphasis] for protecting compelling states interests" (520).

Significance

The clear significance of this case is that the Court said the *voir dire* presumptively is open because it is, in effect, part of the trial itself. In other words, the Court ruled the First Amendment implicitly guarantees the press a right to sit in a courtroom while prospective jurors are being examined. The public and the press, however, have only a qualified implicit right of access because it can be overruled, in certain situations, by important implicit privacy rights or interests of jurors. Nevertheless, when closing the *voir dire,* the trial court should institute the least restrictive means possible to protect privacy interests, and it should do so only after presenting specific findings supporting the closure.

The Court's recognition here of privacy rights held by jurors is similar to its ascription in *Globe Newspaper Co.* v. *Superior Court* (1982) of privacy rights held by witnesses. Both forms of privacy interests are insufficient in themselves to compel closing a trial or any part of it. To force closure, these rights must be shown to constitute a "compelling governmental interest," and the trial court must consider alternatives that do not threaten the First Amendment implicit guarantee of press access to criminal trials. Moreover, a court can close only those portions that threaten this particular and specific "compelling" interest. In particular, the Court noted that one of the actions a trial judge can take is to allow those jurors concerned about privacy to express their concerns on the record in a judge's chamber with counsel for both parties being the only additional persons present.

While it is entirely possible, the Court asserted, that "valid privacy interests" may invoke a constitutionally legitimate requirement that part of the transcript should be sealed or the name of a juror withheld, before taking such actions trial judges first must consider alternatives to closure and total suppression of the transcript and then articulate "with specificity" their resulting findings.

One effect of this ruling is extending the boundaries of a trial to include the questioning of prospective jurors. Such a limited extension still leaves unanswered, though, the question first raised in *Gannett* v. *DePasquale* (1979) of whether the implicit First Amendment right of public access to criminal trials includes pretrial maneuvers taking place before jurors are questioned. Although, while considering the Sixth Amendment, the Court addressed in *Waller* v. *Georgia* (1984) the issue of when a trial begins, the answer to this question as it relates to the First Amendment comes two years later in *Press-Enterprise* v. *Superior Court* (1986).

Waller v. Georgia

Guy Waller
v.
State of Georgia

Docket No. 83-321

Clarence Cole, et al.
v.
State of Georgia

Docket No. 83-322

467 U.S. 39, 81 L.Ed.2d 31, 104 S.Ct. 2210 (1984)
Argued March 27, 1984. Decided May 21, 1984.

Background

Although the Supreme Court had ruled earlier, in *Gannett* v. *DePasquale* (1979), that Sixth Amendment rights were personal to the accused and did not apply to the general public and so not to the media, it had never before considered the impact of denying to the accused the Sixth Amendment right to a public trial. Here, a pretrial proceeding was closed over the objections of the accused (all thirty-six of them). The specific question facing the Court was whether the Sixth Amendment right to a public trial applies to the particular pretrial proceeding at issue: a suppression of evidence hearing.

The Court also was asked to address several related questions. May a suppression hearing be closed—over the objection of the accused—to protect asserted privacy rights of unindicted persons whose telephone conversations were recorded on police wiretaps? Are privacy interests of these persons substantial? If so, should an attempt be made to protect those interests by means short of closure? If no such means can be found, then should closure be ordered only while the tapes are being played and not for the entire suppression hearing?

Based on a series of rulings that begins with *Nebraska* v. *Stuart* (1976) and includes *Gannett* v. *DePasquale* (1979), *Richmond* v. *Virginia* (1980), *Globe* v. *Superior Court* (1982), and *Press-Enterprise Co.* v. *Riverside* (1984), Guy Waller and Clarence Cole argued that suppression hearings should be closed only after a finding of compelling justification and unavoidable necessity. The trial court, they said, made no finding that the privacy interests at stake in this case were substantial enough to warrant closure or that means short of closure were unavailable to protect such interests.

The state, in contrast, said it had compelling interests in having the courtroom closed based on statutory requirements that evidence obtained as a result of electronic surveillance shall not be subject to publication.

This case has implications important to the media primarily because the Court formulated guidelines for determining the degree of explicit Sixth Amendment protections granted to the accused from guidelines promulgated earlier relating to implicit First Amendment rights of the public to gain access to pretrial proceedings. Thus, as a result of the deliberate connection made here by the Court, future developments in Sixth Amendment law may have an impact on First Amendment rights to observe criminal proceedings.

Circumstances

Between June 1981 and January 1982, Guy Waller, Clarence Cole, and several others operated in the metropolitan Atlanta area a lottery based on the daily stock and bond volume of the New York Stock Exchange. Gambling information was transmitted electronically and stored in Cole's computer.

In response, law enforcement officials undertook an extensive program of electronic surveillance, during which more than forty telephone lines were tapped and more than 800 hours of telephone conversations recorded. Using simultaneously executed search warrants in January 1982, the Georgia police gained evidence to indict and charge on February 9, thirty-six persons, including Waller and Cole, with violations of the Georgia Racketeer Influenced and Corrupt Organizations (RICO) Act and with commercial gambling and communicating gambling information.

With search warrants authorizing seizure of "tangible evidence of the crimes of commercial gambling," Georgia police swept through more than 150 homes in twelve counties across the state. The warrants specifically authorized seizure of "money, betting slips, lottery ribbons, lists of bettors; documents containing information related to gambling computers and other information storage and retrieval devices; telecopiers and other facsimile reproduction devices; telephone and other related communication devices; radio frequency scanners and other radio communication devices . . . tangible evidence of the crimes of commercial gambling, communicating gambling information and keeping a gambling place."

Despite the fairly limited scope of these warrants, law enforcement officers "just went in and took everything in sight." Among the things seized were gas and electric bills, cemetery deeds, love letters, children's drawings, Christmas cards, school report cards, wedding portraits, and bounced checks. According to Waller's and Cole's attorneys, the police also seized a blind man's rent money, envelopes for contributions to the Reverend Billy Graham, and a booklet advertising incense and candles. More than 350 boxes of material were seized.

Waller, Cole, and thirteen others moved to suppress the evidence gained from the wiretaps. When the trial court scheduled a hearing on the motion, the state moved to close the hearing to the public, saying that, to "validate" the seizure of certain electronically gathered evidence, it would have to use wiretap tapes that threatened to invade the privacy of persons not indicted.

During hearings on the two motions, the state argued that, in order to use the same information from the wiretaps in subsequent prosecutions against other defendants and to protect the privacy rights of those persons not on trial, the hearing to suppress the wiretaps should be closed. An open hearing, it argued, would "taint" such evidence according to a Georgia statute forbidding the use of wiretap evidence not " 'necessary and essential" to the case. Agreeing that presentation of wiretap evidence at the hearing on the motion to suppress would amount to publication and so would taint the evidence and make it inadmissible in future prosecutions of other offenders, the trial court, over the objection of the defendants, closed the hearing to the public and the press.

During the seven-day suppression hearing "less than two-and-one-half hours were devoted to playing tapes of intercepted telephone conversations" (42), and none of the tapes included unindicted persons. After nearly three days of deliberation, the jury acquitted five of the defendants on all counts; acquitted all others, including Waller and Cole of the RICO count; but convicted them both of commercial gambling and communicating gambling information. Cole and Waller were sentenced to three years' imprisonment and two years' probation and ordered to pay a $20,000 fine.

The Georgia Supreme Court ruled in 1983 that the privacy rights overruled Sixth Amendment rights to public proceedings other than a trial. Two questions are presented to the Court: the trial court's order granting the state's motion to close the suppression hearing and its order partly overruling defendant's motions to suppress all evidence seized during the January raids.

Summary of the Court's Analysis

Justice Lewis F. Powell, Jr. writes for unanimous court.
Chief Justice Warren E. Burger and Justices William J. Brennan,
Byron R. White, Thurgood Marshall, Harry A. Blackmun, William H.
Rehnquist, John Paul Stevens, and Sandra Day O'Connor join.

Justice Powell says this case focuses on three questions: (1) Does an accused person's right to a public trial, as guaranteed by the Sixth Amendment, also apply to a suppression hearing held before a jury is given evidence? (2) If the Sixth Amendment right to a public trial does indeed extend to open suppression hearings, then was that right violated for Waller and Cole? (3) What is the appropriate remedy for such a violation?

When considering the first question, Powell notes there are several precedents, among them *Globe Newspaper Co.* v. *Superior Court* (1982); *Richmond Newspapers, Inc.* v. *Virginia* (1980); *Press-Enterprise Co.* v. *Superior Court* (1984); and *Gannett Co.* v. *DePasquale* (1979). All of these cases assert, says Powell, that the right to a public trial may be considered less important, in certain cases, than other rights, such as the right to a fair trial or the right to privacy. Such instances will be rare, he speculates, and courts should take special care when balancing these interests.

If there exist implicit First Amendment rights to an open trial, then certainly, Powell reasons, there are explicit Sixth Amendment rights as well. Moreover, these rights clearly extend to a suppression hearing. He writes, "These . . . interests are no less pressing in a hearing to suppress wrongfully seized evidence. . . . Suppression hearings often are as important as the trial itself" (46). "A suppression hearing often resembles a bench trial" (46), he notes, with witnesses and arguments by lawyers.

In fact, Powell says there are "particularly strong" reasons for opening suppression hearings. For one thing, challenging the legality of how evidence is seized often means attacking "the conduct of the police and prosecutor" (47). "The public," Powell writes, "has a strong interest in exposing substantial allegations of police misconduct to . . . public scrutiny" (47). Consequently, the justices unanimously "hold that under the Sixth Amendment any closure of a suppression hearing over the objections of the accused must meet the tests set out in *Press-Enterprise* [1984] and its predecessors" (47).

Powell summarizes those tests in four parts. First, in order to close the hearing, an "overriding interest" must be presented. Second, no more of the hearing should be closed than is necessary to protect that interest. In addition, "the trial court must consider reasonable alternatives to closing the proceedings, and it must make findings adequate to support the closure" (48). Georgia failed these tests. First, although the state cited a right to privacy as the overriding interest, it did not specifically identify just exactly whose privacy was threatened and how the hearing would threaten their privacy. In any case, the order to close the entire hearing was much too broad to protect the interests of selected persons. Moreover, the trial court did not consider alternatives. Powell suggests two. Georgia could have presented in the judge's private chambers more detail supporting its request for closure or only those selected portions of the hearing that might threaten privacy rights could be closed. Thus this "closure was far more extensive than necessary" (49).

Waller and Cole ask for a new trial as the remedy for this violation of the Constitution. Georgia feels a new suppression hearing would be sufficient. Powell asserts, "The remedy should be appropriate to the violation" (50).

The Court, therefore, orders a new suppression hearing with only those selected portions, if any, closed that the state court feels is necessary based on any overriding interests that may still exist at the time of the new hearing. "A new trial need be held only if a new, public suppression hearing results in the suppression of material evidence not suppressed at the first trial," Powell concludes (50).

Ruling

Powell writes, "The judgements below are reversed, and the cases remanded for further proceedings not inconsistent with this opinion" (50).

Significance

The first significant aspect of this case is the assertion that the explicit Sixth Amendment right to a public trial extends to suppression hearings. The Court extended this right for four main reasons. First, suppression hearings are very similar to trials. Second, a suppression hearing may be the only trial certain defendants ever get, as would be the case for those who plead guilty after the hearing. In addition, these hearings are more likely than trials to result in an evaluation of the conduct of police and prosecutors. Finally, the public has a strong interest, the Court said, in seeing that the conduct of these persons is open to public scrutiny.

This case is also significant for other reasons. The Court reaffirmed its position that, in certain circumstances, the right to a public trial can be overruled by other rights or interests, such as the right to a fair trial and the right to privacy. In this case the privacy interests, although declared insufficient by the Court, were said to reside in those innocent persons mentioned in tape recordings of telephone conversations.

A significant aspect of this case, therefore, is the list of tests that the Courts said must be met in order to close a suppression hearing: (1) An overriding interest must be asserted, (2) reasonable alternatives to closure must be considered, (3) adequate findings must be presented to support closure, and (4) the closure should be no broader than necessary to protect the overriding interest. This list gives coherence to various disjunctive requirements asserted in several previous decisions.

Patton v. Yount

Ernest S. Patton,
Superintendent, SCI-Camp Hill
and Leroy S. Zimmerman,
Attorney General of Pennsylvania
v.
Jon E. Yount

Docket No. 83-95
467 U.S. 1025, 81 L.Ed.2d 847, 104 S.Ct. 2885 (1984)

Argued February 28, 1984. Decided June 26, 1984.

Background

In *Reynolds* v. *U.S.* (1878), the Court first said determining impartiality (or the lack thereof) in a member of a jury is a mixed question of law and fact and that the trial court's determination of impartiality can be overruled only if a "clear" or "manifest" error was committed. The Court here disagrees about the scope of these two questions and about the meaning of granting deference to a trial court's answers.

Justice Stevens in dissent asserted that the question of fact is to be limited to a determination of whether the juror's testimony is true while the determination of how strongly an opinion is held is a matter of law. He also said only the trial court's finding of truth is due the deference of fact. The majority of the Court, however, said that the question of fact includes determining both the truthfulness and the depth of a juror's opinion; whereas the question of law centers upon applying the correct standard of impartiality. The deference to fact, according to the Court, applies, therefore, to both the truthfulness and the depth of a prospective juror's opinion about the guilt of an accused.

The words of Justice Holmes in *Holt* v. *U.S.* (1910) should not be overlooked. He wrote in avowed reference to *Reynolds*, "The finding of the trial court upon the strength of the juryman's opinion *and* [emphasis added] his partiality or impartiality ought not to be set aside by a reviewing court unless the error is manifest" (248). Thus, Holmes appears to limit the question of fact to "the strength of the juryman's opinion" and the question of law to "his partiality or impartiality." Moreover, he grants deference on both questions to the trial judge.

Circumstances

The fact that Jon E. Yount had spent eighteen years behind bars before the Court issued this ruling is unmistakable evidence that a complex series of events preceded the ruling in this case.

The legal wheels began moving at 5:45 A.M., on April 29, 1966, when Yount, 28, walked into the Pennsylvania State Police Substation at DuBois and confessed he had choked, hit with a wrench, and murdered Pamela Sue Rimer, an 18-year-old former student of his at the DuBois Area High School. Her body had been found the night before in a wooded area adjoining a road leading from her school bus stop to her rural home in Luthersburg, Clearfield County. An autopsy revealed that death was the result of shock, loss of blood, and strangulation from an excess of blood in her lungs. The medical examination revealed numerous wounds about the girl's head from a blunt weapon, three slashes across her throat, and cuts by a sharp instrument—such as a small Boy Scout pocket knife—on the fingers of her left hand. Although the girl's body was not fully clothed when found, the autopsy produced no indication of sexual assault.

Yount, who had no prior criminal record, was married and the father of two children; he held an M.Ed. and was a teacher of mathematics for eight years and chemistry for two years at DuBois Area High School. Clearfield County's population then was 74,619; two newspapers, the Clearfield *Progress* (circulation 16,250) and the DuBois *Courier Express* (circulation 9,500), and local radio and television stations closely covered the events.

Rimer was an honors student and chemistry was a favorite subject. She was known as "Bunny," played first chair clarinet in the school band, and was the only girl of nine students in Yount's advanced math class. Her brother Douglas was killed three years earlier in a tragic farm accident at age 10.

In his confessions—which contain several different, but fairly similar, versions of this story—Yount said he was looking for some land to buy where he would have room to hunt and fish. He picked up Pamela while he was driving down the road that led to her house and asked her to show him some land; when she turned down his request and tried to get out of the car, he held on to her coat and then got the wrench and hit her.

Because the police refused to release Yount's confession to the press, it was not published until it was read at his arraignment three days later. After his first trial, from September 28 to October 7, 1966, Yount was found guilty of rape and first-degree murder. The jury recommended life imprisonment. The Supreme Court of Pennsylvania reversed Yount's conviction on the basis of *Miranda* v. *State of Arizona* (1966), which had been decided between the date of Yount's arrest and the date of his trial, saying the police failed to inform him properly, before his confession, of his right to an attorney.

At his second trial, which began on November 17, 1970, the court disallowed that portion of the confession obtained after Yount was in legal custody. His move for a change of venue was denied in spite of his assertion that "publication of prejudicial information could not be eradicated from the minds of prospective jurors" (1027). Judge John Cherry said that "the articles were merely reported events without editorial comment" (1028). On November 20 Yount was convicted a second time of first-degree murder and resentenced to life imprisonment. The rape charge was not retried.

Nearly 98 percent of the prospective jurors and all but one seated juror for the second trial had read about the case. More than 90 percent of those questioned had discussed the case or heard others express opinions about it, and 84 percent admitted holding an opinion related to Yount's guilt. Nevertheless, nine of the seated jurors were selected without challenge of any kind. The remaining three jurors, although challenged for cause, indicated either that they had no fixed opinion or that they could enter the jury box with an open mind.

Yount's request for a third trial—on the basis of prejudicial pretrial publicity before the second one—was denied because the court said "no publicity had been given to the case between trials, and that little public interest was shown during the second trial" (1028). The Pennsylvania Supreme Court affirmed, so Yount filed a petition for a writ of habeas corpus in the United States District Court.

The District Court rejected a magistrate's recommendation that the petition be granted, saying, "The pretrial publicity was not vicious, excessive, nor officially sponsored, and . . . the jurors were able to set aside any preconceived notions of guilt" (1028). The Court of Appeals for the Third Circuit reversed, saying the publicity made a fair trial in Clearfield County impossible. This court had a special problem with a juror named Hrin who indicated that he would need to be shown evidence before he would change his mind about Yount's guilt. The court said this attitude "stripped" Yount "of the presumption of innocence" (1031).

Summary of the Court's Analysis

Justice Lewis F. Powell, Jr., writes for the Court.
Chief Justice Warren E. Burger and Justices Byron R. White,
Harry A. Blackmun, William H. Rehnquist,
and Sandra Day O'Connor join.

Justice Powell says the Court grants certiorari in order to consider "the problem of pervasive media publicity that now arises so frequently in the trial of sensational criminal cases" (1031).

It is true, Powell notes at first, that *Irvin* v. *Dowd* (1961), held that "adverse pretrial publicity can create such a presumption of prejudice in a community that the juror's claims that they can be impartial should not be believed" (1031). It is also true, he notes in contrast, that "the trial court's findings of impartiality might be overturned only for 'manifest error' [referring to *Irvin* where the Court quotes from *Holt* v. *U.S.* (1910), which, in turn, quotes from *Reynolds* v. *U.S.* (1878), the original source of these words]" (1031). Thus, Powell says the Court will review the circumstances to discover what, if anything, the appeals court missed in its analysis of manifest error.

Powell begins his observations by pointing out that the "extensive adverse publicity" reached its height before the first trial. Second, much of the publicity for the second trial consisted of "extremely brief announcements of the trial dates and scheduling [information] such as are common in rural newspapers" (1032). In addition, the news stories "were purely factual articles generally discussing not the crime or prior prosecution, but the prolonged process of jury selection" (1031). Most telling, though, according to Powell, is the "lapse in time" with the result that most veniremen "simply had let the details of the case slip from their mind" (1033).

Powell writes, "The record suggests that their [the jurors'] passions had not been inflamed, nor their thoughts biased" (1034). He continues, "It is clear that the passage of time between a first and a second trial . . . clearly rebuts any presumption of partiality or prejudice that existed at the time of the initial trial" (1035).

Having dealt with the issue of the impartiality of the jury as a whole, Powell turns to the challenges of individual jurors, looking at two alternates and a juror named Hrin. Immediately, the Court rejects the appeals court's contention that the question of prejudiced jurors in this case is a mixed one of law and facts in this case. Instead, in a federal habeas corpus case, Powell asserts that the relevant statute indicates "it is plainly one of historical fact: did a juror swear that he could set aside any opinion he might hold and decide the case on the evidence, and should the juror's protestation of impartiality have been believed" (1036). In a footnote, the Court points out that the relevant law (28 U.S.C. Section 2254 [d]) is clear. The legal standard for constitutionally accepted partiality is plainly defined in the law; the question here is whether or not certain individual jurors did meet in fact that standard.

While it is true, Powell admits, that the three jurors gave "ambiguous and at times contradictory" testimony, he notes they are "lay persons" who "had no briefings by lawyers," who "may never have been subjected to the type of leading questions and cross-examination tactics," and so who "cannot be expected invariably to express themselves carefully or even consistently" (1039). Moreover, the essential point, says Powell, is that "only the trial judge could tell which of these answers was said with the greatest comprehension and certainty" (1040). He writes, "The trial judge properly may choose to believe those statements that were the most fully articulated or that appeared to have been least influenced by leading" (1039).

Ruling

Powell writes:

We concluded that the voir dire . . . did not reveal the kind of "wave of public passion" that would have made a fair trial unlikely by the jury that was empaneled as a whole. We also conclude that the ambiguity in the testimony of the cited jurors who were challenged for cause is insufficient to overcome the presumption of correctness owed to the trial court's findings. We therefore reverse. (1040)

Justice John Paul Stevens writes a dissenting opinion.
Justice William J. Brennan, Jr., joins.

Stevens says he will deal with five points: (1) the news coverage, (2) the examination of jurors, (3) the court of appeals decision relating to the jury as a whole, (4) juror Hrin, and (5) the "more profound issue that a case of this kind raises" (1041).

Stevens notes first that the "lapse in time" was not as important as the Court said in "softening" opinions about guilt because the time lapse was not very long. He writes, "There were in effect, three chapters in the relevant news coverage: the stories about the crime itself and the first trial in 1966; the stories and events surrounding the State Supreme Court's reversal of the first conviction in 1969; and the stories that were published in 1970 immediately before the trial began" (1041).

He uses the *voir dire* of the wife of a minister to illustrate the impact of these three "chapters" of publicity. She indicated that the people in her church expected her to convict Yount. "Her testimony," writes Stevens, "repudiates the notion that the community had all but forgotten the Yount case" (1044).

Concerning the jury as a whole, Stevens notes that all but two of the 163 veniremen questioned "had read or heard about the case" (1045). He continues, "Of the 121 dismissed for cause, 96 testified that they had firm opinions that could not be changed regardless of what evidence might be presented" (1045).

Turning to juror Hrin, Stevens writes, "Hrin's testimony clearly is sufficient to overcome the presumption of correctness" (1049) that the relevant statute says is a judgment to be made by the trial judge. He continues, "Contrary to the Court, I believe that whether a juror has a disqualified opinion is a mixed question of law and fact" (1051). The question of fact, he says, is simply a determination of whether a juror is telling the truth. The question of law is whether a juror's truthful statement reflects bias. The relevant statute (28 U.S.C.S. Section 2254[d]), he argues, asserts that only the factual determination is to be granted a presumption of correctness. The problem with granting "an elected judge" a "presumption of correctness" in determining the legal standard, Stevens asserts, is the judge's concern "about the community's reactions to his disposition of highly publicized cases" (1053).

Finally, Stevens turns to what he considers the more profound issue" raised in this case. He writes, "Of much greater importance is our dedication to the principle that guilt or innocence of a criminal offense in our society is not to be decided by executive fiat or by popular vote" (1054). Stevens feels the Court granted certiorari, not because an important legal principle is at issue, but because of the facts: specifically, "the conviction of a confessed high school teacher had been set aside by an appellate court" (1053). He says the Court responded on an "emotional" level to the "desire" of the "residents of Clearfield County" "to do something about such an apparent miscarriage of justice" (1053).

Significance

The difference between impartiality in an individual juror and in the jury as a whole (or the jury panel, as it is sometimes called) represent the two areas of significance for this case.

The issue of unconstitutional prejudice in the panel arises out of concerns about widespread and intense pretrial media coverage. The Court said the questioning of Yount's prospective jurors did not "reveal the kind of 'wave of public passion' that would have made a fair trial unlikely by the jury that was empaneled as a whole.'" Significantly, the Court gives two reasons for believing that the publicity did not "fatally infect" the community with unconstitutional prejudice against Yount. The first is that the news coverage was mainly factual and not inflammatory. The second is that too much time passed between the height of the publicity and the questioning of prospective jurors. The Court said evidence of how time ameliorates prejudice is that the persons questioned could only vaguely remember information from the publicity. These conclusions reaffirm similar ones in *Stroble* v. *California* (1952) and *Murphy* v. *Florida* (1975).

The issue of individual juror prejudice produced a conflict within the Court. It was in *Reynolds* v. *U.S.* (1878) that the Court first said determining impartiality in a member of a jury is a mixed question of law and fact. The Court said here that *Irvin* v. *Dowd* (1961) correctly asked a mixed question about a jury panel because 28 U.S.C.S. Section 2254(d)—which was added to federal law after *Reynolds* was decided—does not address the jury panel. Since this statute does apply to an individual juror, however, the Court said that federal habeas corpus cases should focus only on the question of fact. That question, it said, includes determining both the truthfulness and the depth of a juror's opinion; whereas the question of law centers upon applying the correct standard of impartiality. The cited statutory deference due to the trial judge's determination of fact, according to the Court, applies, therefore, to both the truthfulness and the depth of a prospective juror's opinion about the guilt of an accused. In Yount's case the Court concluded that "the ambiguity in the testimony of the cited jurors who were challenged for cause is insufficient to overcome the presumption of correctness owed to the trial court's findings."

Stevens in dissent asserted that the question of fact is limited to a determination of whether the juror's testimony is true while the determination of how strongly an opinion is held is a matter of law. Consequently, he asserted that the trial court's deference of fact is limited to a determination of whether or not an individual juror told the truth.

Press-Enterprise Co. v. Superior Court

Press-Enterprise Company

v.

Superior Court of California for the County of Riverside

Docket No. 84-1560

478 U.S. 1, 92 L.Ed.2d 1, 106 S.Ct. 2735 (1986)

Argued February 26, 1986. Decided June 30, 1986.

Background

The Court comes full circle with this case. Questions focusing on the openness of trials and trial-related proceedings were first addressed specifically in *Gannett* v. *DePasquale* (1979). The Court ruled there that the public and so the press have no Sixth Amendment right to attend pretrial hearings. The Sixth Amendment, according to the Court, is personal to the accused.

Then in *Richmond Newspapers, Inc.* v. *Virginia* (1980), the Court ruled that the public and so also the press do have, however, a First Amendment right to attend trials, provided there is no constitutionally valid specific evidence presented asserting an overriding interest. Later, in *Press-Enterprise Co.* v. *Superior Court* (1984), the Court said the public and therefore the press, absent other overriding interests, also have a First Amendment right to attend the *voir dire* of prospective jurors. In the present case the Court extends that First Amendment right to all pretrial hearings.

The heart of the issue in both *Press-Enterprise* cases is defining what events associated with a trial are covered by implicit First Amendment rights guaranteeing access to public information. In the first *Press-Enterprise* case (1984) the First Amendment rights of access to public information were extended to the questioning of jurors. In the second (1986) these rights are extended to pretrial hearings. Some journalists are seeking to extend these rights to the very beginning of what they assert might broadly be called the trial process, including access to reports of arrests written by police officers.

The right asserted to support closed hearings in the first *Press-Enterprise* case was the privacy of jurors, a right not specifically mentioned in the Constitution; the right in this case—to a fair trial—is fundamental and can be found stated explicitly in the Sixth Amendment.

Therefore, in opposition to the newspaper company, the Court asserted that, while there may be some procedural similarities between a trial and a preliminary hearing, the two are functionally dissimilar and serve vastly different societal goals. The purpose of a trial, it argued, is to determine guilt and innocence. In contrast, the purpose of preliminary hearings is to protect the liberty of the accused. Thus, the right to a preliminary hearing is a personal right guaranteeing the accused an opportunity to be free from unwarranted criminal prosecutions and from publicity of evidence introduced at such hearings to support allegations of criminal conduct.

Circumstances

A complaint was filed on December 23, 1981, in municipal court, Riverside Judicial District, Riverside County, California, against Robert Rubane Diaz, alleging twelve counts of murder under California Penal Code, Section 190.2(a)(3), which authorizes the death penalty. The state said Diaz murdered twelve hospital patients by administering overdoses of lidocaine, a drug commonly used as an antiarrhythmic medication. It suppresses and prevents rhythm disturbances (irregular heart beats) arising from the ventricle (lower part) of the heart.

About six months later Diaz was granted his motion asking a California magistrate to close his July 6, 1982, preliminary hearing in the Riverside Municipal Court to the public under California Penal Code, Section 868.

The motion was unopposed. At the conclusion of a forty-one-day hearing, the Press-Enterprise Company unsuccessfully sought release of the transcript. The state on January 21, 1983, later joined by Press-Enterprise on February 7, unsuccessfully petitioned the Superior Court to release the transcript. On February 10 Diaz filed a motion in opposition, claiming the release of the transcripts would result in prejudicial publicity, jeopardizing his right to an impartial jury.

Following the refusal by the Superior Court to release the transcript on the basis of a threat to a fair trial, Press-Enterprise filed a writ of mandamus with the California Court of Appeals, Fourth Appellate District, Division Two. That court at first denied the writ, but then the court set a hearing on it after being ordered to do so by the California Supreme Court. After Diaz waived his right to a jury trial, the Court of Appeals declared the controversy moot and then denied the writ.

On appeal, the California Supreme Court denied the writ, saying the First Amendment right of access to trials does not extend to preliminary hearings. This court said the statutory right of access under California Penal Code Section 868 could be denied upon the showing of a "reasonable likelihood of substantial prejudice" to the defendant's right to a fair trial unless the prosecution could sustain its resulting burden of showing by a "preponderance of the evidence that there is no such reasonable probability of prejudice" (6).

Summary of the Court's Analysis

Chief Justice Warren E. Burger writes for the Court.
Justices Harry A. Blackmun, William J. Brennan, Jr.,
Thurgood Marshall, Sandra Day O'Connor, Lewis F. Powell, Jr.,
and Byron R. White join.

As is often true in cases like this, the Court first addresses the issue of jurisdiction. Referring to *Gannett* v. *DePasquale* (1979) and *Globe* v. *Superior Court* (1982), Chief Justice Burger notes that here again the Court is faced with a controversy that, although settled, is " 'capable of repetition, yet evading review' " (6). Thus the Court asserts jurisdiction and turns to the merits of the case.

Burger begins his analysis of the merits by pointing out that the right to an open trial is shared by the accused and the public, both having an interest in fairness. He states that, in the past, the Court has recognized, first, the presumptive openness of trials and, second, the role of the public in guaranteeing fairness. Although "these are considerations of experience and logic," writes Burger, "there are some limited circumstances in which the right to a fair trial might be undermined by publicity" (9).

As a general rule, however, Burger concludes there is a right of access "to preliminary hearings as conducted in California" (10). First, these hearings traditionally have been open in that state. Second, Burger writes, "Public access to criminal trials and the selection of jurors is essential to the proper functioning of the criminal justice system. California preliminary hearings are sufficiently like a trial to justify the same conclusion" (11). The mere fact that a criminal cannot be convicted in a preliminary trial in California is not a sufficient basis to distinguish it for the purposes of openness from the trial itself. He writes, "We therefore conclude that the qualified First Amendment right of access to criminal proceedings applies to preliminary hearings as they are conducted in California" (13).

Next, Burger turns to the conditions necessary for denying access. There must be "specific, on the record, findings," he asserts, "demonstrating that 'closure is essential to preserve higher values and is narrowly tailored to serve that interest' " (13, 14). Moreover, in the case of an asserted interest in a fair trial, the following are particular requirements to closure. Burger writes:

> The preliminary hearing shall be closed only if specific findings are made demonstrating that first, there is a substantial probability that the defendant's right to a fair trial will be prejudiced by publicity that closure would prevent and, second, reasonable alternatives to closure cannot adequately protect the defendant's free trial rights. (14)

Moreover, the California Supreme Court's requirement of a "reasonable likelihood" of prejudice, writes Burger, "places a lesser burden on the defendant than the 'substantial probability' test which we hold is called for by the First Amendment" (14). A mere "risk of prejudice," Burger asserts, "does not automatically justify refusing public access to hearing" (15).

Ruling

Burger writes, "The First Amendment right of access cannot be overcome by the conclusory assertion that publicity might deprive the defendant of that right [to a fair trial]. And any limitation 'must be narrowly tailored to serve that interest'" (15). He concludes, "Accordingly, the judgment of the California Supreme Court is reversed" (15).

Justice John Paul Stevens writes a dissenting opinion.
Justice William H. Rehnquist joins.

Stevens outlines what he considers to be the "constitutional question" this way: "Whether members of the public have a First Amendment right to insist upon access to the transcript of a preliminary hearing during the period before the public trial" (15). Before answering this question, Stevens makes some observations. First, the transcript presents only one side of the story, the prosecution's. Second, the prosecutor in this case did not oppose the motion of closure. Third, "the Magistrate had earlier rejected less restrictive alternatives to sealing the transcript" (16). Stevens asserts, therefore, "The trial judge had an obvious and legitimate reason for refusing to make the transcript public any sooner than he did" (17). He writes, "In my opinion, the judge's decision did not violate the First Amendment either" (17).

Stevens points out that he supports "a proper construction of the First Amendment" to embrace "a right of access to information about the conduct of public affairs" (18). He writes, "Neither our elected nor our appointed representatives may abridge the free flow of information simply to protect their own activities from public scrutiny" (19). Nevertheless, Stevens feels the First Amendment right of access to information is much narrower than the First Amendment right to disseminate information. It is narrowed, in part, by "the risk of prejudice to the defendant's right to a fair trial" (20).

When reviewing the relevant history, Stevens notes, "It is uncontroverted that a common law right of access did not inhere in preliminary proceedings at the time the First Amendment was adopted, and that the Framers and ratifiers of that provision could not have intended such proceedings to remain open" (22). He says the historical evidence for open proceedings are "too little" and the Court relies on it "too much" (25).

Stevens finishes his analyses by outlining the Court's reasons for opening the proceeding, "It [quoting now from *Press-Enterprise Co.* v. *Riverside*, I (1984)] 'is often the final and most important step in the criminal proceeding'; that it provides 'the sole occasion for public observation of the criminal justice system'; that it lacks the protective presence of a jury; and that closure denies an outlet for community catharsis" (25). He concludes that these reasons can be applied to "the traditionally secret grand jury with as much force as it applies to the California preliminary hearing" (26).

Thus, he asserts, "The constitutionally-grounded fair trial interests of the accused if he is bound over for trial, and the reputational interests of the accused if he is not, provide a substantial reason for delaying access to the transcript for at least the short time before the trial" (29).

Significance

The assertion of a First Amendment right of access to a preliminary hearing constitutes the significance of this case. Although not absolute, the Court says the public and therefore the press have a right to attend and to read the transcripts of such hearings.

In order to close some part of a preliminary hearing, the trial court must present specific, on the record, findings demonstrating that closure is essential to preserve higher values. These findings must also show that the closure is narrowly tailored to serve those particular values or interests.

The Court also noted that when a fair trial is put forth as the overriding interest, then the preliminary hearing shall be closed only if specific findings are made demonstrating that, first, there is a substantial probability the defendant's right to a fair trial will be prejudiced by publicity that closure would prevent and, second, reasonable alternatives to closure cannot protect adequately the defendant's free trial rights.

In addition, the California Supreme Court's requirement of a "reasonable likelihood" of prejudice is too weak to support closure according to the Court. Likelihood of prejudice places a lesser burden on the defendant than the substantial probability test the Court says is called for by the First Amendment. Echoing Justice Holmes in *Holt* v. *U.S.* (1910), the Court asserts that a mere risk of prejudice does not automatically justify refusing public access to hearings. Instead, there must be a showing that, without closure, there exists a substantial probability that the defendant's fair trial will be unconstitutionally prejudiced by publicity.

Mu'Min v. Virginia

Dawud Majid Mu'Min
v.
Virginia

Docket No. 90-5193
500 U.S. ___, 114 L.Ed.2d 493, 111 S.Ct. 1899 (1991)
Argued February 20, 1991. Decided May 20, 1991.

Background

Roots for this case reach back to *Mima Queen* v. *Hepburn* (1813), a case about slavery. Objecting to the dismissal of a juror named James Reed, Mima Queen and her child petitioned the Court to reverse a decision denying her freedom. During the *voir dire* of Queen's trial, Reed had "avowed his detestation of slavery to be such that in a doubtful case he would find a verdict for Queen and her child" (297). He said he would also decide for them if the evidence were equal on both sides. The trial judge dismissed Reed for failure to be "indifferent," and Queen appealed his dismissal to the Court. Chief Justice John Marshall acknowledged that "the difficulty of obtaining jurors whose minds are entirely uninfluenced by opinions previously formed is undoubtedly considerable" (297). Nonetheless, he concluded, "Yet it was desirable to submit the case to those who felt no bias either way; and therefore the court exercised a sound discretion in not permitting him to be sworn" (297). So Queen lost her appeal because the Court felt jurors should "stand perfectly indifferent between the parties" (297).

The Court's ruling in *Queen* later played an important role in *Connors* v. *U.S.* (1895), that was influential, in turn, upon *Mu'Min*. James Connors was convicted of stealing a ballot box in Denver, Colorado. He appealed in no small part because the judge at his trial refused to ask the jurors seven questions he had prepared, all dealing with the jurors' participation in the 1890 election. The following question was of special interest to Connors: "'Would your political affiliations or party predilections tend to bias your judgment in this case either for or against this defendant'" (412). After quoting at length Marshall's remarks from *Queen* about the "sound discretion" of the trial judge, Justice John M. Harlan admitted, "A suitable inquiry is permissible in order to ascertain whether the juror has any bias, opinion, or prejudice that would affect or control the fair determination by him of the issues to be tried" (413). He added, "That inquiry is conducted under the supervision of the court, and a great deal must, of necessity, be left to its sound discretion" (413).

Concerning Connors's question about political affiliation, Harlan writes, "In the absence of any statement tending to show that there was some special reason or ground for putting that question to particular jurors called into the jury box for examination, it cannot be said that the court erred in disallowing it" (414). Such a question would be proper, Harlan asserts, only if jurors indicated that the case appeared to be "involving the interests of political parties rather than the enforcement of a law designed for the protection of the public against frauds in elections" (415). For a second time, the Court reaffirmed the "sound discretion" of the trial judge. In addition, the Court set forth a condition under which it would have been proper to ask prospective members of the jury a particular question. Later, the Court is to continue this practice of setting up guidelines governing the trial judge's questioning of jurors about specific issues or events by trial judges.

Of two major issues arising in this case from the conflict between a free press and fair trial, the first one is the problem of determining whether jurors are telling the truth when they say they are impartial. Important early attempts to deal with this issue can be found in *Queen* and *Connors*, where the Court supported the "sound discretion" of trial judges. Eventually, support for "sound discretion" evolved into a "special deference" that must be given by the appellate courts to a trial judge's evaluation of the credibility of prospective jurors. The reason for this deference is a judge's special advantage of being able to observe the demeanor of jurors when they assert their impartiality. Appellate judges, in contrast, can only read the record; they are unable to watch prospective jurors respond to questions. Therefore, only in the instance of an egregious mistake (what the Court calls "manifest error") can an appellate court overturn the trial judge's evaluation of impartiality.

In *Mu'Min* the dissenting opinion challenges this long-standing deference to the evaluations arrived at by the "sound discretion" of trial judges. The dissent asks what special actions must trial judges take in order to merit deference to their judgment. Is there some minimum effort these judges must make to earn respect for their evaluation of jury impartiality, or should an appellate court unquestioningly trust the judges' "sound discretion"? This group of dissenting justices asserts unequivocally that trial judges cannot expect special deference in all instances. They contend that, when a prospective juror admits some knowledge of pretrial publicity, then trial judges must question each juror individually (1) about the nature and extent of the particular juror's knowledge (that is, about the content of what that person knows) and (2) about the impact of that knowledge on the juror's attitude toward the defendant's innocence. The dissent contends that judges who do not take these two actions forfeit the privilege of being granted special deference to their judgment about a particular juror's impartiality.

One justice in a lone dissent says trial judges need not necessarily take these two specific actions. Instead, the judge must only do something—that is, make some minimum effort of some kind—more than allowing prospective jurors who are aware of pretrial publicity to assert their impartiality simply by silently and passively not responding in the affirmative when asked if they are biased against the defendant.

The majority, in contrast, says the judge may question the prospective jurors in groups and is not required to ask questions about the content of prospective jurors' knowledge of pretrial publicity merely because they have avowed some vague knowledge of the case.

A second issue focuses, not on the individual juror, but on the community from which prospective jurors are to be drawn. This issue can be summed up in a question: When is mass media publicity so pervasive that no juror's assertion of impartiality can be believed by any reasonable judge? One justice in a concurring opinion says that the Court should respect the answers of trial judges because they live in the area where the publicity is disseminated. A group of three dissenters, in contrast, asserts that, when the publicity is intense, widespread, and potentially damaging to a fair trial, then the trial judge has an obligation to ask prospective jurors questions about the content of their knowledge of the pretrial publicity.

These two issue are raised by the sixty-four questions that Dawud Majid Mu'Min requested his trial judge ask prospective jurors. Mu'Min wanted the judge to ask individual prospective jurors questions about the content of their knowledge of the publicity about his crime. Only in this way, asserted Mu'Min, could the judge adequately evaluate a juror's assertion of impartiality. The judge refused and Mu'Min appealed.

One other argument by Virginia should not be overlooked. The Commonwealth said that, even when the Court held that the opportunity for specific *voir dire* inquiry is guaranteed by the Constitution, those rulings require only questions pertaining directly to the prospective jurors' assessment of their impartiality, not their factual knowledge of events. Calling attention to what was heard or read outside of court, argued the Commonwealth, might suggest to a juror that out-of-court statements are relevant. Such questions could serve to refresh a juror's recollection of the news accounts, make the events more vivid in the juror's mind, and even unwittingly suggest to a juror the existence of other, more damaging news accounts.

Circumstances

In 1973, when Dawud Majid Mu'Min was 19 years old, he was convicted of first-degree murder of a cab driver in Brayson County, Virginia, and sentenced to forty-eight years in prison. Fifteen years later, in the spring of

1988, he was assigned to Haymarket Correctional Unit 26, a minimum security institution in Prince William County, Virginia.

On September 22, 1988, Mu'Min was working on a public highway with a Department of Transportation work crew. When the work crew broke for lunch, Mu'Min crossed a fence, walked along Interstate Route 95 for about a mile to Ashdale Plaza, a shopping center, and entered Dale City Floors, a carpet and flooring store owned and operated by Mrs. Gladys Nopwasky.

Mu'Min claimed he asked Mrs. Nopwasky about oriental carpets, challenged her prices, and then entered into a heated argument with her, after which he said he stabbed and killed, but did not rape, her. (The knife he used was made earlier with grinding equipment at the prison shop, where he sharpened a metal spike to which he attached a wooden handle.) After taking all the money from the cash drawer, four dollars in coins, he wiped off his finger prints wherever he could, returned to the work crew, washed the blood from his shoes, put his bloody shirt in a plastic bag, and threw it into a trash can. He threw away the knife somewhere along the highway. He was charged following an anonymous letter sent to the authorities by another inmate.

A customer discovered Mrs. Nopwasky's body. Her blouse and bra had been pushed up to expose her breasts; her clothes had been removed from her waist down; her face was so badly beaten and bloodied that she was unrecognizable. An autopsy revealed that her face, neck, chest, and left arm had been stabbed or cut sixteen times. Two wounds were fatal, those in the lower neck and left upper chest. She also suffered numerous "blunt-force trauma injuries" consistent with blows from a fist, causing a laceration on her forehead and bruises over a large portion of her face.

Not surprisingly, the event attracted much attention from the media. Consequently, Mu'Min requested on January 30, 1989, a change of venue. After the motion was denied, he submitted on April 14 a list of proposed *voir dire* questions. This motion was denied as was a request for individual *voir dire*.

Mu'Min produced forty-seven newspaper stories supporting his motion for a change of venue. The Court noted that the following items were covered in these articles: "details of the murder and investigation," "information about" his "prior criminal record," "the fact that he had been rejected for parole six times," "accounts of alleged prison infractions," "details about the prior murder for which Mu'Min was serving his sentence," "a comment that the death penalty had not been available when Mu'Min was convicted for this earlier murder," "indications that Mu'Min had confessed to killing Gladys Nopwasky," "alleged laxity in the supervision of prison gangs," and arguments "for reform of the prison work-crew system" (L.Ed.2d 501).

Instead, the judge asked some questions of the entire panel and other questions to groups of four at a time. In addition, the judge refused to ask any of Mu'Min's "proposed questions relating to the content of news items that potential jurors might have read or seen" (L.Ed.2d 502), and he announced a decision to delay ruling on a request for a change of venue until after questioning the prospective jurors.

During collective questioning, sixteen of the twenty-six prospective jurors said they had "acquired . . . information about the alleged offense or the accused [Mu'Min] from the news media" (L.Ed.2d 502), but only one, a man, said he could not, as a consequence, remain an impartial juror willing to base an opinion of guilt or innocence only on information presented in court. The judge then denied Mu'Min's motion to dismiss the other fifteen jurors and rejected a renewed motion for a change of venue.

During the questioning in groups of four, jurors who mentioned they had gained some information about the case from an outside source were asked if they thought this information would prevent them from remaining impartial. According to Rehnquist, "All swore that they could enter the jury box with an open mind and wait until the entire case was presented before reaching a conclusion as to guilt or innocence" (L.Ed.2d 503). He takes care to note, "One juror who equivocated as to whether she could enter the jury box with an open mind was removed *sua sponte* [on his own without being asked] by the trial judge" (L.Ed.2d 503).

Eight of the twelve seated jurors said "they had read or heard something about the case" (L.Ed.2d 500) although they also denied having "formed an opinion based on the outside information" and asserted that this knowledge would not "affect their ability to determine petitioner's [Mu'Min's] guilt or innocence based solely on the evidence presented at trial" (L.Ed.2d 500).

Mu'Min was convicted of first-degree murder in 1989 and sentenced to death. Upon appeal, the Supreme Court of Virginia, by a split vote, affirmed, as does the Court.

Summary of the Court's Analysis

Chief Justice William H. Rehnquist writes for the Court.
Justices Byron R. White, Sandra Day O'Connor, Antonin Scalia,
and David H. Souter join.

Chief Justice Rehnquist begins his analysis by noting that the Court's authority over the questioning of jurors serving state courts is "limited to enforcing the commands of the United States Constitution" (L.Ed.2d 503), whereas federal courts are "subject to this Court's supervisory power" (L.Ed.2d 503). Next, he reviews three opinions related to each of these two areas of government—state and federal. All six cases focus on questions designed to determine the racial bias of a prospective juror.

Beginning with federal courts, Rehnquist points out that, in *Connors* v. *U.S.* (1895), the Court ruled the trial judge must be given a "'great deal'" of "'sound discretion'" in determining "'whether the juror has any bias, opinion, or prejudice that would affect or control the fair determination by him'" of guilt or innocence (L.Ed.2d 504). Then, in *Aldridge* v. *U.S.* (1931), the Court ruled that a trial judge committed a reversible error when he failed to ask members of the jury "whether any of them might be prejudiced against the defendant because of his race" (L.Ed.2d 504). Finally, in *Rosales-Lopez* v. *U.S.* (1981), the Court ruled that questions about "racial or ethnic prejudice" need only be asked when "the defendant was accused of a violent crime and the defendant and the victim were members of different racial or ethnic groups" (L.Ed.2d 504).

Moving to the state courts, Rehnquist notes first that, in *Ham* v. *South Carolina* (1973), "the Due Process Clause of the Fourteenth Amendment required the court" to ask questions the defendant had submitted about racial bias, but not those he submitted related to prejudice against persons wearing beards (L.Ed.2d 504). Then, in *Ristaino* v. *Ross* (1976), the Court ruled it was not necessary for "a state court trial judge to question prospective jurors as to racial prejudice in every case where the races of the defendant and the victim differ" (L.Ed.2d 504). Finally, in *Turner* v. *Murray* (1986), the Court "held that in a capital case involving a charge of murder of a white person by a black defendant such questions must be asked" (L.Ed.2d 504).

Rehnquist concludes from his review of both federal and state court requirements that two themes emerge. The first is that "the possibility of racial prejudice against a black defendant charged with a violent crime against a white person is sufficiently real that the Fourteenth Amendment requires that inquiry be made into racial prejudice" (L.Ed.2d 505). The second is that "the trial court retains great latitude in deciding what questions should be asked of prospective jurors" (L.Ed.2d 505).

Not satisfied with the general requirement in *Aldridge* asserting broadly that the "Court 'cover the subject'" (L.Ed.2d 505), Mu'Min wants the trial court to ask specific questions about each prospective juror's knowledge of the content of pretrial publicity. Such questions, Rehnquist admits, may help the defendant to use peremptory challenges more effectively. "But, since peremptory challenges are not required by the Constitution" (L.Ed.2d 505), Rehnquist says it therefore does not require content questions. Moreover, asking content questions may require questioning prospective jurors individually in order to avoid exposing one juror to the pretrial publicity known to another juror. Asking jurors to fill out written questionnaires also is unacceptable to the Court because they "would not give counsel or the court any exposure to the demeanor of the juror in the course of answering the content questions" (L.Ed.2d 505).

Content questions may also help the trial judge learn whether jurors can be believed when they assert that they have not formed an opinion about the defendant's guilt or innocence, Rehnquist notes. Nevertheless, failing to ask questions that may be helpful, according to the Court, is not such a serious error that it reaches the level of being an unconstitutional fault. "To be Constitutionally compelled," Rehnquist asserts, failure to ask questions must "render the defendant's trial fundamentally unfair" (L.Ed.2d 506).

The Court's earlier ruling in *Aldridge* requiring inquiry about racial prejudice in certain circumstances, Rehnquist says, was based on "a unanimous body of state court precedents" (L.Ed.2d 506). "On the subject of pretrial publicity, however, there is no similar consensus, or even weight of authority, favoring petitioner's [Mu'Min's] position," he points out (L.Ed.2d 506).

Emphasizing the Court's long-standing reliance on the trial judge's evaluation of prospective jurors, Rehnquist notes, "The judge of that court sits in the locale where the publicity is said to have had its effect, and brings to his evaluation of any such claim [of unconstitutional prejudice] his own perception of the depth and extent of news stories that might influence a juror" (L.Ed.2d 507).

Next Rehnquist distinguishes Mu'Min's trial from Leslie Irvin's, whose appeal resulted in the Court's 1961 ruling that jurors' unsupported assertions that they are not prejudiced may not be sufficient to declare them impartial (see *Irving* v. *Dowd* [1961]). Whereas in Irvin's case eight of the twelve jurors "had formed an opinion as to guilt," in Mu'Min's case eight of the twelve said "they had read or heard something about the case, but none . . . indicated that he had formed an opinion as to guilt" (L.Ed.2d 507).

Turning to *Patton* v. *Yount* (1984), Rehnquist notes, "A trial court's finding of juror impartiality may be overturned only for "'manifest error'" (L.Ed.2d 508). Again he distinguishes Mu'Min's trial from Irvin's. "The cases differ both in the kind of community in which the coverage took place and in the extent of media coverage," he writes (L.Ed.2d 508). In Washington, Rehnquist notes, "hundreds of murders" are committed each year, and the news reports, while "unfavorable" and "substantial," "did not contain the same sort of damaging information" as did those about Irvin, which "included details of . . . [his] confessions" and "numerous opinions as to his guilt" (L.Ed.2d 508). "Much of the pretrial publicity [before Mu'Min's trial]," Rehnquist says, "was aimed at the Department of Corrections and the criminal justice system in general" (L.Ed.2d 508).

Mu'Min supported his appeal in part with the American Bar Association's Standards for Criminal Justice, which require the trial judge, when, in the opinion of the court, there is a "'substantial possibility'" that jurors would have been exposed to considerable pretrial publicity, to ask each juror what he or she has read or heard about the case (L.Ed.2d 508). These standards, Rehnquist admits, assert that a juror can be challenged for cause "if he has been exposed to and remembers 'highly significant information' or 'other incriminating matters that may be inadmissible in evidence'" (L.Ed.2d 509).

The constitutional standard put forth in *Patton* (1984), Rehnquist points out, is different. There the Court said "'the relevant question is not whether the community remembered the case, but whether the jurors . . . had such fixed opinions that they could not judge impartially the guilt of the defendant'" (L.Ed.2d 509). Moreover, in *Irvin*, Rehnquist adds, the Court asserted that jurors do not "'have to be totally ignorant of the facts and issues involved' [*Irvin*, 722]" (L.Ed.2d 509).

Ruling

After affirming the sufficiency of the *voir dire* of Mu'Min's prospective jurors, Rehnquist concludes:

> For the reasons previously stated, we hold that the Due Process Clause of the Fourteenth Amendment does not reach this far [that is, so far as to "require questioning of individual jurors about facts or experiences that might have led to racial bias"], and that the *voir dire* examination conducted by the trial court in this case was consistent with that provision. The judgment of the Supreme Court of Virginia is accordingly affirmed. (L.Ed.2d 510)

Justice Sandra Day O'Connor writes a concurring opinion.

O'Connor opens her opinion with this assertion: "But the question we decide today is not whether the jurors who ultimately convicted Mu'Min had previously read or heard anything about the case" (L.Ed.2d 510). She continues, "Nor is the question whether jurors who read that Mu'Min had confessed to the murder should have been disqualified as a matter of law" (L.Ed.2d 510). As she sees it, "The only question before us is whether the trial court erred by crediting the assurances of eight jurors they could put aside what they had read or heard and render a fair verdict based on the evidence" (L.Ed.2d 510).

One essential consideration here, says O'Connor, is that the trial judge determined that the jurors' assurances of impartiality were credible. Although she admits that he "could have done more" to identify "the information to which each individual juror had been exposed," such an effort held little promise of extra value because, in part, "the trial judge himself was familiar with the potentially prejudicial publicity to which the jurors might have been exposed" (L.Ed.2d 511). Consequently, O'Connor feels the Sixth Amendment does not require asking content questions in order to form an adequate basis for a trial judge to evaluate the credibility of prospective jurors' assertions that, in spite of some exposure to pretrial publicity, they can remain impartial (L.Ed.2d 511).

Justice Thurgood Marshall writes a dissenting opinion.
Justices Harry A. Blackmun and John Paul Stevens join.

Not one to mince words, Marshall writes at the outset, "Today's decision turns a critical constitutional guarantee—the Sixth Amendment's right to an impartial jury—into a hollow formality" (L.Ed.2d 511). "The majority's reasoning is unacceptable," he continues. "A trial court cannot realistically assess the juror's impartiality without first establishing what the juror already has learned about the case" (L.Ed.2d 511).

The first point Marshall addresses is the extent of the pretrial publicity. "The majority . . . ," he writes, "seeks to minimize the impact of the pretrial publicity by arguing that it was not as extensive as in other cases that have come before the court" (L.Ed.2d 511). This observation, he contends, "is completely beside the point" (L.Ed.2d 511). "The simple fact of the matter is that *two-thirds* [emphasis Marshall's] of the persons on Mu'Min's jury admitted having read or heard about the case" (L.Ed.2d 511, 512).

After reviewing much of the publicity, Marshall notes, "Area residents following the controversy were told in no uncertain terms that their local officials [specifically, a local congressman and his opponent in the 1988 election, an opponent who was a member of the Virginia House of Delegates] were already convinced of Mu'Min's guilt" (L.Ed.2d 514).

Marshall phrases the main issue this way: "The question before us is whether, in light of the charged atmosphere that surrounded this case, the trial court was constitutionally obliged to ask the eight jurors who admitted exposure to pretrial publicity to identify precisely *what* [emphasis Marshall's] they had read, seen, or heard" (L.Ed.2d 514). After reviewing decisions related to the Court's protection of the Sixth Amendment guarantee to trial by an impartial jury, Marshall observes, "We have never indicated the type of *voir dire* that the trial court must undertake in order for its findings to merit this 'special deference' [of having the Court respect its decision that jurors were not prejudiced by pretrial publicity]" (L.Ed.2d 515).

As Marshall sees the issue, the trial court, in order to "merit this 'special deference'" by the Court for its conclusions about jurors' impartiality, "must do more than elicit a simple profession of open-mindedness before swearing that person into the jury" (L.Ed.2d 515). "The fact that the defendant bears the burden of establishing juror partiality . . . ," Marshall writes, "makes it all the more imperative that the defendant be entitled to meaningful examination at jury selection in order to elicit potential biases possessed by prospective jurors" (L.Ed.2d 516). He asserts, "Once a prospective juror admits exposure to pretrial publicity, content questioning must be part of the *voir dire* for at least three reasons" (L.Ed.2d 516).

The first reason, Marshall writes, is that "content questioning is necessary to determine whether the type and extent of publicity to which a prospective juror has been exposed would disqualify the juror as a matter of law"

(L.Ed.2d 516). "But unless the trial court asks a prospective juror exactly *what* [emphasis Marshall's] he had read or heard about a case," he continues, "the court will not be able to determine whether the juror comes under this class [of persons unconstitutionally prejudiced by the mere amount and intensity of pretrial publicity]" (L.Ed.2d 516).

Marshall moves on, "Second, even when pretrial publicity is not so extreme to make a juror's exposure to it *per se* disqualifying, content questioning is still essential to give legal depth to the trial court's finding of impartiality" (L.Ed.2d 517). He says the trial court, "by asking the prospective juror . . . what he had read or heard about the case and what corresponding impressions he has formed," would be "able to confirm that the impartiality that the juror professes is the same impartiality that the Sixth Amendment demands" (L.Ed.2d 517).

The third point stresses facilitation of "accurate trial court factfinding" (L.Ed.2d 517). Marshall asserts that "the precise content" of the pretrial publicity that prospective jurors acknowledge they are aware of is "essential to an accurate assessment of whether the prospective juror's profession of impartiality is believable" (L.Ed.2d 517). He contends that, if a trial court fails to explore the "precise content" of pretrial publicity a prospective juror admits to being aware of, then that judge should lose his "deference" upon appeal (L.Ed.2d 517).

Basically, Justice O'Connor's concurring opinion, Marshall says, argues that the trial judge in this case did not need to ask content questions because, being a resident of the geographical area the prospective jurors were selected from, he was thoroughly familiar with the pretrial publicity. He terms her position "perplexing," saying, "The judge's awareness of the contents of the extraordinarily prejudicial stories written about Mu'Min is not a substitute for knowledge of whether the *prospective jurors* [emphasis Marshall's] were aware of the content of these stories" (L.Ed.2d 518). He adds, "The trial judge's awareness of these stories makes even more inexcusable his unwillingness to seat the jurors without first ascertaining what they had read about the case" (L.Ed.2d 518).

The final point Marshall addresses is the majority's assertion that "content questioning should be rejected because it would unduly burden trial courts" (L.Ed.2d 519). To this he responds, "Numerous Federal Circuits and States have adopted the sorts of procedures for screening juror bias that the majority disparages as being excessively intrusive" (L.Ed.2d 519).

Marshall concludes, "The procedures undertaken in this case amounted to no more than the trial court going though the motions. I cannot accept that a defendant's Sixth Amendment right to an impartial jury means so little. I dissent" (L.Ed.2d 512).

He closes his opinion by reiterating his objection to the death penalty as "cruel and unusual punishment prohibited by the Eighth and Fourteenth Amendments" (L.Ed.2d 520).

Justice Anthony M. Kennedy writes a dissenting opinion.

The distinction between bias in individual jurors and bias in a jury as a whole constitutes the focus of Kennedy's dissent. He feels that this case is not concerned about the effect of massive pretrial publicity upon all prospective jurors, but rather only about the impartiality of those eight seated jurors who said they were familiar with at least some of the publicity. Marshall's dissent, he asserts, fails "to note the distinction between two quite different questions we have addressed. He appears to conflate the two categories of cases" (L.Ed.2d 521, 522).

Kennedy fears that instituting a rule disqualifying all prospective jurors who have been exposed "to a certain level of publicity" would result in virtual immunity from trial" for certain defendants in "celebrated cases" (L.Ed.2d 522).

The majority is also wrong in believing that the trial judge questioned the prospective jurors closely enough "for an informed ruling that the jurors were qualified to sit" (L.Ed.2d 522). Kennedy continues, "In my view, a juror's acknowledgement of exposure to pretrial publicity initiates a duty to assess that individual juror's ability to be impartial" (L.Ed.2d 522). Supporting Marshall, he writes, "Our willingness to accord substantial deference to a trial court's finding of juror impartiality rests on our expectation that the trial court will conduct a sufficient *voir dire* to determine the credibility of a juror professing to be impartial" (L.Ed.2d 522). Limiting his point and supporting O'Connor, he writes, "Any need for content questioning disappears if the trial judge evaluating juror impartiality assumes a worst-case hypothesis that the jurors have read or seen all of the pretrial publicity" (L.Ed.2d 523).

Kennedy's primary objection to the *voir dire* in this case is that, since the questions were asked to groups of four jurors, "individual jurors attested to their own impartiality by saying nothing" (L.Ed.2d 523). He adds, "In my judgment, findings of impartiality must be based on something more than the mere silence of the individual in response to questions asked *en masse*" (L.Ed.2d 523).

Significance

Not insignificant is the fact that four members of the Court asserted that, when prospective jurors acknowledge they are aware of pretrial publicity, then the trial judge must do more than accept a silent denial from them as a group when asked if their knowledge makes them prejudiced against the defendant. This dissent demonstrates some of the difficulties residing in the problems of how to know when jurors are telling the truth or when they are honestly unaware of their own prejudices.

It is also significant that the Court relied on law and not psychology to solve this problem. Although the Court disagreed on what trial judges must do to determine when prospective jurors are truthfully and creditably asserting their impartiality, no member questioned the judge's ability ultimately to make that determination without the help of special psychological techniques.

Perhaps the greatest significance, however, is the Court's ruling that the Due Process Clause of the Fourteenth Amendment does not require in all cases questioning individual jurors about facts or experiences that might have led to racial bias. On the one hand, the Court asserts that the possibility of racial prejudice against a black defendant charged with a violent crime against a white person is sufficiently real that the Fourteenth Amendment requires some inquiry be made into racial prejudice. On the other hand, the Court reaffirmed its long-standing opinion that the trial court retains great latitude in deciding what questions should be asked of prospective jurors. Thus, the Constitution, asserts the majority, does not require trial judges to ask questions about the content of prospective jurors' knowledge of pretrial publicity that is prejudicial against the defendant.

Appendix A

ALPHABETICAL LIST OF PRIMARY U.S. SUPREME COURT CASES RELATED TO FREE PRESS–FAIR TRIAL CONFLICT

1. *David D. Beck* v. *Washington*
   Docket No. 1962-40
   369 U.S. 541, 8 L.Ed.2d 98, 82 S.Ct. 955 (1962)

2. *Aaron Burr* v. *The United States of America*
   Docket No. 14692g, 25 Fed. Cas. 49 (1807)

3. *Noel Chandler and Robert Granger* v. *State of Florida*
   Docket No. 79-1260
   449 U.S. 560, 66 L.Ed.2d 740, 101 S.Ct. 802 (1981)

4. *Billie Sol Estes* v. *State of Texas*
   Docket No. 1965-256
   381 U.S. 532, 14 L.Ed.2d 543, 85 S.Ct. 1628 (1965)

5. *Gannett Co., Inc.* v. *Daniel A. DePasquale, et al.*
   Docket No. 77-1301
   443 U.S. 368, 61 L.Ed.2d 608, 99 S.Ct. 2898 (1979)

6. *Globe Newspaper Company* v. *Superior Court for the County of Norfolk*
   Docket No. 81-611
   457 U.S. 596, 73 L.Ed.2d 248, 102 S.Ct. 2613 (1982)

7. *James H. Holt* v. *The United States*
   Docket No. 1910-231
   218 U.S. 245, 54 L.Ed. 1021, 31 S.Ct. 2 (1910)

8. *Frederick Hopt* v. *People of the Territory of Utah*
   Docket No. 1887-1099
   120 U.S. 430, 30 L.Ed. 708, 7 S.Ct. 614 (1887)

9. *Leslie Irvin* v. *A. F. Dowd, Warden*
   Docket No. 1960-41
   366 U.S. 717, 6 L.Ed.2d 751, 81 S.Ct. 1639 (1961)

10. *Howard R. Marshall* v. *United States of America*
    Docket No. 1959-383
    360 U.S. 310, 3 L.Ed.2d 1250, 79 S.Ct. 1171 (1959)

11. *Clyde Mattox* v. *The United States*
    Docket No. 1892-1008
    146 U.S. 140, 36 L.Ed. 917, 13 S.Ct. 50 (1892)

12. *Dawud Majid Mu'Min* v. *Virginia*
    Docket No. 90-5193
    500 U.S. ___, 114 L.Ed.2d 493, 111 S.Ct. 1899 (1991)

13. *Jack Roland Murphy* v. *State of Florida*
    Docket No. 74-5116
    421 U.S. 794, 44 L.Ed.2d 589, 95 S.Ct. 2031 (1975)

14. *Nebraska Press Association, et al.* v. *Hugh Stuart, Judge,*
    District Court of Lincoln County, Nebraska, et al.
    Docket No. 75-817
    427 U.S. 539, 49 L.Ed.2d 683, 96 S.Ct. 2791 (1976)

15. *Ernest S. Patton, Superintendent, SCI-Camp Hill and Leroy S.*
    Zimmerman, Attorney General of Pennsylvania v. *Jon E. Yount*
    Docket No. 83-95
    467 U.S. 1025, 81 L.Ed.2d 847, 104 S.Ct. 2885 (1984)

16. *Press-Enterprise Company* v. *Superior Court of California,*
    Riverside County
    Docket No. 82-556
    464 U.S. 501, 78 L.Ed.2d 629, 104 S.Ct. 819 (1984)

17. *Press-Enterprise Company* v. *Superior Court of California*
    for the County of Riverside
    Docket No. 84-1560
    478 U.S. 1, 92 L.Ed.2d 1, 106 S.Ct. 2735 (1986)

18. *George Reynolds* v. *United States*
    Docket No. 1878-180
    98 U.S. 145, 25 L.Ed. 244, 8 Otto 10 (1878)

19. *Richmond Newspapers, Inc., et al.* v. *Commonwealth of Virginia*
    Docket No. 79-243
    448 U.S. 555, 65 L.Ed.2d 973, 100 S.Ct. 2814 (1980)

20. *Wilbert Rideau* v. *State of Louisiana*
    Docket No. 1963-630
    373 U.S. 723, 10 L.Ed.2d 663, 83 S.Ct. 1417 (1963)

21. *Samuel Shepherd and Walter Irvin* v. *State of Florida*
    Docket No. 1951-420
    341 U.S. 50, 95 L.Ed. 740, 71 S.Ct. 549 (1951)

22. *Samuel H. Sheppard* v. *E. L. Maxwell, Warden*
    Docket No. 1966-490
    384 U.S. 333, 16 L.Ed.2d 600, 86 S.Ct. 1507 (1966)

23. *James A. Simmons* v. *United States*
    Docket No. 1891-1296
    142 U.S. 148, 35 L.Ed. 968, 12 S.Ct. 171 (1891)

24. *August Spies* v. *The State of Illinois*
    Docket No. 1887-09
    123 U.S. 131, 31 L.Ed. 80, 85 S.Ct. 21 (1887)

25. *Fred Stroble* v. *State of California*
    Docket No. 1952-373
    343 U.S. 181, 96 L.Ed. 872, 72 S.Ct. 599 (1952)

26. *Robert F. Stroud* v. *The United States of America*
    Docket No. 1919-276
    251 U.S. 15, 64 L.Ed. 103, 40 S.Ct. 50 (1919)

27. *Charles Thiede* v. *People of the Territory of Utah*
    Docket No. 1895-633
    159 U.S. 510, 401 L.Ed. 237, 16 S.Ct. 62 (1895)

28. *The United States* v. *Thomas Reid and Edward Clements*
    53 U.S. 361, 13 L.Ed. 1023, 12 Howard 361 (1851)

29. *United States of America, ex rel. David Darcy* v. *Earl D. Handy, Warden of Bucks County Prison, Dr. Fred S. Baldi, Warden of the Western State Penitentiary, and Carl H. Fleckenstine, United States Marshal for the Middle District of Pennsylvania*
    Docket No. 1956-323
    351 U.S. 454, 100 L.Ed. 1331, 76 S.Ct. 965 (1956)

30. *Guy Waller, et al.* v. *State of Georgia*
    Docket Nos. 83-321 and 83-322
    467 U.S. 39, 81 L.Ed.2d 31, 104 S.Ct. 2210 (1984)

Appendix B

SUPPORTING CASES

Presented in this section are direct quotations from a carefully selected collection of important supporting cases cited in the primary ones. For the most part, the supporting cases focus on the topics of contempt, access, due process, a free press, and the definition of an impartial jury.

Adams v. *U.S.*, 317 U.S. 269, 87 L.Ed. 268, 63 S.Ct. 236 (1942).

But procedural devices rooted in experience were written into the Bill of Rights not as abstract rubrics in an elegant code but in order to assure fairness and justice before any person could be deprived of "life, liberty or property" (267). It is not asking too much that the burden of showing essential unfairness be sustained by him who claims such injustice and seeks to have the result set aside, and that it be sustained not as a matter of speculation but as a demonstrable reality (277).

Adamson v. *California*, 332 U.S. 46, 91 L.Ed. 1903, 67 S.Ct. 1672 (1947).

It is a settled law that the clause of the Fifth Amendment, protecting a person against being compelled to be a witness against himself, is not made effective by the Fourteenth Amendment as a protection against state action on the ground that freedom from testimonial compulsion is a right of national citizenship, or because it is a personal privilege or immunity secured by the Federal Constitution as one of the rights of man that are listed in the Bill of Rights (50, 51). As a matter of words, this [first sentence of the Fourteenth Amendment] leaves a state free to abridge, within the limits of the due process clause, the privileges and immunities flowing from state citizenship (52, 53). A right to a fair trial is a right admittedly protected by the due process clause of the Fourteenth Amendment (53). The purpose of due process is not to protect an accused against a proper conviction, but against an unfair conviction (57).

Aldridge v. *U.S.*, 283 U.S. 308, 75 L.Ed. 1054, 51 S.Ct. 470 (1931).

In accordance with the existing practice, the questions to the prospective jurors were put by the court and the court had a broad discretion as to the questions to be asked. The exercise of this discretion, and the restriction upon inquiries at the request of counsel, were subject to the essential demands of fairness (310). If the defendant was entitled to have the jurors asked whether they had any racial prejudice, by reason of the fact that the defendant was a negro, and the deceased a white man, which would prevent their giving a fair and impartial verdict, we cannot properly disregard the court's refusal merely because of the form in which the inquiry was presented (311).

Backus v. *Fort Street Union Depot,* 169 U.S. 557, 42 L.Ed. 853, 18 S.Ct. 445 (1898).

These are questions of procedure which do not enter into or form the basis of fundamental right. All that is essential is that some appropriate way, before some properly constituted tribunal, inquiry shall be made as to the amount of compensation, and when this has been provided there is that due process of law which is required by the Federal Constitution (569).

Baldwin v. *Kansas,* 129 U.S. 52, 32 L.Ed. 640, 9 S.Ct. 193 (1889).

The question whether the evidence in the case was sufficient to justify the verdict of the jury, and the question whether the Constitution of the State of Kansas was complied with or not . . . are not federal questions which this court can review (57).

Barker v. *Wingo,* 407 U.S. 514, 33 L.Ed.2d 101, 92 S.Ct. 2182 (1972).

The right to a speedy trial is generically different from any of the other rights enshrined in the Constitution for the protection of the accused. In addition to the general concern that all accused persons be treated according to decent and fair procedures, there is a societal interest in providing a speedy trial which exists separate from, and at times in opposition to, the interests of the accused (519). A second difference . . . is that deprivation of the right may work to the accused's advantage (521). Finally . . . the right to a speedy trial is a more vague concept than other procedural rights (521). We can . . . identify some of the factors courts should assess in determining whether a particular defendant has been deprived of his right . . . : Length of delay, the reason for the delay, the defendant's assertion of his right, and prejudice to the defendant (530).

Barron v. *Baltimore,* 32 U.S. 243, 8 L.Ed. 672, 7 Peter 243 (1833).

The plaintiff in error [John Barron] contends that it [his writ in error] comes within that clause in the Fifth Amendment to the Constitution which inhibits the taking of private property for public use without just compensation. He insists that this amendment, being in favor of the liberty of the citizen, ought to be so construed as to restrain the legislative power of a State as well as that of the United States (247). The counsel for the plaintiff in error insists that the Constitution was intended to secure the people of the several States against the undue exercise of power by their respective

State governments (248). If the original Constitution, in the ninth and tenth sections of the first article, draws this plan and marked the line of discrimination between the limitations it imposes on the powers of the general government and on those of the States; if in every inhibition intended to act on State power, words are employed which directly express that intent, some strong reasonmust be assigned for departing from this safe and judicious course in framing the amendments, before that departure can be assumed (249). We search in vain for that reason (249). Had the framers of these [ten] amendments intended them to be limitations on the powers of the State governments they would have imitated the framers of the original Constitution and have expressed that intention (250). These amendments contain no expression indicating an intention to apply them to the State governments. This court cannot so apply them (250). This court, therefore, has no jurisdiction in the cause, and it is dismissed (251).

Benton v. *Maryland*, 395 U.S. 784, 33 L.Ed.2d 707, 89 S.Ct. 2056 (1969).

We hold that the Double Jeopardy Clause of the Fifth Amendment is applicable to the States through the Fourteenth Amendment (787). Once it is decided that a particular Bill of Rights guarantee is "fundamental to the American scheme of justice," the same constitutional standards apply against both the state and Federal Government (795).

Branzburg v. *Hayes*, 408 U.S. 665, 33 L.Ed.2d 626, 92 S.Ct. 2646 (1972).

The issue in these cases is whether requiring newsmen to appear and testify before state or federal grand juries abridges the freedom of speech and press guaranteed by the First Amendment. We hold that it does not (667).

Bridges v. *California*, 314 U.S. 252, 86 L.Ed. 192, 62 S.Ct. 190 (1941).

The assumption that respect for the judiciary can be won by shielding judges from published criticism wrongly appraises the character of American public opinion. For it is a prized American privilege to speak one's mind, although not always with perfect good taste on all public institutions. And an enforced silence, however limited, solely in the name of preserving the dignity of the bench, would probably engender resentment, suspicion, and contempt much more than it would enhance respect (270–271). Legal trials are not like elections, to be won through the use of the meeting-hall, the radio, and the newspaper. But we cannot start with the assumption that . . . it is necessary for judges to have a contempt power by which they can close all channels of public expression to all matters which touch upon pending cases (271).

Brown v. *Mississippi*, 297 U.S. 278, 80 L.Ed. 682, 56 S.Ct. 461 (1936).

But the freedom of the State in establishing its policy is the freedom of constitutional government and is limited by the requirement of due process of law. Because a State may dispense with a jury trial, it does not follow that it may substitute trial by ordeal (286).

Buchalter v. *N.Y.,* 319 U.S. 427, 87 L.Ed. 1492, 67 S.Ct. 1129 (1943).

The due process clause of the Fourteenth Amendment requires that action by a state through any of its agencies must "be consistent with the fundamental principles of liberty and justice which lie at the base of our civil and political institutions, which are not infrequently designated as 'law of the land'" (429) [quoting in part from *Herbert* v. *Louisiana,* 272 U.S. 312 (1926)]. But the Amendment does not draw unto itself the provisions of state constitutions or state laws. It leaves the states free to enforce their criminal laws under such statutory provisions and common law doctrines as they deem appropriate (429–430).

Burr v. *U.S.,* 8 U.S. 455, 2 L.Ed. 677, 4 Cranch 455 (1807).

[*Note:* The material referenced in this citation is not the famous Marshall opinion describing an impartial juror. Instead, the documents referred to here include the following: affidavits of James Wilson, Commander in Chief of the U.S. Army, and of William Eaton, Attorney; depositions of James Lowry Donaldson and Lieutenant William Wilson; and an "Opinion on the Motion to Introduce Certain Evidence in the Trial of Aaron Burr for Treason, Pronounced Monday, August 31, 1807."]

Cassell v. *Texas,* 339 U.S. 282, 94 L.Ed. 839, 70 S.Ct. 629 (1950).

The statements of the jury commissioners that they chose only whom they knew, and that they knew no eligible Negroes in an area where Negroes made up so large a proportion of the population, prove intentional exclusion that is discrimination in violation of petitioner's constitutional rights (290).

Central Land Co. v. *Laidley,* 159 U.S. 103, 40 L.Ed. 91, 16 S.Ct. 80 (1895).

When the parties have been fully heard in the regular course of judicial proceedings, an erroneous decision of a state court does not deprive the unsuccessful party of his property without due process of law, within the 14th Amendment of the Constitution of the United States (112).

Chambers v. *Florida,* 309 U.S. 227, 84 L.Ed. 716, 60 S.Ct. 472 (1940).

From the popular hatred . . . of violations of the "law of the land" evolved the fundamental idea that no man's life, liberty or property be forfeited as criminal punishment for violation of that law until there had been a change fairly made and fairly tried in a public tribunal free of prejudice, passion, excitement, and tyrannical power (236, 237). This requirement—of conforming to fundamental standards of procedure in criminal trials—was made operative against the States by the Fourteenth Amendment (238).

Chappell v. *Bradshaw,* 128 U.S. 132, 32 L.Ed. 369, 9 S.Ct. 40 (1888).

To give this court jurisdiction to review the judgment of a state court under section 709 of the Revised Statutes, because of the denial by a state court of any title, right, privilege or immunity claimed under the Constitution or any treaty of the United States, it must appear on the record that such title, right, privilege, or immunity was "specially set up or claimed" at the proper time and in the proper way (132).

Connors v. *U.S.,* 158 U.S. 408, 39 L.Ed. 1033, 15 S.Ct. 951 (1895).

It is quite true, as suggested by the accused, that he was entitled to be tried by an impartial jury, that is, by jurors who had no bias or prejudice that would prevent them from returning a verdict according to the law and evidence. It is equally true that a suitable inquiry is permissible in order to ascertain whether the juror had any bias, opinion, or prejudice that would affect or control the fair determination by him of the issues to be tried. That inquiry is conducted under the supervision of the court, and a great deal must, of necessity, be left to its sound discretion. This is the rule in civil cases, and the same rule must be applied in criminal cases (413).

Costello v. *U.S.,* 350 U.S. 359, 362, 100 L.Ed. 397, 76 S.Ct. 406 (1956).

The basic purpose of the English grand jury was to provide a fair method for instituting criminal proceedings against persons believed to have committed crime (362).

Craig v. *Harney,* 331 U.S. 367, 91 L.Ed. 1546, 67 S.Ct. 1249 (1946).

A trial is a public event. What transpires in the courtroom is public property. If a transcript of the court proceedings had been published, we suppose none would claim that the judge could punish the publisher for contempt. Those who see and hear what transpires can report with impunity. There is no special prerequisite of the judiciary which enables it, as distinguished from other institutions of democratic government, to suppress, edit, or censor events which transpire in proceedings before it (374).

Davidson v. *New Orleans,* 96 U.S. 97, 24 L.Ed. 616, 6 Otto 97 (1878).

The equivalent of the phrase "due process of law," according to Lord Coke, is found in the words "law of the land," in the Great Charter [Magna Carta] (101). It must be confessed, however, that the constitutional meaning or value of the phrase "due process of law," remains to-day without that satisfactory precision of definition which judicial decisions have given to nearly all the other guarantees of personal rights found in the Constitutions of the several States and of the United States (101, 102). It is not possible to hold that . . . a fair trial in a court of justice, according to the modes or proceedings applicable to such case, that he [appellant] has been deprived of that property without due process of law (105). The part complaining here appeared, and had a full and fair hearing in the court of the first instance, and afterwards in the Supreme Court. If this be not due process of law, then the words can have no definite meaning as used in the Constitution (105, 106). [From Justice Bradly's separate opinion:] We are entitled, under the XIV Amendment, not only to see that there is some process of law, but "due process of law" . . . and that, in judging, what is "due process of law" . . . [a process] is found to be suitable or admissible in the special case it will be adjudged to be "due process of law;" but if found to be arbitrary, oppressive and unjust, it may be declared to be not "due process of law" (107).

Dennis v. *U.S.,* 339 U.S. 162, 94 L.Ed. 734, 70 S.Ct. 519 (1950).

In fact both the Wood and Fraizer Cases this Court stressed that while impaneling a jury, the Trial Court has a serious duty to determine the question of actual bias, and a broad discretion in its ruling on challenges therefore. We reaffirm those principles. In exercising its discretion, the trial court must be zealous to protect the rights of an accused (168).

Duncan v. *Louisiana,* 391 U.S. 145, 20 L.Ed.2d 491, 88 S.Ct. 1444 (1968).

Because we believe that trial by jury in criminal cases is fundamental to the American scheme of justice, we hold that the Fourteenth Amendment guarantees a right of jury trial in all criminal cases which—were they to be tried in a federal court—would come within the Sixth Amendment's guarantee (149). *Maxwell* v. *Dow,* 176 U.S. 581 (1900) held that no provision of the Bill of Rights applied to the States—a proposition long since repudiated (155).

FBI v. *Abramson,* 456 U.S. 615, 72 L.Ed.2d 376, 102 S.Ct. 2054 (1982).

The sole question in this case is whether information contained in records compiled for law enforcement purposes loses that exempt status when it is incorporated into records compiled for purposes other than law enforcement (618). We reject the argument that the legitimate interests in protecting information from disclosure under Exemption 7 are satisfied by other exemptions when a record has been recompiled for a non-law-enforcement purpose (629). The reasons for a Section 7 exemption may well remain intact even though information in a law enforcement record is recompiled in another document for a non-law-enforcement function (630). The statutory language is reasonably construable to protect that part of an otherwise non-exempt compilation which essentially reproduces and is substantially the equivalent of all or part of an earlier record made for law enforcement uses (625).

Fraizer v. *U.S.,* 335 U.S. 497, 93 L.Ed. 187, 69 S.Ct. 201 (1948).

In each case a broad discretion and duty reside in the court to see that the jury as finally selected is subject to no solid basis of objection on the score of impartiality (198).

Frank v. *Mangum,* 237 U.S. 309, 59 L.Ed. 969, 25 S.Ct. 528 (1915).

Mere errors in point of law, however serious, committed by a criminal court in the exercise of its jurisdiction over a case properly submitted to it cannot be reviewed by habeas corpus (326). The due process of law guaranteed by the 14th Amendment has regard to substance of right, and not to matters of form or procedure (332). This familiar phrase [due process] does not mean that the operations of the state government shall be conducted without error or fault in any particular case, nor that the Federal courts may substitute their judgment for that of the state courts, or exercise any general review over their proceedings, but only that the fundamental rights of the prisoner shall not be taken from him arbitrarily or without the right to be heard according to the usual course of law in such cases (334, 335). [Holmes in dissent:] Whatever disagreement there may be as to the scope of the phrase "due process of law," there can be no doubt that it embraces the fundamental conception of a fair trial, with opportunity to be heard (347). Any judge who has sat with juries knows that in spite of forms they are extremely likely to be impregnated by the environing atmosphere (349).

Gideon v. *Wainwright*, 372 U.S. 335, 9 L.Ed.2d 799, 83 S.Ct. 792 (1963).

Those guarantees of the Bill of Rights which are fundamental safeguards of liberty immune from federal abridgment are equally protected against state invasion by the Due Process Clause of the Fourteenth Amendment (341). A provision of the Bill of Rights which is "fundamental and essential to a fair trial" is made obligatory upon the States by the Fourteenth Amendment (342). The right of one charged with crime to counsel may not be deemed important in some countries, but it is in ours. From the very beginning, our state and national constitutions and laws have laid great emphasis on procedural and substantive safeguards designed to assure fair trials before impartial tribunals in which every defendant stands equal before the law. This noble ideal cannot be realized if the poor man charged with crime has to face his accusers without a lawyer to assist him (344).

Gitlow v. *New York*, 268 U.S. 652, 69 L.Ed. 1138, 45 S.Ct. 625 (1923).
For present purposes we may and do assume that freedom of speech and of the press—which are protected by the 1st Amendment from abridgment by Congress—are among the fundamental personal rights and "liberties" protected by the due process clause of the 14th Amendment from impairment by the states (666).

Ham v. *South Carolina*, 409 U.S. 524, 35 L.Ed. 46, 93 S.Ct. 848 (1973).

The Fourteenth Amendment required the judge in this case to interrogate the jurors upon the subject of racial prejudice. The essential fairness required by the Due Process Clause of the Fourteenth Amendment requires that under the facts shown by this record the petitioner be permitted to have the jurors interrogated on the issue of racial bias (409).

Hayes v. *Missouri*, 120 U.S. 68, 30 L.Ed. 578, 7 S.Ct. 350 (1887).

The right to a trial by an impartial jury . . . implies that the jurors shall be free from all bias for or against the accused (69, 70). Impartiality requires not only freedom from any bias against the accused, but also from prejudice against his prosecution. Between him and the State the scales are to be evenly held (70). The right to challenge is the right to reject, not to select a juror. If from those who remain, an impartial jury is obtained, the constitutional right of the accused is maintained (71). The accused cannot complain if he is still tried by an impartial jury. He can demand nothing more (71).

Herbert v. *Louisiana,* 272 U.S. 312, 71 L.Ed. 270, 47 S.Ct. 103 (1926).

The due process of law clause in the 14th Amendment does not take up the statutes of several states and make them the test of what it requires; nor does it enable this court to revise the decisions of state courts on the questions of state law. What it does require is that state action, whether through one agency or another, shall be consistent with the fundamental principles of liberty and justice which lie at the base of all our civil and political institutions and not infrequently are designated as "law of the land." Those principles are applicable alike in all the states and do not depend upon or vary with local legislation (316, 317).

Hurtado v. *California,* 110 U.S. 516, 28 L.Ed. 232, 4 S.Ct. 111 (1884).

The proposition of law we are asked to affirm is that an indictment of prosecution or presentment by a grand jury, as known to the common law of England, is essential to that "due process of law," when applied to prosecutions for felonies, which is secured and guaranteed by this provision [14th Amendment] of the Constitution of the United States, and which accordingly it is forbidden to the States respectively to dispense with in the administration of criminal law (520). The question . . . involves a consideration of what additional restrictions upon the legislative policy of States have been imposed by the 14th Amendment to the Constitution of the United States (520). If in the adoption of that [14th] Amendment it had been part of its purpose to perpetuate the institution of the grand jury in all the States, it would have embodied, as did the 5th Amendment, express declarations to that effect. Due process in the latter refers to that law of the land which derives its authority from the legislative powers conferred upon Congress by the Constitution of the United States, exercised within the limits therein prescribed, and interpreted according to the principles of the common law. In the 14th Amendment, by parity of reason, it refers to that law of the land in each State, which derives its authority from the inherent and reserved powers of the State exerted within the limits of those fundamental principles of liberty and justice which lie at the base of all our civil and political institutions (535). Arbitrary power . . . is not law (535). Any legal proceeding enforced by public authority . . . in furtherance of the general public good, which regards and preserves these principles of liberty and justice, must be held to be due process of law (537). By these principles, we are unable to say that the substitution for a presentment or indictment by a grand jury of the proceeding by information, after examination and commitment by a magistrate, certifying to the probable guilt of the defendant, with the right on his part to the aid of counsel, and to the cross examination of the witnesses produced for the prosecution, is not due process of law (538).

Klopfer v. *North Carolina,* 386 U.S. 213, 18 L.Ed.2d 1, 87 S.Ct. 988 (1967).

We hold here that the right to a speedy trial is as fundamental as any of the rights secured by the Sixth Amendment (223).

Landmark Communications v. *Virginia,* 435 U.S. 829, 56 L.Ed.2d 1, 98 S.Ct. 1535 (1978).

The operations of the courts and the judicial conduct of judges are matters of utmost public concern (839). The public interest is not served by discussion of unfounded allegations of misconduct which defames honest judges and serves only to demean the administration of justice (840). Neither the Commonwealth's interest in protecting the reputation of its judges, nor its interest in maintaining the institutional integrity of its courts is sufficient to justify the subsequent punishment of speech at issue here (841). Speech cannot be punished when the purpose is simply "to protect the court as a mystical entity or the judges as individual or as anointed priests set apart from the community" (842). Properly applied the [clear and present danger] test requires a court to make its own inquiry into the imminence and magnitude of the danger said to flow from the particular utterance and then to balance the character of the evil, as well as its likelihood, against the need for free and unfettered expression (842, 843). It is true that some risk of injury to the judge under inquiry, to the system of justice, or to the operation of the Judicial Review Commission may be posed by premature disclosure, but the danger . . . here falls far short of [clear and present] (845). We conclude that the publication Virginia seeks to punish under its statute lies near the core of the First Amendment, and the Commonwealth's interests advanced by the imposition of criminal sanctions are insufficient to justify the actual and potential encroachments on freedom of speech and of the press which follow therefrom (838).

Leeper v. *Texas,* 139 U.S. 462, 35 L.Ed. 225, 11 S.Ct. 577 (1891).

That to give this court jurisdiction to review the judgement of a state court under section 709 of the Revised Statutes, because of the denial by the state court of any right, title, privilege or immunity claimed under the Constitution, or any treaty or statute of the United States, it must appear on the record that such title, right, privilege or immunity was specially set up or claimed at the proper time and in the proper way (467). By the Fourteenth Amendment the powers of the States in dealing with crime within their borders are not limited, except that no State can deprive particular persons, or classes of persons, of equal and impartial justice under the law; that law in its regular course of administration through courts of justice is due process, and when secured by the law of the State the constitutional requirement is satisfied; and that due process is so secured by laws operating on all alike, and not subjecting the individual to the arbitrary exercise of the powers of government unrestrained by the established principles of private right and distributive justice (467, 468).

Lisenba v. *California*, 314 U.S. 219, 86 L.Ed. 166, 62 S.Ct. 280 (1941).

[For significance, see Background section of *Stroble* v. *California* (1952).]

Malloy v. *Hogan*, 378 U.S. 1, 12 L.Ed.2d 653, 84 S.Ct. 1489 (1964).

We hold today that the Fifth Amendment's exception from compulsory self-incrimination is also protected by the Fourteenth Amendment against abridgment by the States (377). The Fourteenth Amendment secures against state invasion the same privilege that the Fifth Amendment guarantees against federal infringement—the right of a person to remain silent unless he chooses to speak in the unfettered exercise of his own will, and to suffer not penalty, as held in *Twining* [which this case now overrules], for such silence (378).

Mapp v. *Ohio*, 367 U.S. 643, 6 L.Ed.2d 1081, 81 S.Ct. 1684 (1961).

Since the Fourth Amendment's right of privacy has been declared enforceable against the States through the Due Process Clause of the Fourteenth, it is enforceable against them by the same sanction of exclusion as is used against the Federal Government (655). Moreover, our holding that the exclusionary rule is an essential part of both the Fourth and Fourteenth Amendments . . . makes very good sense (367).

Maryland v. *Baltimore Radio Show*, 338 U.S. 912, 94 L.Ed. 562, 70 S.Ct. 252 (1950).

One of the demands of a democratic society is that the public should know what goes on in courts by being told by the press what happens there, to the end that the public may judge whether our system of criminal justice is fair and right (920).

Miami Herald v. *Tornillo*, 418 U.S. 241, 41 L.Ed.2d 730, 94 S.Ct. 2831 (1974).

A compulsion to publish that which "reason" tells them not be published is unconstitutional. A responsible press is an undoubtedly desirable goal, but press responsibility is not mandated by the Constitution and like many other virtues it cannot be legislated (256). A newspaper is more than a passive receptacle or conduit for news, comment, and advertising. The choice of material to go into a newspaper, and the decisions made as to limitations on the size and content of the paper, and treatment of public issues and public officials—whether fair or unfair—constitutes the exercise of editorial control and judgment (258).

Milligan, Ex Parte, 71 U.S. 2, 18 L.Ed. 281, 4 Wallace 2 (1866).

It is the birthright of every American citizen, when charged with a crime, to be tried and punished according to law (L.Ed. 295). The great minds of the country have differed on the correct interpretation to be given to various provisions of the Federal Constitution; . . . but until recently no one ever doubted that the right of trial by jury was fortified in the organic law against the power of attack. It is now assaulted; but if ideas can be expressed in words, and language has any meaning, this right—one of the most valuable in a free country—is preserved to every one accused of crime who is not attached to the army or navy or militia in actual service (L.Ed. 296). All other persons, citizens of the States where the courts are open, if charged with a crime, are guaranteed the inestimable privilege of trial by jury. This privilege is a vital principle, underlying the whole administration of criminal justice; it is not held by sufferance, and cannot be frittered away on any plea of state or political necessity (L.Ed. 296).

Milwaukee Electric Railway & Light Co. v. *Wisconsin, ex. rel. city of Milwaukee,* 252 U.S. 100, 64 L.Ed. 476, 40 S.Ct. 306 (1920).

The Fourteenth Amendment does not, in guaranteeing equal protection of the laws, assure uniformity of judicial decisions . . . any more than, in guaranteeing due process, it assures immunity from judicial error (106).

Mima Queen v. *Hepburn,* 11 U.S. 290, 3 L.Ed. 348, 7 Cranch 290 (1813).

It is certainly much to be desired that jurors should enter upon their duties with minds entirely free from every prejudice. Perhaps on general and public questions it is scarcely possible to avoid receiving some prepossessions and where a private right depends on such a question the difficulty of obtaining jurors whose minds are entirely uninfluenced by opinions previously formed is undoubtedly considerable. Yet they ought to be superior to every exception, they ought to stand perfectly indifferent between the parties and although the bias which was acknowledged in this case might not perhaps have been so strong as to render it positively improper to allow the juror to be sworn on the jury, yet it was desirable to submit the case to those who felt no bias either way, and therefore the court exercised a sound discretion in not permitting him to be sworn (297, 298).

Miranda v. *State of Arizona,* 384 U.S. 436, 16 L.Ed.2d 694, 86 S.Ct. 265 (1966).

The prosecution may not use statements . . . stemming from custodial interrogation of the defendant unless it demonstrates the use of procedural safeguards effective to secure the privilege against self-incrimination. By custodial interrogation, we mean questioning initiated by law enforcement officers after a person has been taken into custody or otherwise deprived of his freedom of action in any significant way. As for the procedural safeguards to be employed . . . the following measures are required. Prior to any questioning, the person must be warned that he has a right to remain silent, that any statement he does make may be used as evidence against him, and that he has a right to the presence of an attorney, either retained or appointed. The defendant may waive effectuation of these rights, provided the waiver is made voluntarily, knowingly and intelligently.

Missouri v. *Lewis,* 101 U.S. 22, 25 L.Ed. 989, 11 Otto 22 (1880).

The 14th Amendment does not profess to procure to all persons in the United States the benefit of the same laws and the same remedies. Great diversity in these respects may exist in two states separated by only an imaginary line (31).

Mooney v. *Holohan,* 294 U.S. 103, 79 L.Ed. 791, 55 S.Ct. 340 (1935).

That requirement [of due process], in safeguarding the liberty of the citizen against deprivation through action of the State, embodies the fundamental conceptions of justice which lie at the base of our civil and political institutions. It is a requirement that cannot be deemed to be satisfied by mere notice and hearing if the State has contrived a conviction through the pretence of a trial which in truth is but used as a means of depriving a defendant of liberty through a deliberate deception of court and jury by the presentation of testimony known to be perjured (112).

Moore v. *Dempsey,* 261 U.S. 87, 67 L.Ed. 543, 43 S.Ct. 265 (1923).

But it is the case that the whole proceeding is a mask—that counsel, jury, and judge were swept to the fatal end by an irresistible wave of public passion, and that the state courts failed to correct the wrong—[then] neither perfection in the machinery for correction nor the possibility that the trial court and counsel saw no other way of avoiding an immediate outbreak of the mob can prevent this court from securing the petitioners their constitutional rights (90).

Murchison, In Re, 349 U.S. 133, 99 L.Ed. 942, 75 S.Ct. 623 (1955).

A fair trial in a fair tribunal is a basic requirement of due process. Fairness of course requires an absence of actual bias in the trial of cases. But our system has always endeavored to prevent the probability of unfairness (136).

Murry v. *Hoboken,* 59 U.S. 272, 25 L.Ed. 372, 18 Howard 272 (1856).

The words "due process of law," were undoubtedly intended to convey the same meaning as the words "by the law of the land," in Magna Carta. Lord Coke . . . says they mean due process of law. The constitutions which had been adopted by the several States before the formation of the federal Constitution . . . generally contained the words, "but by the judgment of his peers, or the law of the land" (276). The Constitution contains no description of those processes which it [due process] was intended to allow or forbid. It does not even declare what principles are to be applied to ascertain whether it be due process. It is manifest that it was not left to the legislative power to enact any process which might be devised. The article is a restraint on the legislative as well as on the executive and judicial powers of government (276). For though "due process of law" generally implies and includes . . . regular allegations to some settled course of judicial proceedings, yet this is not universally true (280).

Nye v. *U.S.*, 313 U.S. 33, 85 L.Ed. 1172, 61 S.Ct. 810 (1941).

The [U.S.] Act of March 2, 1831 [Section 268 of the Judicial Code, 28 U.S.C.A., Section 385] gave the court no power to punish a newspaper publisher for contempt for publishing an "offensive" article relative to a pending case (50). It is not sufficient that the misbehavior charged has some direct relation to the work of the court. "Near" in this context [of the act] juxtaposed to "presence," suggests physical proximity, not relevancy (49).

Offutt v. *United States*, 348 U.S. 11, 99 L.Ed. 11, 75 S.Ct. 11 (1954).

Therefore, justice must satisfy the appearance of justice (14).

Oklahoma Publishing Co. v. *District Court*, 430 U.S. 308, 51 L.Ed.2d 355, 97 S.Ct. 1045 (1977).

The First and Fourteenth Amendments will not permit a state court to prohibit the publication of widely disseminated information obtained at court proceedings which were in fact open to the public (310).

Oliver, In Re, 333 U.S. 257, 92 L.Ed. 682, 68 S.Ct. 499 (1948).

Whatever other benefits the guarantee to an accused that his trial be conducted in public may confer upon our society, the guarantee has always been recognized as a safeguard against any attempt to employ our courts as instruments of persecution. The knowledge that every criminal trial is subject to contemporaneous review in the forum of public opinion is an effective restraint on possible abuse of judicial power (270). We further hold that failure to afford the petitioner a reasonable opportunity to defend himself against the charge of false and evasive swearing was a denial of due process of law. A person's right to reasonable notice of a charge against him, and an opportunity to be heard in his defense—a right to his day in court—are basic in our system of jurisprudence; and these rights, include as a minimum, a right to examine the witnesses against him, to offer testimony, and to be represented by counsel (273). It is the "law of the land" that no man's life, liberty or property shall be forfeited as a punishment until there has been a charge fairly made and fairly tried in a public tribunal (278).

Palko v. *Connecticut*, 302 U.S. 319, 82 L.Ed. 288, 58 S.Ct. 149 (1937).

We have said that in appellant's view the Fourteenth Amendment is to be taken as embodying the prohibition of the Fifth. His thesis is even broader. Whatever would be a violation of the original bill of rights (Amendments 1 to 8) if done by the federal government is now equally unlawful by force of the Fourteenth Amendment if done by a state. There is no such general rule (323). On the other hand, the due process clause of the Fourteenth Amendment may make it unlawful for a state to abridge by its statutes the freedom of speech which the First Amendment safeguards against encroachment by the Congress (324). Immunities that are valid as against the federal government by force of the specific pledges of particular amendments have been found to be implicit in the concept of *ordered liberty* [emphasis added], and thus, through the Fourteenth Amendment, become valid as against the states (324, 325). There emerges the perception of a rationalizing principle which gives to discrete instances a proper order and coherence. The right to trial by jury and the immunity from prosecution except as the result of an indictment may have value and importance. Even, so they are not of the very essence of a scheme of ordered liberty. To abolish them is not to violate a "principle of justice so rooted in the traditions and conscience of our people as to be ranked as fundamental" [*Snyder* v. *Massachusetts* (1934)] (325). We reach a different plane of social and moral values when we pass to the privileges and immunities that have been taken over from the earlier articles of the federal bill of rights and brought within the Fourteenth Amendment by a process of absorption. If the Fourteenth Amendment has absorbed them, the process of absorption has had its source in the belief that neither liberty nor justice would exist if they were sacrificed (326). Our survey of cases serves, we think, to justify the statement that the dividing line between them, if not unfaltering throughout its course, has been true for the most part to a unifying principle. Is that kind of double jeopardy to which the statute has subjected him a hardship so acute and shocking that our polity will not endure it? Does it violate those "Fundamental principles of liberty and justice which lie at the base of all our civil and political institutions"? [*Herbert* v. *Louisiana,* 272 U.S. 312 (1926)]. The answer surely must be "no" (328).

Patterson v. *Colorado,* 205 U.S. 454, 51 L.Ed. 879, 27 S.Ct. 556 (1907).

A publication likely to reach the eye of a jury, declaring a witness in a pending cause a perjurer, would be none the less a contempt that it was true. It would tend to obstruct the administration of justice, because even a correct conclusion is not to be reached in that way, if our system of trials is to be maintained. The theory of our system is that the conclusions to be reached in a case will be induced only by evidence and argument in open court, and not by any outside influence, whether of private talk or public print (462).

Pennekamp v. *Florida,* 328 U.S. 331, 90 L.Ed. 1295, 66 S.Ct. 1029 (1945).

We must, therefore, weigh the right of free speech . . . against the danger of the coercion and intimidation of court (346). It does not follow that public comment of every character upon pending trials or legal proceedings may be as free as a similar comment after complete disposal of the litigation (346). Courts must have the power to protect the interests of prisoners and litigants before them from unseemly efforts to pervert judicial action (347). Freedom of discussion should be given the widest range compatible with the essential requirement of the fair and orderly administration of justice (347). It is suggested . . . a judge may be influenced by a desire to placate the accusing newspaper to retain public esteem and secure reelection presumably at the cost of unfair rulings against an accused. For this [a clear and present danger to justice] to follow, there must be a judge of less than ordinary fortitude without friends or support or a powerful and vindictive newspaper, bent upon a rule or ruin policy, and a public unconcerned with or uninterested in the truth or the protection of their judicial institutions. (349).

Perez v. *U.S.,* 22 U.S. 579, 6 L.Ed. 165, 9 Wheat 579 (1824).

We think . . . the law has invested courts of justice with the authority to discharge a jury from giving any verdict, whenever in their opinion . . . there is a manifest necessity for the act, or the ends of public justice would otherwise be defeated. They are to exercise a sound discretion on the subject; and it is impossible to define all the circumstances which would render it proper to interfere. To be sure, the power ought to be used with the greatest caution . . . and, in capital cases especially, courts should be extremely careful how they interfere with any of the chances of life, in favor of the prisoner. But, after all, they have the right to order the discharge: and the security which the public have for the faithful, sound and conscientious exercise of this discretion, rests in this, as in other cases, upon the responsibility of the judges under their oaths of office (580).

Powell v. *Alabama,* 287 U.S. 45, 77 L.Ed. 158, 53 S.Ct. 55 (1932). [Known as the *Scottsboro* case]

The right to the aid of counsel is of this fundamental character (68). It has never been doubted by this court, or any other, so far as we know, that notice and hearing are preliminary steps essential to the passing of an enforceable judgment, and that they, together with a legally competent tribunal having jurisdiction of the case, constitute basic elements of the constitutional requirement of due process of law (68). The right to be heard would be, in many cases, of little avail if it did not comprehend the right to be heard by counsel (68, 69). The failure of the trial court to make an effective appointment of counsel was likewise a denial of due process within the meaning of the Fourteenth Amendment (71).

Rawlings v. *Georgia,* 201 U.S. 638, 50 L.Ed. 899, 26 S.Ct. 560 (1908).

At the argument before us the not uncommon misconception seemed to prevail that the requirement of due process of law took up the special provisions of the state Constitutions and laws into the 14th Amendment for the purposes of the case, so that this court would revise the decision of state court that the local provisions had been complied with. This is a mistake. If the state Constitution and laws as construed by the state court are consistent with the 14th Amendment, we can go no further. The only question for us is whether a state could authorize the course of proceedings adopted, if that course were prescribed by its Constitution in express terms (639, 640). The exclusion was not the result of race or class prejudice. Even when persons liable to jury duty under the state law are excluded, it is no ground for challenge to the array, if a sufficient number of unexceptional persons are present. But if the state law itself should exclude certain classes on the bona fide ground that it was for the good of the community that their regular work should not be interrupted, there is nothing in the 14th Amendment to prevent it (640).

Ristaino v. *Ross,* 424 U.S. 589, 47 L.Ed.2d 258, 96 S.Ct. 1017 (1976).

The Constitution does not always entitle a defendant to have questions posed during voir dire specifically directed to matters that conceivably might prejudice veniremen against him (594).

Rosales-Lopez v. *U.S.,* 451 U.S. 182, 68 L.Ed.2d 22, 101 S.Ct. 1629 (1981).

There is no constitutional presumption of juror bias for or against members of any particular racial or ethnic group (190). Only when there are more substantial indications of the likelihood of racial or ethnic prejudice affecting the jurors in a particular case does the trial court's denial of a defendant's request to examine the jurors' ability to deal impartially with this subject amount to an unconstitutional abuse of discretion (190). The decision as to whether the total circumstances suggest a reasonable possibility that racial or ethnic prejudice will affect the jury remains primarily with the trial court (192).

Schneider v. *Irvington,* 308 U.S. 147, 84 L.Ed. 155, 60 S.Ct. 146 (1939).

The freedom of speech and of the press secured by the First Amendment against abridgment by the United States is similarly secured to all persons by the Fourteenth against abridgment by a state (160). Although a municipality may enact regulation in the interest of the public safety, health, welfare or convenience, they may not abridge the individual liberties secured by the Constitution to those who wish to speak, write or circulate information or opinion (160). This Court has characterized the freedom of speech and that of the press as fundamental personal rights and liberties (161).

Singer v. *U.S.,* 380 U.S. 24, 13 L.Ed.2d 630, 85 S.Ct. 783 (1965).

A defendant's only constitutional right concerning the method of trial is to an impartial trial by jury. We find no constitutional impediment to conditioning a waiver of this right on the consent of the prosecuting attorney and the trial judge when, if either refuses to consent, the result is simply that the defendant is subject to an impartial trial by jury—the very thing that the Constitution guarantees (36).

Smith v. *Daily Mail Publishing Company,* 443 U.S. 97, 61 L.Ed.2d 399, 99 S.Ct. 2667 (1979).

State action to punish the publication of truthful information seldom can satisfy constitutional standards (102). There is no evidence to demonstrate that the imposition of criminal penalties is necessary to protect the confidentiality of juvenile proceedings (105). The asserted state interest [confidentiality of juvenile records] cannot justify the statute's imposition of criminal sanctions on this type of publication (106).

Snyder v. *Massachusetts,* 291 U.S. 105, 78 L.Ed. 677, 54 S.Ct. 330 (1934).

The Commonwealth of Massachusetts is free to regulate the procedure of its courts in accordance with its own conception of policy and fairness unless in so doing it offends some principle of justice so rooted in the traditions and conscience of our people as to be ranked as fundamental (105).

Southeastern Promotions, Ltd. v. *Conrad,* 420 U.S. 559, 43 L.Ed.2d 448, 95 S.Ct. 1239 (1975).

It is established, of course, that the Fourteenth Amendment has made applicable to the states the First Amendment's guarantee of free speech (547).

Southern Pacific Terminal Co. v. *ICC,* 219 U.S. 498, 55 L.Ed. 310, 31 S.Ct. 279 (1911).

The question involved in the orders of the Interstate Commerce Commission are usually continuing . . . and these considerations ought not to be, as they might be, defeated by short-term orders, capable of repetition, yet evading review (515).

Thornhill v. *Alabama,* 310 U.S. 88, 84 L.Ed. 1093, 60 S.Ct. 736 (1940).

The freedom of speech and of the press, which are secured by the First Amendment against abridgment by the United States, are among the fundamental rights and liberties which are secured to all persons by the Fourteenth Amendment against abridgment by a state (95). The freedom of speech and of the press guaranteed by the Constitution embraces at the least the liberty to discuss publicly and truthfully matters of public concern without previous restraint or fear of subsequent punishment (101, 102). The dissemination of information concerning the facts of a labor dispute must be regarded as within that area of free discussion that is guaranteed by the Constitution (102).

Toledo Newspaper Co. v. *United States,* 247 U.S. 425, 62 L.Ed. 1195, 38 S.Ct. 560 (1918).

The sacred obligation of courts [is] to preserve their right to discharge their duties free from unlawful and unworthy influences, and in doing so, if need be, to clear from the pathway leading to the performance of this great duty all unwarranted attempts to pervert, obstruct, or distort judgment (416). However complete is the right of the press to state public things and discuss them, that right, as every other right enjoyed in human society, is subject to the restraints which separate right from wrongdoing (419, 420). It is said that there is no proof that the mind of the judge was influenced . . . by the publication . . . but here again, not the influence upon the mind of the particular judge is the criterion, but the reasonable tendency of the acts done to influence or bring about the baleful result is the test (421).

Tracy v. *Ginzberg,* 205 U.S. 170, 51 L.Ed. 755, 27 S.Ct. 461 (1907).

The 14th Amendment did not impair the authority of the states, by their judicial tribunals, and according to their settled usages and established modes of procedure, to determine finally, for the parties before them controverted questions as to the ownership of property, which did not involve any right secured by the Federal Constitution, or by any valid act of Congress or by any treaty. Within the meaning of that Amendment, a deprivation of property without due process of law occurs when it results from the arbitrary exercise of power inconsistent with "those settled usages and modes of proceeding (178, quoting in part from *Murry* v. *Hoboken,* 1856).

Turner v. *Louisiana,* 379 U.S. 466, 13 L.Ed.2d 424, 85 S.Ct. 546 (1965).

In the constitutional sense, trial by jury in a criminal case necessarily implies at the very least that the "evidence developed" shall come from the witness stand in a public courtroom where there is full judicial protection of the defendant's right of confrontation, of cross-examination, and of counsel (472, 473). It would be blinking reality not to recognize the extreme prejudice inherent in this continual association throughout the trial between the jurors and these two key witnesses for the prosecution (473).

Turner v. *Murray,* 476 U.S. 28, 90 L.Ed.2d 27, 106 S.Ct. 624 (1986).

We hold that a capital defendant accused of an interracial crime is entitled to have prospective jurors informed of the race of the victim and questioned on the issue of racial bias (36, 37). Also, a defendant cannot complain of a judge's failure to question the venire on racial prejudice unless the defendant has specifically requested such an inquiry (37).

Twining v. *New Jersey,* 201 U.S. 78, 53 L.Ed. 97, 29 S.Ct. 14 (1908).

We conclude, therefore, that the exemption from compulsory self-incrimination is not a privilege or immunity of national citizenship guaranteed by this clause of the 14th Amendment against abridgement by the states. The defendants, however, do not stop here. They appeal to another clause of the 14th Amendment, and insist that the self-incrimination which they allege the instruction to the jury compelled was a denial of due process of law. If this is so, it is not because those rights are enumerated in the first eight Amendments, but because they are of such a nature that they are included in the conception of due process of law (99).The words "due process of law" were intended to secure the individual from the arbitrary exercise of the power of government unrestrained by the established principles of private rights and distributive justice (101).The privilege was not conceived to be inherent in due process of law, but, on the other hand, a right separate, independent, and outside of due process (110).We think that the exemption from compulsory self-exemption from compulsory self-incrimination in the courts of the States is not secured by any part of the Federal Constitution (114).

Virginia v. *Rives,* 100 U.S. 313, 25 L.Ed. 667, 10 Otto 313 (1880).

The provisions of the 14th Amendment . . . have reference to state action exclusively, and not to any private individuals. It is the State which is prohibited from denying to any persons within its jurisdiction the equal protection of the law (318). Denials of equal rights in the action of the judicial tribunals of the State are left to the advisory powers of this court (322).The assertions . . . that the grand jury by which the petitioners were indicted, as well as the jury summoned to try them, were composed wholly of the white race . . . falls short of showing that any civil right was denied, or that there had been any discrimination against the defendants because of their color (322). It *is* [emphasis in original] a right to which every colored man is entitled, that, in the selection of jurors to pass upon his life, liberty, or property, there shall be no exclusion of his race, and not discrimination against them because of their color. But this is a different thing from the right . . . to have a jury composed in part of colored men. A mixed jury in a particular case is not essential to the equal protection of the law. . . . It is not, therefore, guaranteed by the 14th Amendment (322, 323).

Wainwright v. *Witt,* 469 U.S. 412, 83 L.Ed.2d 841, 105 S.Ct. 844 (1985).

The question whether a venireman is biased has traditionally been determined through voir dire culminating in a finding by the trial judge concerning the venireman's state of mind. We also noted that such a finding is based upon determinations of demeanor and credibility that are peculiarly within a trial judge's province. Such determinations were entitled to deference even on direct review (428).

Walker v. *Sauvinet,* 92 U.S. 90, 23 L.Ed. 678, 2 Otto 90 (1876).

The States so far as this [the Seventh] Amendment is concerned, are left to regulate trials in their own courts in their own way. A trial by jury in suits at common law pending in the State Courts is not, therefore, a privilege or immunity of national citizenship, which the States are forbidden by the Fourteenth Amendment (92). Due process of law . . . does not necessarily imply that all trials in the state courts affecting the property of persons must be by jury. This requirement of the Constitution is met, if the trial is had according to the settled course of judicial proceedings (92, 93). Due process of law is process due according to the law of the land. This process in the States is regulated by the law of the State. Our power over that law is only to determine whether it is in conflict with the supreme law of the land; that is to say, with the Constitution and laws of the United States made in pursuance thereof, or with any treaty made under the authority of the United States (93).

Wall Ex Parte, 107 U.S. 265, 27 L.Ed. 552, 17 Otto 265 (1883).

The action of the court in cases within its jurisdiction is due process of law. It is a regular and lawful method of proceeding, practiced from time immemorial (288–289). It is a mistaken idea that due process of law requires a plenary suit and a trial by jury, in all cases where property or personal rights are involved (289). In all cases that kind of procedure is due process which is suitable and proper to the nature of the case and sanctioned by the established customs and usages of the courts (289).

Weinstein v. *Bradford,* 423 U.S. 147, 46 L.Ed.2d 350, 96 S.Ct. 347 (1975).

Sosna v. *Iowa,* 419 U.S. 393, 42 L.Ed.2d 532, 95 S.Ct. 553 (1975) decided that in the absence of a class action, the "capable of repetition, but evading review" doctrine was limited to the situation where two elements combined: (1) the challenged action was in its duration too short to be fully litigated prior to its cessation or expiration, and (2) there was a reasonable expectation that the same complaining party would be subjected to the same action again (149).

Wood v. *U.S.,* 299 U.S. 123, 81 L.Ed. 78, 57 S.Ct. 177 (1936).

The [Sixth] Amendment prescribes no specific test. The bias of a prospective juror may be actual or implied; that is, it may be bias in fact or bias conclusively presumed as a matter of law. All persons otherwise qualified for jury service are subject to examination as to actual bias (133). The question here is as to implied bias, a bias attributed in law to the prospective juror regardless of actual partiality (174). Impartiality is not a technical conception. It is a state of mind. For the ascertainment of this mental attitude of appropriate indifference, the constitution lays down no particular tests and procedure is not chained to any ancient and artificial formula (145).

Zurcher v. *Stanford Daily,* 436 U.S. 547, 56 L.Ed.2d 525, 98 S.Ct. 1970 (1978).

Valid warrants may be issued to search *any* [emphasis the Court's] property, whether or not occupied by a third party, at which there is probable cause to believe that fruits, instrumentalities, or evidence of a crime will be found (554). There is no apparent basis in the language of the Amendment for also imposing the requirements for a valid arrest-probable cause to believe that the third party is implicated in the crime (554). It is untenable to conclude that property may not be searched unless its occupant is reasonably suspected of crime and is subject to arrest (559). They [the Framers of the Constitution] did not forbid warrants where the press was involved, did not require special showings that subpoenas would be impractical, and did not insist that the owner of the place to be searched, if connected with the press, must be shown to be implicated in the offense being investigated (565).

BIBLIOGRAPHY

Accetta, Barbara Schoke. "Can Courtroom Doors Be Closed When Minor Victim Testifies in Sex Offense Trials?" *Suffolk University Law Review* 16 (1982): 240–63.

Ambraham, Henry J. *Freedom and the Court: Civil Rights and Liberties in the United States.* 5th ed. New York: American Journal of Legal History, 1988.

Andrews, Lori B. *The Rights of Fair Trial and Free Press.* Chicago, Ill.: The Committee, 1981.

Association of the Bar of the City of New York. *Freedom of the Press and Fair Trial.* New York: Columbia University Press, 1967.

Avrich, Paul. *The Haymarket Tragedy.* Princeton, N.J.: Princeton University Press, 1984.

Beth, Loren P. *The Development of the American Constitution, 1877–1917.* New York: Harper and Row, 1971.

Bodenhamer, David J. *Fair Trial: Rights of the Accused in American History.* New York: Oxford University Press, 1992.

Brigner, Michael. "Cameras in the Courtroom." *Docket Call* 16 (1982): 12–16.

Carey, Steve. "Fair Trial and Free Press." *Montana Law Review* 45 (1984): 323–33.

Carroll, John S., Norbert L. Kerr, James J. Alfini, Frances M. Weaver, Robert J. MacCoun, and Valerie Feldman. "Free Press and Fair Trial." *Law and Human Behavior* 10 (1985): 187–201.

Clark, Todd, and Rebecca J. Novelli. *Fair Trial–Free Press.* Encino, Calif.: Benziger, 1977.

Coke, Sir Edward. *The First Part of the Institutes of the Laws of England, or A Commentary upon Littleton, not the Name of the Author only, but of the Law Itself.* London, 1656. (See also the 13th edition, Dublin: James Moore, 1791.)

Committee on the Operation of the Jury System. *Report on the Free Press–Fair Trial Issue.* Washington, D.C.: Administrative Office of the United States Courts, 1968.

Cook, Fred J. "The Corrupt Society: Part X, Silent Partners of Billie Sol Estes." *The Nation* 196 (1963): 185–96.

Copeland, David. "The Mormon Problem: The Press Reacts to Mormons, Polygamy and *Reynolds* v. *United States* 1879." Paper presented at the annual conference of the American Journalism Historians Association, Philadelphia, October 1991.

Cortner, Richard C. *The Supreme Court and the Second Bill of Rights: The Fourteenth Amendment and the Nationalization of Civil Liberties.* Madison: University of Wisconsin Press, 1981.

Cowen, Zelman. *Fair Trial v. a Free Press.* Santa Barbara, Calif.: Center for the Study of Democratic Institutions, 1965.

Cusenbary, Karen A. "Constitutional Law." *St. Mary's Law Journal* 23 (1991): 541–61.

Danis, Charles W., Jr. "A First and Ninth Amendment Theory of a Right of Access to Criminal Trials." *Western New England Law Review* 2 (1980): 723–58.

David, Henry. *The History of the Haymarket Affair.* New York: Russell and Russell, 1936.

Denniston, Lyle W. *The Reporter and the Law.* New York: Hastings House, 1980.

Denniston, Lyle. "The Struggle Between the First and Sixth Amendments." *California Lawyer* 2 (1982): 42–47.

Drechel, Robert E. "An Alternative View of Media-Judiciary Relations." *Hofstra Law Review* 18 (1989): 1–36.

Dyer, Carolyn Stewart, and Nancy Hauserman. "Electronic Coverage of the Courts." *Georgetown Law Journal* 75 (1987): 1633–1700.

Felsher, Howard, and Michael Rosen. *The Press in the Jury Box.* New York: Macmillan, 1966.

Fergason, Jane Deanne. "The Public's Right to Access Versus the Right to a Fair Trial." *Baylor Law Review* 33 (1981): 191–202.

Foerster, Beth Regier. "Constitutional Law." *Washburn Law Journal* 21 (1981): 419–26.

Fretz, Donald R. *Courts and the News Media.* Reno: National College of the State Judiciary, University of Nevada, 1977.

Frey, Christopher G. "The Imposition of Strict Civil Liability on Media Defendant for Publication of Truthful, Lawfully Obtained Information." *Stetson Law Review* 18 (1988): 119–46.

Friedman, Lawrence M. *A History of American Law.* 2nd ed. New York: Simon and Schuster, 1985.

Friedman, Richard D. "Another Look at Gannett." *District Lawyer* 4 (1981): 315–50.

Frumkin, Arthur S. "The First Amendment and Mandatory Courtroom Closure in *Globe Newspaper Co.* v. *Superior Court.*" *Hastings Constitutional Law Quarterly* 71 (1984): 637–64.

Fulero, Solomon M. "The Role of Behavioral Research in the Free Press–Fair Trial Controversy." *Law and Human Behavior* 11 (1987): 259–64.

Fuoco, Robert J. "The Prejudicial Effects of Cameras in the Courtroom." *Richmond Law Review* 16 (1982): 867–83.

Gaddis, Thomas. *Bird Man of Alcatraz: The Story of Robert F. Stroud.* New York: The New American Library, 1962.

Gillmor, Donald M. *Free Press and Fair Trial.* Washington: Public Affairs Press, 1966.

Graham, Fred P. *The Due Process Revolution: The Warren Court's Impact on Criminal Law.* New York: Hayden Book Company, 1970.

Hagen, Scott A. "Another Episode in the Fair Trial–Free Press Saga." *Utah Law Review* 85 (1985): 739–57.

Hale, William Green. *The Law of the Press.* 2nd ed. St. Paul, Minn.: West Publishing Co., 1933.

Hall, Kermit L. *A Comprehensive Bibliography of American Constitutional and Legal History.* New York: Kraus, 1991.

———. *The Magic Mirror: Law in American History.* New York: Oxford University Press, 1989.

Hall, Kermit L., James W. Ely, Jr., William Wiecek, and Joel Grossman, eds. *The Oxford Companion to the Supreme Court.* New York: Oxford University Press, 1991.

Harris, Robert J. *The Quest for Equality: The Constitution, Congress, and the Supreme Court.* Baton Rouge: Louisiana State University Press, 1960.

Hassett, Joseph M. "A Jury's Pre-trial Knowledge in Historical Perspective." *Law and Contemporary Problems* 43 (1980): 155–68.

Helle, Steve. "Publicity Not Equal to Prejudice." *Media Law Notes* 10 (1983): 6, 7.

Henry, David. *The History of the Haymarket Affair: A Study in the American Social-Revolutionary and Labor Movements.* 2nd ed. New York: Russell and Russell, 1958.

Holdsworth, W. S. *A History of English Law.* London: Methuen and Company, 1952.

Honeyman, Sandra Metzger. "Constitutional Law." *Suffolk University Law Review* 19 (1985): 129–36.

Hyman, Harold, and William C. Wiecek. *Equal Justice Under Law: Constitutional Development, 1835–1875.* New York: Harper and Row, 1982.

Jenks, Edward. *A Short History of English Law from the Earliest Times to the End of the Year 1919.* 2nd ed. Boston: Little, Brown, 1922.

Jones, Robb M. "The Latest Empirical Studies on Pretrial Publicity, Jury Bias, and Judicial Remedies." *American University Law Review* 40 (1991): 841–48.

Kalven, Harry. *The American Jury.* Boston: Little, Brown, 1966.

Kane, Peter E. *Murder, Courts, and the Press.* Carbondale: Southern Illinois University Press, 1986.

Kantor, Steven J. "Public Access to Pretrial Hearings." *Vermont Law Review* 6 (1991): 415–35.

Keenan, Sally M. "A First Amendment Right of the Press and Public to Be Present during the Criminal Trial." *Hofstra Law Review* 11 (1983): 1353–81.

Kelly, Alfred, Winfred Harbison, and Hermand Belz. *The American Constitution: Its Origin and Development.* 6th ed. New York: Norton, 1983.

Kelly, George W. "Richmond Newspapers and the First Amendment Right of Access." *Akron Law Review* 18 (1984): 33–49.

Kelly, Kathleen A. "Voir Dire." *Comment* 5 (1983): 779–93.

Kennedy, James M. "Clarifying the First Amendment Right of Access to Criminal Trials." *Boston College Law Review* 24 (1983): 809–33.

Kennedy, Robert F. *The Enemy Within.* New York: Harper, 1960.

Kerr, Norbert L., Geoffrey P. Kramer, and John S. Carroll. "Pretrial Publicity, Judicial Remedies, and Jury Bias." *Law and Human Behavior* 14 (1990): 409–38.

Kerr, Norbert L., Geoffrey P. Kramer, John S. Carroll, and James J. Alfini. "On the Effectiveness of Voir Dire in Criminal Cases with Prejudicial Pretrial Publicity." *American University Law Review* 40 (1991): 665–726.

Lahav, Pnina. *Press Law in Modern Democracies.* New York: Longman, 1985.

Leoni, Bruno. *Freedom and the Law.* 3rd ed. Indianapolis: Indiana University Press, 1991.

Lomask, Milton. *Aaron Burr: The Conspiracy and Years of Exile, 1805–1836.* New York: Farrar, Staus, and Giroux, 1982.

Malak, Michael P. "First Amendment." *Journal of Criminal Law and Criminology* 75 (1984): 583–608.

Maurer, Wilhelm. *An Inquiry into Anglo-Saxon Mark-Courts.* London: Whittaker and Co., 1855.

McCall, Gregory K. "Cameras in the Criminal Courtroom." *Columbia Law Review* 85 (1985): 1546–72.

McDonald, Forrest. *Novus Ordo Seclorum: The Intellectual Origins of the Constitution.* Lawrence: University of Kansas Press, 1985.

McGill, Norman L. "Juror Impartiality–Prejudicial Publicity. *Southern Illinois University Law Journal* 85 (1985): 565–84.

Minow, Newton N., and Fred H. Cate. "Who Is an Impartial Juror in an Age of Mass Media?" *American University Law Review* 40 (1991): 631–64.

Moore, Lloyd E. *The Jury: Tool of Kings, Palladium of Liberty.* Cincinnati, Ohio: W. H. Anderson Co., 1973.

Nagel, Stuart S. *Legal Policy Analysis.* Lexington, Mass.: Lexington Books, 1977.

New York Times Information Service. *The Courts and the Press.* Parsippany, N. J.: New York Times Information Service, 1979.

Norwood, Edward Andrew. "The Prosecutor and Pretrial Publicity." *Journal of the Legal Profession* 11 (1986): 169–86.

Nowaczewski, Jeanne L. "The First Amendment Right of Access to Civil Trials after *Globe Newspaper Co.* v. *Superior Court.*" *University of Chicago Law Review* 51 (1984): 286–314.

O'Connell, Peter D. "Pretrial Publicity, Change of Venue, Public Opinion Polls." *University of Detroit Law Review* 65 (1988): 169–97.

Pequignot, Margot. "From Estes to Chandler." *Florida State University Law Review* 9 (1981): 315–50.

Pfister, Thomas K. "The Illinois Supreme Court Confronts the Free Speech–Fair Trial Controversy." *John Marshall Law Review* 20 (1987): 581–95.

Pound, Roscoe. *Criminal Justice in America.* New York: H. Holt, 1930.

Puder, Susan. "Protecting the Rape Victim Through Mandatory Closure Statutes." *New York Law School Law Review* 32 (1987): 111–37.

Riley, Richard W. "Constitutional Law–First Amendment." *Villanova Law Review* 32 (1987): 789–811.

Rudinsky, Paul J. "Finding the Path Between an Attorney's First Amendment Right to Free Speech and a Client's Sixth Amendment Right to a Fair Trial." *Willamette Law Review* 22 (1986): 187–200.

Rutland, Robert Allen. *The Birth of the Bill of Rights, 1776-1791.* Chapel Hill: University of North Carolina Press, 1963.

Schmidt, Benno C. *Freedom of the Press vs. Public Access.* New York: Praeger, 1976.

Schwartz, Bernard. *The Great Rights of Mankind: A History of the Bill of Rights.* New York: Oxford University Press, 1977.

Sheppard, Samuel. *Endure and Conquer.* Cleveland: The World Publishing Company, 1966.

Siana, Stephen V. "Constitutional Law–Free Press–Fair Trial." *Villanova Law Review* 28 (1983): 723–40.

Siebert, Frederick Seaton. *Free Press and Fair Trial.* Athens: University of Georgia Press, 1970.

Simon, Rita James. *The Jury: Its Role in American Society.* Lexington, Mass.: Lexington Books, 1980.

Spencer, Christopher C. "Public Access to Criminal Trials." *University of Richmond Law Review* 15 (1981): 741–53.

Spooner, Lysander. *An Essay on the Trial by Jury.* Birmingham, Al.: Bryphon Editions, 1989.

Sprague, William E. *Abridgement of Blackstone's Commentaries.* Detroit, Mich.: 1895.

Steigleman, Walter Allan. *The Newspaperman and the Law.* 1950. Dubuque, Iowa: W. C. Brown. Reprint. Westport, Conn.: Greenwood Press, 1975.

Stewart, Ronald B. *Trial by the Press.* Charlottesville, Va.: Judge Advocate General's School, 1968.

Sullivan, Francis L. *The News Media and Crime Reporting.* Amherst: University of Massachusetts Press, 1982.

Tanielian, Eileen F. "Battle of the Privileges." *Loyola Entertainment Law Journal* 10 (1990): 215–36.

Urofsky, Mel. *A March of Liberty: A Constitutional History of the United States.* New York: Knopf, 1988.

Walker, Samuel. *Popular Justice: A History of American Criminal Justice.* New York: Oxford University Press, 1980.

Webstor, Timothy. "Criminal Procedure: Defendant's Right to Public Jury Selection." *Temple Law Quarterly* 59 (1986): 757–70.

White, G. Edward. *The American Judicial Tradition: Profiles of Leading American Judges.* New York: Oxford University Press, 1976

Willock, Ian Douglas. *The Origins and Development of the Jury in Scotland.* Edinburgh: Stair Society, 1966.

Winters, Glenn R. *Fair Trial–Free Press*. Chicago: American Judicature Society, 1971.

Woodson, James. *News Media Handbook on Virginia Law and Courts*. 3rd ed. Richmond: Virginia State Bar, 1978.

Yang, Iris Ping. "The Richmond Newspapers Case." *U.C. Davis Law Review* 14 (1981): 1081–1104.

Younger, Richard D. *People's Panel: The Grand Jury in the United States, 1641–1941*. Providence: Brown University Press, 1963.

Zavatsky, Michael J. "Rights in Collision." *University of Cincinnati Law Review* 49 (1980): 440–61.

Zimmerman, Diane L. "Overcoming Future Shock." *Duke Law Journal* (1980): 641–708.

INDEX

About the Author

DOUGLAS S. CAMPBELL is Chair of the Department of English, Journalism, and Philosophy at Lock Haven University in Pennsylvania. He is a member of the Law Division of the Association for Education in Journalism and Mass Communication, and he is the author of *The Supreme Court and the Mass Media* (Praeger, 1990).